Transport Economics

Transport Economics

K.J. Button

Gower

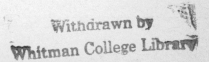

© K.J. Button 1982

First published 1982 by Heinemann Educational Books Limited

Reprinted 1986 by
Gower Publishing Company Limited
Gower House
Croft Road
Aldershot
Hants GU11 3HR
England

ISBN 0-566-05167-2 Pbk
     0-435 84092 4 Hbk

Typeset by Georgia Origination, Liverpool
Printed and bound in Great Britain by
Biddles Ltd, Guildford and King's Lynn

Contents

Preface

This book is intended to show how modern economics can be applied to the transport sector. It is hoped not only that it may serve a useful purpose as a teaching aid for a variety of academic and professional courses, but also that it may be of wide interest to those directly involved in the provision and regulation of transport facilities. The book differs from others in a number of ways, not least in the emphasis that is placed on the interaction of transport with other activities within the broader economy. Further, it is not concerned with specific modes or forms of transport but rather with the movement of goods and people.

The level of exposition should pose few problems for those who have undertaken an introductory course in economic principles. While there are a few equations, in general these are used to reinforce points and readers with only a limited mathematical background can quite easily read over them without losing the thread of an argument. In many cases the equations are for those wishing to apply theory to practical transport problems. Illustrations, examples and case studies are drawn from a wide range of sources.

The writing and preparation of this book has been both time consuming and taxing. My first thanks must go to my wife, Elizabeth, who has once again suffered neglect and lack of attention as I have jotted away upstairs. She has borne the frequent absence of my witty, charming and modest personality with great fortitude. At different times people have read, criticised and commented upon various fragments and sections of the book. They are too numerous for me to mention all by name, but one person who deserves specific mention is Alan Pearman who undertook the onerous task of reading almost the entire manuscript. The efforts of these individuals have considerably improved the final product; it would inevitably have been better still if I had paid more heed to their views. Finally, I must thank Madge Lowe for translating my scribblings into a readable final manuscript.

K.J. Button
September 1981

1 Transport and Economics

1.1 Transport economists

Some years ago in an address to the Chartered Institute of Transport, K.J.W. Alexander (1975) made the sober remark that despite the importance of transport in the economy, '...the number of academic economists who specialise exclusively in transport could probably be counted on two hands. If one adds to these economists the applied economists employed in the transport business and the specialist consultants working exclusively in that field I would be surprised if the total number exceeded sixty or seventy'. In comparison with other sectors of the economy, transport was in the mid 1970s (and still is today) under-researched and poorly understood. This is surprising because transport problems have in the past stimulated major developments in economic theory (e.g. the notion of consumer surplus and refinements of the marginal cost pricing principle) and, more recently, have encouraged work on applied econometrics (e.g. the development of discrete choice models in consumer theory). In part, the relatively small number of specialist transport economists – although they are now slightly more numerous than when Alexander made his speech – may be attributed to the diverse nature of the industry with many sectors comprising numerous small firms without resources to employ full-time specialists. It may also be explained by the tendency, until comparatively recently, for physical planners and transport engineers to dominate substantive investment decision-making within the sector. The emphasis was on the physical manifestation of travel, namely trips and journey numbers, rather than the demand for movement and the ability of the system to meet these aspirations. This situation has gradually changed with innovations in management and planning.

The recent upsurge in interest in transport economics began slowly about twenty years ago, as Rakowski (1976) points out, 'the field had essentially been in a state of semi-dormancy since the 1920s'. The reasons for the renewed research interest in the 1960s, especially in the USA, Radowski attributes to (i) 'the problems of physical distribution and the development of a new field which has come to be called business logistics', (ii) 'expanded interest in all phases of urban transportation' and (iii) 'a great deal of research in the areas of transportation in the developing countries'. Gwilliam (1980) echoes these themes but places particular emphasis on the growing problems of urban transport in the 1960s and the recognition that land-use and transport needed to be considered together, and usually simultaneously, if the problems were to be successfully tackled. As a result of this, he argues, 'the boundaries between transport economics and urban and regional planning were obscured'.

It is important to emphasise at the outset that transport economics is not distinct from all other branches of economics but rather, as our knowledge has increased, it has become difficult, if not impossible, for economists to follow developments in all branches of their discipline and, hence, increased specialisation has occurred. Transport economics has a long history but, as Alexander and Rakowski suggest, it has only recently become a major field of academic study within universities and only recently has a substantial body of specialists emerged.

The scope of each of the sub-disciplines within economics (e.g. agricultural economics, development economics, public sector economics, etc.) is determined not by particular schools or philosophies but rather by the type of subject matter examined and the problems tackled. Transport economists are interested in the economic problems of moving goods and people – they are not normally so concerned with either the industries producing the vehicles and infrastructure (aircraft manufacturing, road construction, ship building, etc.) nor with the very wide implications of transport policy (for example, on the balance of payments). Of course, this does not mean that transport issues are viewed in complete isolation from their wider context but it does mean that the main emphasis and thrust of analysis is directed towards the more immediate transport implications.

The main 'tools' of the transport economist are taken directly from the kit-bag of standard microeconomic theory. Having said this, however, one should add that the actual implements used by transport economists have changed significantly over the years. The pre-war emphasis centred on the transport industries (i.e. the railways, road haulage, shipping, etc.) and, in particular, on ways in which the transport market could be improved so that conditions of free competition would ensure that maximum benefit would be derived from public and private transport operations. The situation was summarised by one geographer who felt that transport economics at that time was concerned almost entirely with 'matters of organisation, competition and charging, rather than with the effects of transport facilities on economic activities' (O'Connor, 1965). To some extent – particularly in relation to international transport and, to a lesser extent, inter-urban transport – this interest has remained. It has, however, more recently been supplemented, and in some cases replaced, by concern with the wider welfare and spatial implications of transport. Greater emphasis is now placed on the environmental and distributional effects of the transport system and, in some cases, market efficiency is seen as an undesirably narrow criterion upon which to base major decisions. As Alexander argued, in the speech cited above, one of the most important roles for economists is to make clear the overall resource costs of transport rather than just the accounting costs.

Transport economics has, like virtually all other branches of economics, become more quantitative in recent years. The dominant pre-war idea that economics is concerned mainly with establishing broad principles (e.g. that quantity demanded rises, *ceteris paribus*, as price falls) has given way, with the advent of econometric techniques and the computer age together with improved data sources, to attempts at detailed measurement (i.e. a rise of x tons in the quantity demanded will, *ceteris paribus*, follow from a £y fall in unit price). Transport economists are now heavily involved in trying to assess the precise quantitative effect of different policy options and with forecasting likely changes in transport demand. The increasing sophistication of transport operations, combined with both the long lead times which are required for full policy implementation and the financial costs involved, place mounting strains upon economists to produce useful, quantified predictions of future trends.

From the relatively small base of the 1960s, transport economists are now becoming established in both public and private enterprises, in addition to assisting in national transport policy formulation. Their increased interest in the overall welfare consequences of different transport strategies, together with a willingness to attempt some form of quantitative assessment, has led to transport economists becoming closely involved in major urban transport planning exercises. They have an established role in advising on appropriate actions at the national policy formulation level but more recently this has spread down to a more specific function at the local planning level. Transport economists, for example, made a significant contribution to the Greater London Development Plan of the late 1960s and have subsequently been involved in many detailed appraisals of traffic management schemes (both in developed and less developed countries.) The particular advances made in transport investment appraisal – most notably the development of cost-benefit (CBA) techniques as practical tools of analysis – led to the adoption of economic criteria for the assessment of many large scale investment projects in the 1960s and 1970s (e.g. the Third London Airport scheme and the Channel Tunnel). Recent refinements have resulted in rather more standardisation, and uniform CBA procedures are employed as a standard method of small-scale transport project appraisal (e.g. the COBA package used in trunk road investment appraisal).

The dichotomy between the wealth of the industrial nations and the poverty of third world countries has resulted in large-scale programmes being initiated to stimulate the economic development of the third world. Much of this aid has been in the form of monies and resources to improve transport provision. In 1977–9 some 21 per cent of World Bank lending, for example, went on transport projects and overall 16 per cent of total Bank assistance – grants, expertise, etc. – was directed to this sector. Although it is not altogether agreed that aid actually stimulates growth (e.g. see Baur, 1971) nor that, if it does, transport investments are the most suitable projects to finance, it is nevertheless important that within the narrow confines of transport efficiency these monies are spent wisely. Transport economists have become increasingly involved in the third world in transport project appraisal work.

The remainder of this Introduction is concerned with setting the scene for the body of the book. Initially, some of the main economic features of the transport sector are discussed. The intention is, however, not to point to the uniqueness of transport but rather to highlight the particular characteristics of the sector which pose special problems for economists. Recent trends in transport are then reviewed and commented upon. Finally, a detailed contextual section explains the format of the book and outlines briefly the rationale for the structure adopted.

1.2 The economic characteristics of transport

Possibly the most important characteristics of transport is that it is not really demanded in its own right. People wish, in general, to travel so that some benefit can be obtained at the final destination – the trip itself is to be as short as possible. Of course, there are 'joy riders' but they tend to be in the minority. Similarly, users of freight transport perceive transport as a cost in their overall production function and seek to minimise it wherever possible. The derived nature of the demand for transport is often forgotten in everyday debate but it underlies all economics of transport.

While the demand for transport has particular, if not unique, features, certain aspects of supply are entirely peculiar to transport. More specifically part of the plant is 'mobile' – almost by definition – and is entirely different in its characteristics to the fixed plant (e.g. rail-track, airports etc.). The fixed component is usually extremely long-lived and expensive to replace. While most factories in the manufacturing sector may be thought to have a physical life expectancy of a hundred years at most we still use ports and roads constructed in Roman times. Further, few pieces of transport infrastructure have alternative uses: some former waterways have been turned into leisure areas but these tend to be exceptions.

In contrast, most mobile plant is relatively short-lived and replacement usually occurs with physical obsolescence rather than technical obsolescence as with the fixed components. It is also cheap, with the prospect of alternative employment if demand declines in one market; for example, a bus can be transferred to another route or another form of service. Also, unlike fixed plant, the mobile components of transport are generally subject only to minimal scale economies. (Ships and aircraft may be seen as exceptions to this in some cases.) The fixed component, on the other hand, is normally subject to quite substantial economies of scale. Once a rail track is laid the marginal cost of using it falls until some maximum capacity is reached. This means that generally there is a minimum practical size below which the provision of transport infrastructure is non-economical. There are minimum traffic flows, for example, below which it is not economically practical to build motorways.

As Thomson (1974) has pointed out, it is these features of the fixed and mobile components of transport which have influenced the present institutional arrangements in the sector. The high cost of provision, longevity and scale economies associated with the fixed components create tendencies towards monopoly control, while the ease of entry, flexibility and lack of scale effects tend to stimulate competition in the mobile sector. In common with many other countries official reaction in Britain to this situation has tended to be the nationalisation and public ownership of transport infrastructure and the regulation of competition in the mobile sector. Nations differ in the degree to which fixed transport assets are publically owned (there are private railways in other countries while several European states have privately operated motorways) and in the types of regulation imposed on mobile factors but the overall impression is consistent.

While the rationale of directly controlling the provision and sale of the fixed components of transport can be linked to the containment of any monopoly exploitation which may accompany private ownership (although British experience in the nineteenth century suggests that control might equally well be enforced through price regulation), the need to regulate the mobile component stems from another aspect of transport operations. Transport generates considerable external effects (most obvious of which are congestion and pollution); as Thomson (1974) says, it is an engineering industry carried on outside the factory. It is, therefore, felt important at least to contain the harmful effects of transport and at best to ameliorate them. Coupled with this is the imperfect knowledge enjoyed by operators and, in particular, their inability to foresee relatively short-term change in demand. Regulation is, therefore, often justified to ensure that excessive competition at times of depressed demand does not reduce the capacity of the transport system to an extent that it cannot meet higher demand during the upturn. Finally, there are political–economy arguments that transport is a social service which should meet 'need' rather than demand and, hence, traditional market forces need to be supplemented to ensure that this wider, social criterion of transport operations is pursued rather than the simple profit motive.

1.3 Some statistics
Some indications of recent global trends are seen in Table 1.1. The table gives a broad picture of the growth of world transport during recent years. It is quite clear that, despite the limitations of using this

Table 1.1   World transport trends, 1968–77

	1968	1971	1974	1977
Motor vehicles (thousands)				
Cars	170450	206110	246220	285660
Lorries	44750	53660	62720	76410
Merchant shipping				
(thousands gross registered tons)				
Steam	74263	78518	113031	140100
Motor	119880	159684	198291	253548
Civil aviation				
Freight ton-				
kms (millions)	7920	11590	17030	21340
Passenger-				
kms (millions)	310000	406000	546000	691000
Passengers (thousands)	261000	333000	423000	517000

Source: United Nations, *Statistical Yearbook*

type of crude aggregated data, the growth has been substantial. The mercantile marine has more than doubled as has air traffic. The main difficulty with this type of data is the impossibility of devising a common unit of measurement for transport. It is possible to count physical units (e.g. the number of cars or planes) but lack of homogeneity prevents meaningful comparisons over time for individual modes (e.g. an average aircraft ten years ago is different from the average aircraft of today), let alone contrast of trends to be made between modes. Output measures (e.g. tonne-kilometres or passenger-kilometres), although appearing to circumvent problems of comparability over broad categories of transport, in fact tend to be equally inadequate. Such measures, in particular, ignore the quality and costs of alternatives. Despite these comments it is still possible to look at official statistics and obtain a general feel for the transport situation evolving in the more parochial context of Great Britain.

Transport forms a major component of the national output and accounts for between 15 and 20 per cent of national expenditure in Great Britain. A substantial part of this (12.4 per cent in 1975) is accounted for by consumer expenditure, the remainder is undertaken by firms. Table 1.2 gives a more detailed breakdown of the sums involved over the 1970s and it is apparent that, even after allowing for the considerable inflation over the period, the amount spent on

Table 1.2 Expenditure on transport in the United Kingdom, 1968–78

£ million

	1968	1970	1972	1974	1976	1978
Passenger						
Buses and coaches	412	457	555	669	1058	1294
Motoring	3032	3460	4811	5982	8936	12343
Taxis and hire cabs	46	66	94	126	189	276
Rail	230	288	356	413	636	890
All passenger	3720	4271	5816	7190	10819	15303
Freight						
Road	3363	4212	5293	7757	9501	10448
Rail	269	279	260	290	416	517
Inland waterways	5	6	7	9	13	16
All freight	3637	4497	5560	8056	9930	10981
All inland transport, of which	7357	8768	11376	15246	20749	26284
Road	6853	8195	10753	14534	19684	24861
Rail	499	567	616	703	1052	1407

Source: Department of Transport, *Transport Statistics*

Table 1.3   Trends in transport in the United Kingdom 1968-78

	1968	1870	1972	1974	1976	1978
Passenger traffic (thousand million passenger-kms)						
Bus and coach	59	56	55	54	53	52
Car and motor cycle	286	330	347	350	363	390
Pedal cycle	6	5	4	4	4	4
Road sub-total	351	391	406	408	420	446
Rail	34	36	35	36	33	35
Air	1.9	2.0	2.2	2.3	2.3	2.4
Total	387	429	443	446	455	483
Freight traffic (thousand million tonne-kms)						
Road	79	85	87.5	89.9	95.6	99.1
Rail	24	26.8	23.4	22	20.6	20.0
Coastal shipping	24.5	23.2	21.3	20.4	20	—
Inland waterways	0.2	0.1	0.1	0.1	0.1	0.1
Pipeline	2.5	3.0	3.5	5.3	5.7	9.9
Total	130.2	138.2	135.7	137.6	142	129.1[a]

[a] Does not include coastal shipping.

Source: Department of Transport, *Transport Statistics*

transport is rising. Some of the increase may be caused by higher transport prices *vis-à-vis* other goods bought in the economy but, as can be seen in Table 1.3, there is also ample evidence that the main cause of the upward trend in expenditure is the marked rise in the amount of travel undertaken and in the physical quantity of goods moved and the distances over which they are moved. As a rough guide (and making some allowance for short-term fluctuations which are not immediately apparent from Table 1.3), passenger transport has grown by about 30 per cent over the 1970s while freight transport has risen by around 20 per cent.

Tables 1.2 and 1.3 also reveal another important set of trends, namely the changing relative and absolute roles played by the different, individual modes of transport. It is quite clear that travel by road has risen substantially. Car and motor cycle travel dominate personal transport both in terms of traffic carried and monies expended. We also see that the dominance of private (i.e. motor car and motor cycle) transport over public modes is increasing both relatively and absolutely over time. As we see in Chapter 2 the rise in private transport use is closely related to higher car ownership levels – although the question of cause and effect is a complex one.

Table 1.4 draws upon Family Expenditure Survey data to show another interesting aspect of passenger transport, namely the use

Table 1.4 Personal expenditure on transport by income group, UK, 1972

Households	All goods and services (%)	Rail (%)	Bus (%)	Car (%)
Poorest 20%	7.9	5.0	9.3	1.7
Second quintile	14.7	8.8	18.6	11.1
Third quintile	19.0	13.5	20.9	17.5
Fourth quintile	23.8	21.7	24.4	27.5
Richest 20%	34.6	51.0	26.9	42.3
Total	100	100	100	100

Source: Pryke and Dodgson, 1975

made by different income groups of the various modes. The railway mode is clearly used primarily by those in the higher income groups, as is the private car. In contrast bus transport is used disproportionately more by the poorer sectors of the community. The table ignores business account travel which is likely to benefit the higher income groups.

Tables 1.2 and 1.3 also show that inland freight transport is increasingly being dominated by road haulage which is, over time, taking a larger share of the total market. Also we notice that pipelines are gradually emerging as an important form of transport. Physical limits to the type of commodities which can be carried in this way, however, are likely to prevent pipelines from ever becoming more than a minority mode of transport. Rail transport tends to be declining irrespective of whether measured in absolute physical tonne-kilometres or in the real monetary value of the revenues obtained.

While these aggregate data reveal interesting trends they nevertheless hide quite important details. In particular, on the freight side the tonne-kilometres statistics do not show that much of the increase in road haulage is attributable to longer hauls in larger vehicles. The average length of haul by road rose by over 5 per cent between 1967 and 1977 while the average vehicle capacity increased from 9.5 tons in 1973 to 10.3 tons in 1976. The explanation of this probably is in the greater geographical concentration of industry which has occurred, with a small number of production units now supplying the whole country rather than numerous small factories meeting the needs of local markets. Personal trips have also increased in length from an average of 6.1 miles in 1965 to 6.6 miles in 1975. Much of this is accounted for by longer journeys to work, the average length of which rose from 4.8 miles to 5.8 miles over the period.

Table 1.5 Employment by sector in the UK

	1978 (mid-year)			
	Private sector	Public sector	Total employment	
				as % of total employed labour force
	thousands	thousands	thousands	
Agriculture, forestry and fishing	643	10	653	2.6
Mining and quarrying	57	287	344	1.4
Manufacturing	6951	472	7423	29.8
Construction	1473	185	1658	6.6
Gas, electricity and water	13	337	350	1.4
Transport and communication	564	961	1525	6.1
Other services	7844	4813	12657	50.8
Total civilian employment	17545	7065	24610	98.7
HM Forces and Women's Services	–	318	318	1.3
Total employed labour force	17545	7383	24928	100.0

Note: Components may not add to total because of rounding
Source: Central Statistical Office, *Annual Abstracts of Statistics*, London, HMSO, 1979.

Table 1.6 *Actual and forecast public expenditure in the UK, 1978/9–1983/4*

£ million at 1979 survey prices

	1978/79	1979/80	1981/82	1983/84
Defence	7 502	7 723	8 240	8 740
Overseas aid and other overseas services:				
Overseas aid	795	794	730	680
EEC contributions	774	919	1 150	1 550
Other overseas services	393	432	400	400
Agriculture, fisheries, food and forestry	897	944	920	890
Industry, energy, trade and employment	3 203	2 969	2 390	1 760
Government lending to nationalised industries	693	1 900	300	− 550
Roads and transport	2 975	3 073	2 780	2 690
Housing	5 256	5 372	3 840	2 790
Other environmental services	3 330	3 273	3 040	2 880
Law, order and protective services	2 329	2 446	2 600	2 700
Education and science, arts and libraries	9 516	9 654	9 010	8 670
Health and personal social services	9 023	9 067	9 230	9 500
Social security	18 266	18 890	19 800	19 600
Other public services	958	1 014	990	940
Common services	1 022	1 047	1 070	1 120
Northern Ireland	2 233	2 200	2 110	2 070
Total programmes	69 165	71 716	68 600	66 400

Source: HM Treasury, 'The Government's Expenditure Plans 1980/81 to 1983/84', HMSO, Cmnd 784

The public sector plays an important role in transport. It both provides and maintains a considerable amount of infrastructure as well as being responsible for those modes operating within the nationalised transport sector. Total employment in the different sectors of the economy (for 1978) is shown in Table 1.5 together with the share employed in the public sector. It is clear that transport is responsible for a substantial number of jobs in the national economy and that the public contribution is significant. Additionally, in financial terms public expenditure on transport forms a major component of total UK public expenditure both at the local and national levels. Table 1.6 gives some indication of the general trends over recent years. It is worth noting that over 50 per cent (in fact 57 per cent in 1979/80) of the public expenditure on roads and transport is by local rather than central government. These figures are, however, likely to hide some transport expenditures and should, thus, be seen as lower limits. Transport, for instance, accounts, or is directly responsible, for additional expenditures under items such as law and order, environmental services and health. Also monies are lent to the nationalised transport industries. As we see from projections of future expenditure, it is intended to reduce public spending on transport in line with macroeconomic policies, but it will still remain an important item in absolute terms.

External transport has also increased (Table 1.7) although reliance on physical measures often obscures the value or importance of goods traffic. Table 1.7 provides an indication of this measurement problem. Great Britain is typical of a developed economy which tends to import low value, bulk raw materials and exports high value, non-bulk manufactures. This explains the wide difference in the inward and outward flows of shipped tonnage. The growth in air traffic is due, to a large extent, to the growth of international tourism rather than an expansion of business travel.

Table 1.7   International transport to and from the United Kingdom

	1968	1971	1973	1975	1978
Foreign sea					
Traffic (thousand tonnes)					
Inwards	175 606	201 990	219 516	175 327	152 774
Outwards	41 696	48 741	53 515	50 200	90 685
Foreign air					
movements (thousand passengers)					
Inwards	4 617	5 858	6 298	7 826	9 893
Outwards	4 620	5 878	6 240	7 843	9 876

Source: Department of Transport, *Transport Statistics, Great Britain 1968–78*, London, HMSO, 1979

1.4 The framework of the book

The remainder of the book is concerned with the application of economic theory to the transport sector. Unlike other books which often concentrate on particular modes of transport (e.g. Joy (1973) on the railways or Sturmey (1975) on shipping) or specific sectors (e.g. Thomson and Hunter (1973) on the nationalised transport industries) one of the main aims of this book is to show that many problems in transport are common to all modes (albeit with minor variations). Consequently, the approach is to show how economic theory may be applied to improve the overall efficiency of the transport sector; examples are, therefore, drawn from all forms of transport. Also while it is unavoidable, not to say desirable, that official transport policy must be implicitly incorporated in the analysis, this is not a book about transport policy. It is felt useful, on occasions, to give brief details of institutional arrangements since they can influence the type of economic analysis to apply (e.g. a thumb-nail sketch of the historical and institutional framework of urban transport planning is included for this purpose), but, again, this is primarily for contextual reasons. The final chapter *is* concerned with policy and institutions, but at a rather abstract level and certainly is not intended to offer a critique of British transport policy; this is a topic covered much more thoroughly by Gwilliam and Mackie (1975).

At the theoretical level the discussion is couched in terms of verbal and diagramatic analysis. Mathematical expressions are not shunned but equations are included rather as references, permitting readers to look up practical working models should they subsequently wish to undertake their own empirical investigations. There are virtually no mathematical derivations, but important equations are 'talked around' and the reader should find no difficulty in following the book even if his/her mathematical education has been neglected. Those interested in mathematical extensions of the arguments on specific topics are referred to the major references. A knowledge of microeconomic theory is assumed, but not beyond that contained in a standard introductory text such as Lipsey (1979).

The book begins by looking at the role of transport in the national economy and its interaction with other sectors of the economy, especially the land market. This interaction is often neglected in the literature but is central to understanding the role of transport in society. This is followed by a related chapter concerned with the benefits of transport and methods of measuring these benefits, drawing particularly upon the tools of welfare economics. While Chapters 2 and 3 are essentially demand-orientated, the two following chapters are concerned with cost and supply aspects (costs here being seen both in terms of conventional financial cost problems and, also, in terms of wider external costs). The accountancy costs of running transport are now recognised as offering too narrow a picture of the overall social costs associated with the movement of goods and persons.

The remaining chapters concentrate on optimising the size and use made of the transport sector both in the short term and in the longer term. Methods of pricing are reviewed in the context of the particular nature of transport activities with, once again, emphasis being directed to the wider social dimension as well as to narrow commercial criteria. Chapter 7, in particular, looks at methods of optimising the environmental effects of transport on society in general.

Longer-term planning and investment decisions are considered in some detail. This is because of both the complexities of the issues involved and the size of the potential resource wastage if the wrong decision is taken. The sheer costs involved are also enormous, particularly where major pieces of new infrastructure are under consideration – e.g. a Third London Airport or a Channel Tunnel. The long working life of projects means that it is important to be able to forecast the future demands likely to be placed on the infrastructure, and consequently, in Chapter 9, some space is devoted to economic demand forecasting techniques. The emphasis is, once again, focused on the economic assumptions involved rather than the econometric and estimation problems which may be encountered.

The final chapters of the book take a much broader view of transport, considering both the role that transport policy may play in general economic development – within the UK and in less developed countries – and the influence that official transport policy exercises over the sector. The latter discussion is particularly concerned with the relative merits of central co-ordination and direction of transport *vis-à-vis* the use of the market mechanisms and competitive processes.

While each chapter is extensively referenced throughout to permit readers to follow up specific points in more detail should they wish, it has also been thought useful to mention a few key references and some indication of further reading at the end of each chapter. These references are annotated and are really designed to help student readers. The intention is that they should be references to material which is relatively accessible to most readers rather than obscure reports, working papers, etc. which are often extremely difficult for those outside official circles or the academic sphere to obtain. The lists of key references are kept short so that the main items are immediately apparent to those interested.

1.5 Further reading and references

The official *Transport Statistics* (HMSO, London) published annually is an extremely useful source of up-to-date information on trends in United Kingdom transport. The United Nations' *Statistical Yearbook* offers wide-ranging, but rather less reliable, data on developments in world transport. A useful source of historical data for Great Britain is Munby and Watson (1978), which is an invaluable reference work.

Useful general introductions to transport economics include Sharp (1973) and Nash (1976); the former provides a general overview of basic principles while the latter is more concerned with the specific question of public versus private transport. Both offer a good background to this book. At the more advanced level Thomson and Hunter's (1973) book on the nationalised sectors of transport, although now somewhat dated, provides a good basis for the study of the institutional aspects of transport economics. Button (1979) offers an annotated bibliography, together with about 130 references, of recent contributions in the field of transport economics.

References

Alexander, K.J.W. (1975), 'Some economic problems of the transport industry', *Chartered Institute of Transport Journal*, Vol. 36, pp. 306–308, 321.

Baur, P. (1971), *Dissent on Development*, London, Weidenfeld and Nicolson.

Button, K.J. (1979), 'Recent developments in transport economics', *British Review of Economic Issues*, Vol. 2, pp. 14–34.

Gwilliam, K.M. (1980), Review of 'Transport Economics', *Economic Journal*, Vol. 90, pp. 677–8.

Gwilliam, K.M. and Mackie, P.J. (1975), *Economics and Transport Policy*, London, Allen & Unwin.

Joy, S. (1973), *The Train that Ran Away*, London, Ian Allen.

Lipsey, R.G. (1979), *An Introduction to Positive Economics*, 5th edn., London, Weidenfeld and Nicolson.

Munby, D.L. and Watson, A.H. (1978), *Inland Transport Statistics Great Britain 1900–1970*, Oxford, Oxford University Press.

Nash, C.A. (1976), *Public versus Private Transport*, London, Macmillan.

O'Connor, A.M. (1965), *Railways and Development in Uganda*, Nairobi, Oxford University Press for the East African Institute of Social Research.

Pryke, R. and Dodgson, J. (1975), *The Rail Problems*, London, Martin Robertson.

Rakowski, J.P. (1976), *Transportation Economics: A Guide to Information Sources*, Detroit, Gale Research Co.

Sharp, C.H. (1973), *Transport Economics*, London, Macmillan.

Sturmey, S.G. (1975), *Shipping Economics: Collected Papers*, London, Macmillan.

Thomson, A.W.J. and Hunter, L.C. (1973), *The Nationalised Transport Industries*, London, Heinemann.

Thomson, J.M. (1974), *Modern Transport Economics*, Harmondsworth, Penguin.

2 Movement, Transport and Location

2.1 The desire for movement

Robert Louis Stevenson once said, 'For my part, I travel not to any-where, but to go. I travel for travel's sake. The great affair is to move.' (from *Travels with a Donkey*). He is very much in the minority; few people travel for the sheer joy of it, although some modes of transport do arouse feelings of excitement, romance or sentiment. Most individuals travel because they wish to benefit from the social, recreational, educational, employment and other oppor-tunities which become accessible with movement. Similarly, freight transport opens up opportunities for greater efficiency in production and permits extensive geographical specialisation with the accompanying benefits of increased division of labour. More simply, transport permits the spatial disadvantages of separation to be reduced.

In more detail, Thomson (1974) provides a helpful classification of seven main reasons why people in the modern world desire to transport either themselves or their property:

(1) The heterogeneity of the earth's surface means that no one part of it is capable of providing all the products people wish for. An acceptable bundle of such goods can only be obtained by either moving around collecting them or having them brought to you.

(2) The continuation of modern society and the high levels of material well-being rely upon a degree of productive special-isation. Industry requires a multiplicity of diverse inputs which must be collected from wide-ranging sources and also, to permit the necessary level of specialisation, extensive market areas must be tapped and served.

(3) In addition to specialisation, high quality transport permits the

exploitation of other major economies of scale. There are essentially technical economies associated with high levels of output and include automation, bulk handling, research and development activities, mass marketing, purpose-built equipment, etc.

(4) Transport has always served a political and military role. Internally, a country seeks good transport both to permit more effective defence of its borders and to improve the political cohesion of the nation. The Romans were certainly well aware of this and most of their road building was to this end. Externally, good transport permits a country to dominate any colonial or subservient provinces, while more aggressive states require transport to pursue their expansionist policies. Politically, the ownership of expensive, modern transport infrastructure (especially aircraft or mercantile marine) is also treated as a symbol of power and status. In most developed countries the scale of transport required to meet strict needs normally exceeds that required to meet political or military criteria although individual components of a transport system (e.g. specific roads or airports) may be provided explicitly for non-economic reasons.

(5) Without transport, social relationships and contacts are normally very restricted. Transport permits social intercourse, and with it may come a greater understanding of the problems and attitudes of various geographically distant groups. In the developed world the enhancement of social understanding brought about by increased international travel is well recognised, but in many less developed countries the introduction of much more basic transport technology can have profound effects upon the social relationships between inhabitants of formerly isolated towns and villages which are, by Western standards, very close together.

(6) Modern transport has widened cultural opportunities, permitting people to examine the artistic treasures of other countries and to explore their own national heritage. It also allows for the staging of international exhibitions, sports spectaculars, concerts, parades and fairs which stimulate new trends and innovations in the cultural and sporting spheres.

(7) Transport is desired to permit people to live and work apart – specifically it permits the geographical separation of employment from leisure. It increases the life-style options open to

people, giving them a choice among residential locations away from cities but involving a heavy commitment to travel, or ones much closer to the main employment centre but involving short commuting journeys. Transport, quite simply, widens the locational choices open to households.

What becomes apparent from this listing is the close link between location decisions (of both individuals and firms) and the transport system. It is this link we now turn to.

2.2 The 'chicken or egg' problem

In the previous chapter it was suggested that one of the reasons for the surge of interest in transport economics in the 1960s and 1970s was the recognition of the important link between transport and land-use patterns (especially those relating to urban location). The effects of changes in the transport system on land-use tend to be long-term (hence they are often called 'activity shifts') but, given the longevity of much transport infrastructure, such interactions must to some extent concern transport policy-makers. The changes that occur in land-use will also, in turn, by altering the nature and size of the local residential population and industrial base, exert an enormous influence on future transport demand. A major new suburban underground railways system, for example, will immediately attract some travellers away from other modes of transport in addition to encouraging trips to be made by former non-travellers. In the longer term, sites near the underground termini will become desirable while those further away will appear relatively less attractive. There will, therefore, be important implications for residential and employment location patterns. Additionally, changing location and trip-making patterns will alter car ownership decisions.

While these interactions are now fully recognised, it is practically difficult to construct a comprehensive theory which fully reflects all the linkages. The problem is further compounded by the fact that transport and land-use changes are on-going modifications to the spatial economy. There are continual cycles of cause and effect, and it is impossible to decide upon a point where it is sensible to break into this continuum of change. Consequently, from a pragmatic standpoint one has to make a rather careful judgement whether to treat land-use as influenced by transport or vice versa. To some extent the final decision must rest with the questions being considered. Urban and regional scientists tend to treat transport as the influential variable because the focus of attention here is on the spatial dimension. Questions are posed, for example, in terms of why do certain population densities occur or why do specific urban economies interact. In contrast, transport economics usually accepts a given land-use pattern and looks at methods of providing efficient transport services within this constraint. Questions centre, for instance, on problems of aligning routes or controlling traffic flows.

An example of this latter approach which reveals both the methodology of conventional transport economics, but also highlights some of the difficulties in the modelling of urban decision-making, was developed by Kain (1964). This econometric study, looking specifically at public transport subsidies and calibrated using information from a 1953 survey of 40 000 households in Detroit, adopts four steps in its argument:

(1) Workers initially select a residential density in which to live depending upon their income, their preference for a specific plot size and the price of residential land.

(2) Once a location has been selected the decision to purchase a car is treated as dependent upon the local residential density, family income, public transport availability and the composition of the worker's family.

(3) The decision whether to use public transport for the journey to work, besides depending upon the previous decisions regarding location and car ownership, is thought to be influenced by the quality of local public transport, and the demands of non-working members of the household to make use of the car (if one is owned).

(4) Finally the length of journeys is treated as dependent both on previous decisions of the worker and on the price of residential land adjacent to workplaces.

The implied chain of decisions is, therefore, unidirectional and of the following forms:

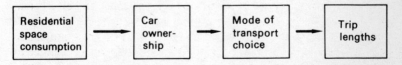

While Kain was clearly aware of the feedbacks from transport to land-use, for a variety of statistical and theoretical reasons he could not adequately reflect them in his model. Besides not allowing for the longer-term feedbacks from travel behaviour to land-use, the sequence takes no account of the influence of public transport quality on the car ownership decision (see Button *et al.*, 1982), or the length of journeys on the longer-term provision of public transport. What the sequence does do, however, is to permit Kain to examine the case for subsidising public transport *within* the current urban land-use framework. The assumptions of the sequential type of framework used by Kain are analogous to the standard *ceteris paribus* assumptions of conventional partial equilibrium microeconomics; they suffer from the same limitations but do provide boundaries within which useful analysis can be conducted.

The majority of this book is concerned exclusively with the transport sector and with short-run travel decisions. It assumes implicitly, therefore, that the causal link runs from land-use to transport and, generally, that land-use is predetermined. It seems inappropriate, however, not to give some brief overview of the approach adopted by spatial scientists; not to do so would in effect ignore the part played by transport in both shaping land-use patterns and determining the size of the market areas served by various industries. In the remainder of this chapter, therefore, we present a brief introductory outline of modern location theory, concentrating primarily on that aspect of theory which gives a central role to transport. The theory is supplemented by some discussion of the applied work which offers quantification of the important role played by transport in this field. Later in the book (in Chapter 10) the subject of transport and locational interaction is touched upon again in the context of economic development.

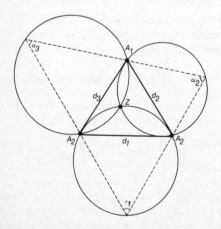

Figure 2.1   Weber's model of industrial location

2.3 Transport and industrial location

The earliest economic theories of industrial location recognised a key role to be played by transport services. As we have seen, provision of good transport permits producers to be separated from both their sources of new materials and also their eventual customers. Weber (Friedrich, 1929) developed one of the first models of location for mobile plant and, within his framework, transport costs determined the location of manufacturing industry. In Figure 2.1 all potential customers are located at A_1 while the two raw materials required by manufacturing industry are located respectively at A_2 and A_3. The ds represent actual distances between the points of raw material supply and final demand. It is assumed that all other factors of production are freely available at all potential production sites and that, topographically, all activities are located on a uniform plain. Transport costs are assumed proportional with respect to both distance covered and weight of goods carried. The location of a manufacturing plant will therefore depend on the relative pulls of the various material locations and the market. The problem is then one of finding the site, Z, for manufacture which minimises total costs, in other words the location which minimises T where:

$$T = a_1 r_{A_1} + a_2 r_{A_2} + a_3 r_{A_3} \tag{2.1}$$

and r_{A_1}, r_{A_2} and r_{A_3} are the *distances from the production site to A_1, A_2 and A_3 respectively.*

a_1 is the physical amount of the final goods consumed at A_1;
a_2 is the physical amount of the raw material available at A_2 required to produce a_1 of the final good; and
a_3 is the physical amount of the raw material available at A_3 required to produce a_1 of the final good.

It is easily seen that if any two of a_1, a_2, a_3 are exceeded by the third, then the location of the production is determined at the site associated with this third variable (e.g. if $a_2 > (a_1 + a_3)$, then production of the final commodity should be at site A_2). If no location is dominant, then graphical methods can be used to find the least-cost site. A second triangle is drawn with sides proportional to a_1, a_2 and a_3 and the three angles measured. We denote the angle opposite the a_1 side by α_1, that opposite a_2 as α_2 and finally that opposite a_3 as α_3. These angles then form the basis for erecting similar triangles around the original locational triangle (see Figure 2.1). Circles are drawn which touch the points of each triangle and the optimal production site Z is then found at the location where all three circles intersect (If Z is found to be outside of the original locational triangle, then it is simple to prove that one of the corner solutions, A_1, A_2, or A_3 is preferable.) This location minimises transport costs as defined in equation 2.1.

This simple analysis implicitly assumes that transport costs are linearly related to distance, but there is ample evidence that there are often considerable diseconomies associated with short hauls and with partially full loads. While Weber originally suggested that one could adjust the sides of the locational triangle to capture this, the situation requires rather more complicated modifications. The difficulty is that in these circumstances location and transport costs are co-determined; without knowledge of the final location (i.e. Z) it is impossible to assess the magnitude, if any, of economies of long-haul transport. There is a suggestion, however, that other things being equal, tapered transport rates (i.e. when the rate per mile declines with distance) tend, in some circumstances, to draw industry to either the source of raw materials or the market for final products.

Suppose that only one raw material is needed to produce the final product (or that the range of raw materials required are located at a single point) and this is to be found at A in Figure 2.2. Further there is no loss of weight in the manufacturing process required to produce the final product which will eventually be sold at M. Either the transport system offers a through service from A to M costing £10 per ton or alternatively there are services from A to the intermediate site B costing £6 per ton and one from B to M also costing £6 per ton. Since we assume no weight loss in production the cost conscious manufacturer is clearly indifferent between A and M but would not select site B (because $(AB + BM) \rangle AM$ in cost terms). Where there are a number of sources of basic inputs or several markets, Palander (1935) has demonstrated that this finding is still valid and that transport costs tapering with distance force the optimal location towards corners of locational space.

To relax the assumption of no weight loss in manufacturing does not remove the disadvantage suffered by B relative to A which is now preferable to location M. (It is possible in this situation for B to be preferred to M if a location at A is impracticable for technical or planning reasons, but this would depend upon the relative importance of the taper *vis-à-vis* the weight loss in manufacture.) Weight loss will only influence the choice between A and M, and this may even be true if different rates are charged not simply by haul length but also by type of commodity. Even if it is more expensive per ton to carry the final product it may still be preferable to locate production facilities at the material source rather than final market. In the

USA, for example, the meat packing industry of the last century was gradually drawn westwards to the main source of beef (initially to Chicago and then to Omaha and Kansas City) even though rail rates per ton mile favoured transport of live animals rather than carcasses. The simple fact was that the dressed meat of a steer weighs only 54 per cent of the live animal weight; hence locations near the raw material were favoured.

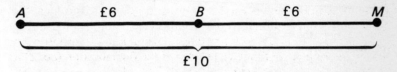

Figure 2.2　The effects of tapered rates on industrial location

Of course, firms do not in general locate in isolation from one another. Losch (1954) has demonstrated that with all firms facing identical production and transport cost schedules, and confronted by a spatially uniform total market, the market would be divided out so that each firm would serve a hexagonal market area. The equilibrium number of firms, and the area served by each, would be determined by transport costs. (A more detailed discussion of market areas is reserved for section 2.5.) The existence of a number of different, but interdependent product markets would, in the Loschian model, tend to encourage concentrations of firms at particular locations.

Discussion of the details of these locational and other models is beyond the scope of this book (although some references for further reading are mentioned at the end of the chapter), but it should be becoming increasingly apparent that transport costs are now recognised to be only one of many factors influencing industrial location. The factors influencing location include (in addition to transport considerations) market structure, demand elasticities, external economies of geographical concentration, expectations of future market changes and processing costs. Greenhutt (1963) suggests that in practice transport costs only become of major importance if freight costs form a large proportion of total costs or differ significantly among potential locations.

While theoretical models of industrial location offer useful insights into the role transport plays, its actual relevance in the real world requires detailed empirical study. If we follow Greenhutt's argument, in many cases transport costs are such a small component of overall production costs that it appears to be more costly to acquire the information necessary to find the least-cost location than

Table 2.1   Transport costs for selected British industries as a percentage of net output (1963)

Industry	%
Watches and clocks	1.08
Engineer's small tools and gauges	1.75
Mens and boys tailored outerwear	1.94
Footwear	2.18
Motor vehicle manufacturing	2.64
Pharmaceutical preparations	2.92
Printing, publishing, etc.	2.92
Tobacco	3.33
Toys, games and sports equipment	5.14
Iron and steel (general)	7.76
Brewing and malting	11.70
Fruit and vegetable products	13.33
Animal and poultry food	17.04
Bricks, fireclay and refractory goods	22.27
Soft drinks, British wines, cider, perry	23.76
Sugar	24.24
Confectionery	24.71
Coal-mining	25.24
Milk products	27.54
Chalk, clay sand and gravel extraction	29.78

Source: Extracted from Edwards, 1970

to suffer the inefficiencies of a sub-optimal situation. (Cook's (1967) study, for example, of industrial location in the Black Country of the Midlands found that many firms were totally ignorant of their transport costs.) One can attempt to isolate such transport cost-insensitive industries by looking at the relative importance of transport costs in their overall costs of production. Table 2.1 offers some estimates of the percentage of the value of net output for a variety of industries attributable to transport costs. It seems reasonable to conclude from this table that, *ceteris paribus*, industries such as watchmaking, footwear, pharmaceuticals, printing, etc. are going to be less influenced in their locational choices by transport considerations than milk products, brick manufacture, soft drinks, confectionery, etc. (In the United States it is often suggested that Gary, Indiana was chosen specifically by US steel to minimise transport costs.) Others such as coal-mining, chalk, clay, sand and gravel extraction represent nodal solutions in the Weberian triangle, with production at the raw material source. Changes in industrial structure over the past thirty years, and especially the movement away from basic industries, would therefore seem to suggest that transport is experiencing a diminishing influence over location decisions – at least at the inter-regional level. This was the picture that emerged when Gudgin (1978) looked at the 1968 Census of Production: he found 'that almost three-quarters of British industry incurs total transport costs at levels of less than 3 per cent of the value of gross output. In 95 per cent of industry, by value of production, the transport costs are less than 5 per cent of total costs'.

As Gwilliam (1979) has pointed out, however, this type of statistic may be giving a slightly distorted impression of the influence of transport factors. In particular, while transport costs may only form a relatively small portion of output costs in many sectors they may, nevertheless, have significant influence on *profits*. Chisholm (1971), for instance, suggests that transport costs may represent as much as 25 per cent of profits in manufacturing industry. Additionally, while transport costs may, on average, be low for some industries they may vary considerably *among* areas. Edwards (1975) suggests that a range of about 20 per cent in transport costs of manufacturing industry by region existed in 1963. It should also be remembered that simple cost estimates may disguise variations in other attributes of transport (speed, regularity, etc.) which can influence decision-makers. The Toothill Report (Scottish Council, 1962), for example, when looking at the real and supposed advantages of Scotland as an industrial location, stressed the importance of rapidity and reliability (rather than cheapness) of transport and communications as a key variable in location choice. Consequently, Gwilliam (1979) concludes, 'Thus location may cause significant *differences* in transport costs, even if transport only accounts for a small proportion of total costs' (emphasis original).

Survey evidence, questioning industrialists about the motivations underlying their locational or re-locational decisions also provides some guide to the importance of transport considerations. There are obvious difficulties in using such results – e.g. the sample may be unrepresentative, respondents offer answers which they hope may further their individual interests, while others offer *ex post* rationalisations of their actions – but some information may be gleaned from them.

In 1973, for instance, the Trade and Industry Sub-Committee of the House of Commons Expenditure Committee (1973), when seeking information about the effectiveness of UK regional economic policy, were told by five of the seventeen major industrial firms interviewed that transport costs were a specific disadvantage for locations in developed areas. While accepting this as objective comment, it is important to note not simply the relatively small number of firms concerned but also their particular nature – e.g. three were car manufacturers and one a large steel tube mill. These were large firms engaged in the production of bulky products whose per unit transport costs were likely to be high. The Armitage Committee (Department of Transport, 1980) recently supported this line and concluded that 'When industry and commerce make decisions about the location of factories or their systems of distribution, it is often less important to reduce transport costs than to reduce other costs such as those of stockholding or to take advantage of the grants for setting up factories in assisted areas'. Such a view is consistent with that of Cameron and Clark (1966), who in their study of seventy-one firms which located in Assisted Areas found that accessibility to main markets was only ranked third as a locational factor (behind the availability of trained labour and local authority co-operation) while local goods transport facilities were listed fifth and accessibility to main suppliers ranked sixth.

One factor which emerges from these studies, and has limited support in econometric work, is that during the post-war phase of full employment and strengthened land-use controls, access to markets and raw material supplies has often been overshadowed in locational decisions by the availability of scarce skilled labour and factory space (e.g. see Trade and Indusry Sub-Committee of the House of Commons Expenditure Committee, 1973). International confirmation of this position is found in the West German context where in a survey of newly located plants conducted in 1971, Fischer (1971) found that accessibility to motorways ranked only fourth in the list of locational criteria.

More localised studies suggest that good *passenger* transport facilities may influence industrial location rather more than the quality of freight transport (Keeble, 1976). This confirms the emphasis that has (at least until the late 1970s) been placed upon the ready availability of trained workers. In retailing and some other activities this argument is further extended to embrace firms' desires to be accessible to customers.

There is now increasing realisation amongst economists that not all firms are concerned with selecting the most cost efficient location for their plant. In many cases provided a site offers, *ceteris parbus*, a location where transport costs are below some threshold, it is considered acceptable. In other cases, the first acceptable location encountered is adopted rather than a protracted search pursued (Townroe, 1971). The influences of social setting and amenities on those who make the decisions about location, and on the staffs whose preferences they have to consider are highlighted in this context by Eversley (1965). Firms often, therefore, adopt 'satisficing' policies in site selection rather than attempting to profit or revenue maximise or cost minimise. Under these conditions the exact role played by transport costs becomes almost impossible to define, but it seems likely that once a location has been chosen, a major rise in transport costs would be necessary to overcome the basic inertia which would seem to accompany such a managerial objective.

2.4 Output, market area and transport costs

Transport costs are not only instrumental in influencing where firms locate, but they also play an important role in determining the market area served by each firm. Transport costs, given the place of industrial location, can determine the total quantity of goods sold and their price and the spatial distribution of this output. Much of the early work looking at market areas was conducted by Losch (1954) but here we focus on a specific transport orientated model which was devised by van Es and Ruijgrok (1974). The simple model treats transport demand as derived from the demand for the final product and assumes all supply and demand curves to be linear. For expositional ease the relevant functions are treated in a manner running counter to economic convention; specifically price is treated as dependent upon demand rather than vice versa. Initially our firm which produces a homogeneous product supplies a single customer who is located some distance from its predetermined site. Hence we have,

$$P^s = a_0 + a_1\, Q^s + P^t \tag{2.2a}$$

$$P^d = b_0 - b_1\, Q^d \tag{2.2b}$$

$$Q^d = Q^s \tag{2.2c}$$

$$P^d = P^s \tag{2.2d}$$

where P^s is the supply price of the commodity;
P^d is the demand price of the commodity;
Q^s is the quantity of the commodity supplied;
Q^d is the quantity of the commodity demanded; and
P^t is a constant transport cost per unit carried to the customer and treated as a cost borne by the supplier.

Manipulation and combination of these equations yields the profit-maximising supply, Q^e, i.e.

$$Q^e = \frac{b_0 - a_0}{a_1 + b_1} - \frac{P^t}{a_1 + b_1} \tag{2.3}$$

It is immediately clear that transport costs exert a negative influence on the quantity the profit-maximising firm ought to supply, i.e. if $P^t = 0$, then the equilibrium output would rise by $\dfrac{P^t}{a_1 + b_1}$. Further we can derive the equilibrium price (P^e) which should be charged to the customer:

$$P^e = \frac{a_1 b_0 + a_0 b_1}{a_1 + b_1} + \frac{b_1 P^t}{a_1 + b_1} \qquad (2.4)$$

Here we see that the transport cost component increases the equilibrium price by $\dfrac{b_1 P^t}{a_1 + b_1}$. The effect of this, together with the effects of transport costs on Q^e, are illustrated graphically in Figure 2.3.

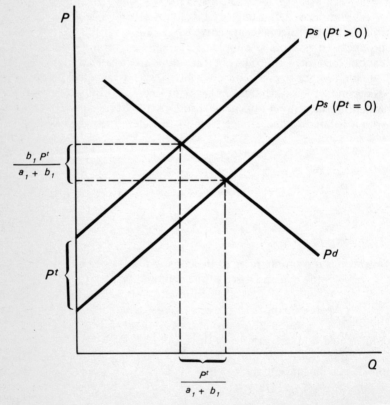

Figure 2.3   The effect of transport costs (P^t) on price and output

The vertical axis shows the final price per unit paid by the customer and the horizontal axis, the quantity of goods sold. The introduction of the transport cost element to the diagram has the effect of pushing the supply curve up from P^s ($P' = 0$) to P^s ($P' > 0$). It is evident that transport cost rises will push up final prices and reduce the quantity sold. The exact impact depends not only upon the magnitude of P' but also the elasticities of supply and demand – greater inelasticity increases the influence on price exerted by transport cost considerations.

To estimate the market area served when potential customers are spread evenly around the production site we will initially assume identical individuals are located at equal distances along a straight road from the site of the supplier. The customers will be confronted by prices which are composed of a fixed factory price reflecting production costs and a variable transport cost dependent upon the distance they live from the production site. Since each customer – by assumption – exhibits a similar demand response it is, therefore, the transport component which determines the amount each will buy. At the edge of the firm's market area, the amount supplied to the marginal customer vanishes to zero (this will be when $P' = b_0 - a_0$). If j customers are served before this limit is reached, then from equation 2.3, we can see that the total sales of the firm (Q^T) will amount to

$$Q^T = \sum_j Q_j^e = j \left[\frac{b_0 - a_0}{a_1 + b_1} \right] - \left[\sum_j P_j' \right] \left[\frac{1}{a_1 + b_1} \right], \tag{2.5}$$

where Q_j^e represents sales to customer j.

This approach can be extended to show the entire geographical area served by the firm. In Figure 2.4 the vertical axis represents the quantity supplied to each customer, on the assumption that the customers are evenly spread over the plane. The amount sold to a customer falls from very high levels ($Q^e = \dfrac{b_0 - a_0}{a_1 + b_1}$) immediately adjacent to the site of supply – where transport costs are zero – and falls to zero when transport costs become excessive. The total amount sold can be measured by calculating the volume of the cone. More formally and for reference the total demand for a commodity can be expressed mathematically as

$$D = b \, \pi \int_0^R f \, (P + T) \, T \, d \, T, \tag{2.6}$$

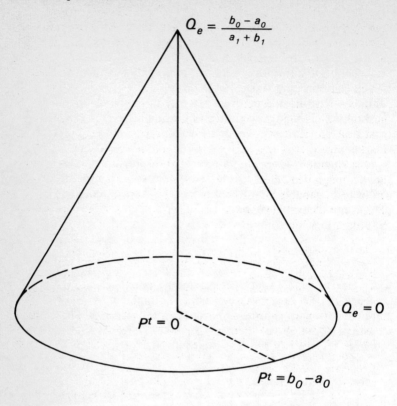

Figure 2.4   The influence of transport costs on market area

where D is total demand as a function of free on board price net of
        mill price P;

    b is twice the population density of a square in which it costs
        1 money unit to ship 1 unit of the commodity along one
        side;

    d $= f(P+T)$, is an individual demand as a function of the
        price of the commodity at the place of consumption;

    P is fob net mill price of the commodity;

    T is freight cost per unit from the factory to the consumer;
        and

    R is the maximum possible transport cost.

While this type of approach (relating the sales, prices and market
area of production to transport costs) is obvious theoretically, inter-

estingly it does rely upon many abstractions from reality for its internal consistency. As with many theories, some of the assumptions associated with the model outline above may be relaxed: it is possible for example to allow for variations in population density, for heterogeneity in consumer tastes, and non-perfectly elastic supply conditions – but this does tend to add complexity to the analysis. The general impression conveyed, however, is always the same, namely that transport costs are key in determining the size of geographical market served by a firm and the total volume of its sales.

One situation where the effects of transport improvements may have a magnified effect on the market area is when the producing industry is capable of exploiting manufacturing scale economies. This is not a novel idea and it was recognised over two centuries ago by Adam Smith (1776):

> The division of labour . . . must always be limited . . . by the extent of the market. When the market is very small, no person can have any encouragement to dedicate himself entirely to one employment . . . (B)y means of water carriage a more extensive market is opened to every sort of industry than that what land carriage alone can afford it . . . A broad-wheeled waggon, attended by two men, and drawn by eight horses, in about six weeks' time carries and brings back between London and Edinburgh near four ton weight of goods. In about the same time, a ship navigated by six or eight good men, and sailing between the ports of London and Leith, frequently carries and brings back two hundred ton weight of goods . . . Were there no other communication between these two places, therefore, but by land carriage . . . they could carry on but a small part of that commerce which at present subsists between them, and consequently give but a small part of that encouragement which they at present mutually afford to each other's industry.

2.5 Urban transport and land values

The previous sections have been concerned with the interaction between transport and the physical, spatial economy but little has been said regarding the way in which transport quality can affect land values. Location, to date, has tended to be viewed in terms of where a firm would locate and the area which would be served. Little has been said about the distribution of land among alternative uses either within one sector, such as manufacturing, or among sectors, notably between industrial and residential use. Early work on this problem can be traced back to von Thünen's (1826) land rent model which attempted to explain differences in agricultural land rent. He argued that concentric zones of crop specialisation would develop around the central market; the key feature of the model being that land rent differentials over homogeneous space are determined entirely by transport cost savings. While the nineteenth century agrarian economy provided the inspiration for 'bid-rent curve' analysis, it is in the context of twentieth century urban development that it has been most fully developed.

Haig (1926) was the first to apply von Thünen's argument in the urban context arguing that, 'Site rents and transportation costs are vitally connected through their relationship to the friction of space. Transportation is the means of reducing that friction, at the cost of time and money. Site rentals are charges which can be made for sites where accessibility may be had with comparatively low transportation costs.' People who are prepared to pay the highest price for improved transport provision (i.e. out-bid rivals) will enjoy the most accessible locations. This approach is clearly dependent upon some very stringent assumptions which need to be spelt out before we proceed further. We focus initially upon the residential location of households. The city under review is seen as a featureless plain with all production, recreational and retailing activities concentrated at a single urban core (the CBD). The population is homogeneous with respect to family size, income, housing demands, etc., but while building costs are invariate to location, transport costs rise with distance from the CBD. With these assumptions, the sum of transport costs plus site rents is constant across the entire city (i.e. if we take a ray out from the CBD to the perimeter of the city and concentrate exclusively on household decisions we have the situation depicted in Figure 2.5. Total site rent in the city may be estimated as the volume of the inverted cone centred on the CBD).

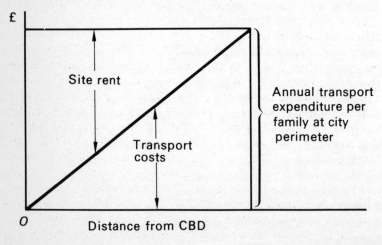

Figure 2.5   The site rent/transport cost trade off

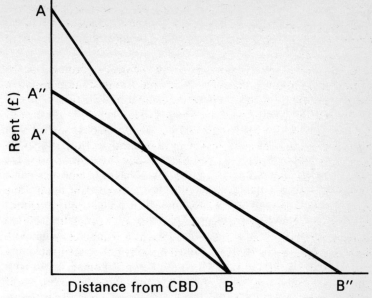

Figure 2.6 Rent gradients before and after a transport improvement

An improvement in the transport system will result in a fall in land values at each location and an outward expansion of the city – the extent of this outward expansion being dependent upon the elasticity of demand for transport services. If the demand for transport is perfectly inelastic then the boundary of the city remains unchanged. If *AB* in Figure 2.6 is the initial rent gradient then, with a perfectly inelastic demand for transport services the result of, say, uniformly lower public transport fares is to shift the gradient to *A'B*. The city's perimeter remains at *B*. With a degree of elasticity, however, the reduced transport cost will encourage longer distance travel to work and recreational activities and the eventual rent gradient is likely to settle at a position such as *A" B"* and the city's boundary to extend out to *B"*. It should be remembered that this simple model assumes that transport costs vary linearly with distance from the CBD and that individuals are identical. If this is not the case then, as Mohring (1961) has pointed out, the precise relation between transport cost and location patterns would be obtained simultaneously rather than sequentially as above. Further, the change in relative site rentals may also result in households wishing to own different size plots of land; this complication is incorporated by allowing for some elasticity in the demand for quantities of land (see Alcaly, 1976).

This model of urban location, which was subsequently greatly refined in a classic paper by Alonso (1964), extends beyond the simple consideration of residential land rent. The priorities of households differ and there is clearly competition in a free-market land economy among the demands of industry, commerce and various classes of households for different sites. In general, there are so called 'agglomeration economies' to be enjoyed by industry and commerce from locating close, both to each other and at the city core – they present an identifiable geographical entity (e.g. medicine in Harley Street, tailoring in Savile Row, etc.), can be easily served by specialised suppliers, provide customers with a comprehensive range of services, etc. Consequently, given the potentially higher revenue associated with a core location, business tends to bid highly for central sites. Poorer people who cannot afford high transport fares and place a relatively low priority on large sites are willing to bid higher rents for inner area locations, while the wealthy will be more inclined to bid a higher rent for suburban locations. Figure 2.7 shows in its upper half the bid-rent curves for three groups of urban land user; business, poor households and wealthy households. We see, in this very simple example, that business will outbid both classes of household for sites near the urban centre (i.e. the CBD will extend from O to B), poorer households will locate adjacent to the CBD (i.e. from B to P) while the wealthy will outbid the other groups for sites at the edge of the city (i.e. from P to W). Traced out into a plane and rotated (as in the lower half of Figure 2.7) a concentric pattern of land-use emerges. The actual boundary *jklm* is the revealed rent function for the city on the basis that land is allocated to the highest bidder. Clearly this is rather a stylised picture of urban land use and rents (Chapter 10 provides some further refinements), but it does offer some insight into the influence transport can have on intra-urban location patterns. Quite simply, high-transport cost activities, *ceteris paribus*, will be located at a close distance to the CBD and low transport cost activities will take locations further away.

Changes in transport costs may affect the amount of land taken up by various activities. The introduction of improved public transport with extremely low fares, for example, may well increase the willingness of poorer households to bid for locations further from the CBD and consequently the central ring of land-use, as we see in Figure 2.8a, may both widen and, more probably, move outwards. Damm *et al.* (1980) found that the construction of the Washington Metro, with its cheap, good quality service, increased the willingness of people to pay for land parcels near metro stations. In the urban

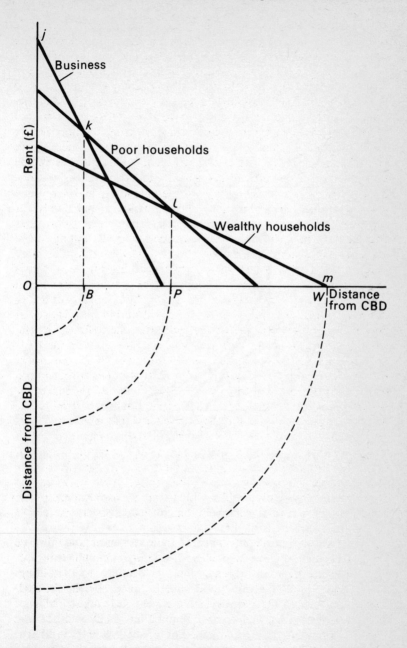

Figure 2.7 Rent-bid curves and concentric urban land use

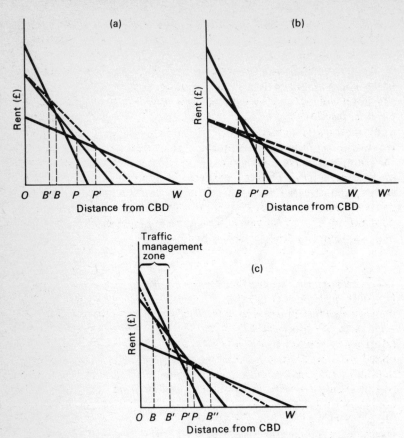

Figure 2.8   The impact of changing transport provision on urban land use

centre retailers were even more willing to offer high rents for sites near metro services. Alternatively the construction of an extensive urban road network is likely to improve the access offered to car-owning, wealthy households, shifting their rent-bid curve upwards and to the right (Figure 2.8b). The ring of land occupied by this group will thus be extended out beyond the original city boundaries (i.e. from *W* to *W'*). Evans (1973), for instance, specifically attributes the 'flight to the suburbs' to 'the large-scale construction of urban motorways which increases commuting speeds and comfort for the commuter' and argues that the only way to get higher income groups back into the central area is to 'Make the transport system slow, cheap and uncomfortable, and not fast, comfortable and expensive.'

Another possibility is that a strict traffic management policy may be introduced in the city centre. Although the exact effect of such a policy depends upon its detailed design we will assume for the sake of illustration that this discourages shoppers etc. from using the CBD. This will reduce the willingness of business to bid for a central site, but it will increase the bidding for outer locations. In Figure 2.8c the final result is that the CBD contracts (to OB') while a sub-centre of business activity emerges, as $P'B''$ in the diagram. Of course, the real world is a little more complicated than these examples suggest; for example we have treated the city in isolation, ignored variations in the geography of the area, assumed away any land-use planning agency, and treated locational change as instantaneous, but it becomes apparent that any attempt at formulating an urban transport policy or any advance in transport engineering will have important implications for urban form.

2.6 Transport and urban wage rates

Not only do transport costs influence urban land-use patterns, but they are also instrumental in determining spatial variations in urban wage rates. As Moses (1962) has pointed out 'the wage differential, positive or negative, a worker is willing to accept is completely determined by the structure of money transport costs'. We will assume that all employment is either concentrated at the city centre or else spread evenly over the surrounding, mainly residential, area. All households are assumed initially to be in equilibrium, all enjoying the same level of welfare. Moreover, all workers are paid identical wages, work the same hours and undertake the same number of commuting trips. Initially then, net monies after work-trip outlays will vary among workers according to the nature of their intra-urban transport costs and the distance of their homes from the CBD. Variations in land values with distance from CBD, as we saw in the previous section, act as an adjustment mechanism to ensure uniformity of welfare. People living away from the urban core will pay more in transport costs, but their land rentals will be correspondingly lower.

In this simple world, however, a worker could improve his well-being by giving up his job at the CBD (and thus saving commuting costs) and work at one of the jobs which are spread evenly over the urban area and which is near his home. He would be willing to accept a lower income in this situation; indeed, he would be willing to sacrifice his wage rate down to the point where it is cut by as much as the commuting costs that are saved. Thus there will be an equilibrium wage at locations nearer home than the CBD which will be lower than the core wage.

The result of this type of approach is the development of an urban wage gradient the shape of which is determined by commuting cost factors. In Figure 2.9 *OW* is the wage paid at the urban centre, of this *WA'* is the travel cost between the boundary of the city, *A* and the CBD. *OA'* is the wage rate required to keep an employee living at *A* in his current occupation if he worked at (or very near) home. The worker living at *A* is, therefore, indifferent between commuting to the CBD and earning *OW* and working at home and earning *OA'*. The *WW'* curve traces out the wage rates at which a worker living at *A* would have to be paid to make him indifferent between working at home and at any intermediate site between *A* and the CBD. (It also shows the wage rates at which people living *between A* and the CBD will be indifferent between working at home and at the core.)

If we introduce the notion of some secondary employment concentration, say at *L*, then reverse commuting may develop. If this sub-centre requires labour which it cannot attract from households to the

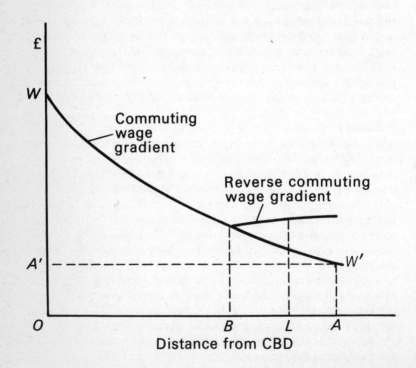

right of L it will need to compensate workers who travel out from areas between L and the CBD. Since the transport system tends to be less costly, in overall terms of money, time and comfort factors (see Chapter 4), for reverse commuting, the reverse commuting wage gradient is likely to be less steep than the commuting wage gradient. The main influence on reverse commuting costs *vis-à-vis* those for commuters are the generally lower levels of traffic congestion away from the CBD.

Just how does the wage gradient theory stand up to empirical investigation? Quite clearly the spread of national wage agreements, combined with imperfections in the land and transport markets (e.g. public transport subsidies and the growth in company cars), makes any exact testing of the theory difficult. American evidence from New York (Segal, 1960) found wages to be higher in suburban counties than at the CBD and, even after allowing for variations in industrial structure, no wage gradient emerged. However, Rees and Schultz (1970) in their study of Chicago found a 'strong positive association of wages with distance travelled to work', but the wage gradient for blue-collar workers had its peak in the area of heavy industrial concentration (the South-west of the city) and sloped downwards towards the North-west. In Britain, Evans (1973) suggests that while a wage gradient can be discerned for Greater London there is little conclusive evidence of one elsewhere. Indeed, in provincial cities, clerical wages are often almost uniform across metropolitan areas. Clerical wages were, however, found to be higher in the City and the West End of London than in the suburbs.

Although these findings are not conclusive, it is clear that the evidence supporting the wage-gradient theory is at least balanced by that rejecting it. The problems are that the studies to date fail to allow for the multiplicity of factors other than transport which affect wage levels. We have already mentioned some of the problems – notably imperfections in certain markets – but to these we must add the tendency for employers to compensate workers for high transport costs by unrecorded payments (free meals, shorter working hours, more flexible time-keeping, etc.). Additionally, in some cities there are unrecorded advantages of working in the city centre (better out-of-work and shopping facilities, increased career potential, etc.). The studies do not, therefore, refute the idea that transport costs influence urban wage patterns, but rather, the situation is more complex than the simple wage gradient theory suggests.

2.7 Further reading and references

Vickerman (1980) offers one of the few attempts to integrate transport, housing and industry within a comprehensive framework. Useful extensions of the conventional partial equilibrium approach to transport and land-use are contained in the following which look at the interaction from the position of regional and urban economics; Richardson (1978, especially Chapter 2), Alcaly (1976) and O'Sullivan (1981, Chapter 2) while, for a more mathematical approach, Richardson (1977, Chapters 2–4) considers the importance of transport in the so-called 'New Urban Economics'. The latter also provides some useful insights into the relationship between urban transport and land values although the potential reader should be forewarned of the mathematical approach employed. Evans (1973) is the most complete work on transport and residential decisions – it is a thorough rewriting of the author's Ph.D. thesis. It is also extremely readable with extensive references. Readers interested in up-to-date empirical studies of the role of transport in industrial location might usefully glance through the contents pages of journals such as *Regional Studies* and *Urban Studies*.

References

Alcaly, R.E. (1976), 'Transportation and urban land values: a review of the theoretical literature', *Land Economics*, Vol. 52, pp. 42–53.

Alonso, W. (1964), *Location and Land Use*, Cambridge, Mass., Harvard University Press.

Button, K.J., Pearman, A.D. and Fowkes A.S. (1982), *Car Ownership Modelling and Forecasting*, Aldershot, Gower Press.

Cameron, G.C. and Clark, B.D. (1966), *Industrial Movement and the Regional Problem*, University of Glasgow Occasional Paper No.6.

Chisholm, M. (1971), 'Freight transport costs, industrial location and regional development', in M. Chisholm and G. Manners (eds.), *Spatial Policy Problems of the British Economy*, Cambridge, Cambridge University Press.

Cook, W.R. (1967), 'Transport decisions of certain firms in the Black Country', *Journal of Transport Economics and Policy*, Vol. 1, pp. 344–56.

Damm, D., Lerman, S.R., Lerner-Lam, E. and Young J. (1980), 'Response of urban real estate values in anticipation of Washington Metro', *Journal of Transport Economics and Policy*, Vol. 14, pp. 315–36.

Department of Transport (1980), *Report of the Inquiry into Lorries, People and the Environment*, London, HMSO.

Edwards, S.L. (1970), 'Transport costs in British industry', *Journal of Transport Economics and Policy*, Vol. 4, pp. 65–83.

Edwards, S.L. (1975), 'Regional variations in freight costs', *Journal of Transport Economics and Policy*, Vol. 9, pp. 115–26.

van Es, J. and Ruijgrok, C.J. (1974), 'Modal choice in freight transport', in E.J. Visser (ed.), *Transport Decisions in an Age of Uncertainty*, The Hague, Martinus Nijhoff.

Evans, A.W. (1973), *The Economics of Residential Location*, London, Macmillan.

Eversley, D.E.S. (1965), 'Social and psychological factors in the determination of industrial location', in T. Wilson (ed.), *Papers on Regional Development*, Oxford, Blackwell.

Fischer, L. (1971), *Die Berucksichtignung Raumordnungs Politiseler Zeilsetviengen in de Verkehrsplanung*, Berlin.

Freidrich, C.J. (1929), *Alfred Weber's Theory of the Location of Industry*, Chicago, Chicago University Press.

Greenhutt, M. (1963), *Microeconomics and the Space Economy*, Chicago, Scott-Foresman.

Gudgin, G. (1978), *Industrial Location Processes and Regional Employment Growth*, Farnborough, Saxon House.

Gwilliam, K.M. (1979), 'Transport infrastructure investments and regional development', in J.K. Bowers (ed.), *Inflation, Development and Integration - Essays in Honour of A.J. Brown*, Leeds, Leeds University Press.

Haig, R.M. (1926), 'Towards an understanding of the Metropolis', *Quarterly Journal of Economics*, no. 40, pp. 179-208.

Kain, J.F. (1964), 'A contribution to the urban transportation debate: an economic model of urban residential and travel behaviour', *Review of Economics and Statistics*, Vol. 47, pp. 55-64.

Keeble, D.E. (1976), *Industrial Location and Planning in the United Kingdom,* London, Methuen.

Losch, A. (1954), *The Economics of Location*, New Haven, Yale University Press.

Mohring, H. (1961), 'Land values and the measurement of highway benefits', *Journal of Political Economy,* Vol. 69, pp. 236-49.

Moses, L.N. (1962), 'Towards a theory of intra-urban wage differentials and their influence on travel behaviour', *Papers of the Regional Science Association*, Vol. 9, pp. 53-63.

O'Sullivan, P. (1981), *Geographical Economics*, Harmondsworth, Penguin.

Palander, T. (1935), *Beitrage zur Standortotheoria*, Uppsala, Almquist and Wiksells, Boktrykeri.

Rees, A. and Shultz, G.P. (1970), *Workers and Wages in an Urban Labour Market*, Chicago, Chicago University Press.

Richardson, H.W. (1977), *The New Urban Economics and Alternatives*, London, Pion.

Richardson, H.W. (1978), *Urban Economics*, Hinsdale, Dryden.

Scottish Council (Development and Industry) (1962), *Report on the Scottish Economy 1960/61*, Edinburgh, HMSO.

Segal, M. (1960), *Wages in the Metropolis*, Cambridge, Mass., Harvard University Press.

Smith, A. (1776), *The Wealth of Nations*, Harmondsworth, Penguin edition, 1970.

Thomson, J.M. (1974), *Modern Transport Economics*, Harmondsworth, Penguin.

von Thünen, J.H. (1826), *Der Isolirte Staat in Beziehung auf Nationale-Konomie und Landwirkschaft*, Stuttgart, Gustav Fischer, 1966 reprint.

Townroe, P.M. (1971), *Industrial Location Decisions: A Study in Management Behaviour*, Centre for Urban and Regional Studies, University of Birmingham.

Trade and Industry Sub-Committee of the House of Commons Expenditure Committee (1973), *Regional Development Incentives Report*, House of Commons Paper 85, London, HMSO.

Vickerman, R.W. (1980), *Spatial Economic Behaviour*, London, Macmillan.

3 The Demand for Transport

3.1 The demand for transport

Chapter 2 looked at the interrelationship between land-use patterns and transport; it thus offered some insights into a few of the factors influencing the demand for transport services. In particular, the chapter laid stress on the derived nature of the demand for the vast majority of transport services, and it is this feature of demand which explains another characteristic of the transport market.

One of the most pronounced characteristics of the demand for transport, for instance, is its regular fluctuation over time. In urban areas, the demand for road space and public transport services is markedly higher in the early morning and late afternoon than during the rest of the day; in the interurban context the demand for passenger transport fluctuates regularly over a year with high seasonal peaks, while with international freight transport (especially shipping) there are long-term cycles in demand. This tendency for peaks and troughs in the demand for transport is a reflection of fluctuations in the demand for the final products made accessible by transport services. In general, people wish to go on holiday in the summer; hence the seasonal peak in the demand for coach, rail and air services, while business finds it helpful to operate standard hours (i.e. from 'nine-to-five') with the consequential concentration of commuter traffic. Longer-term fluctuations in the demand for shipping services reflect the state of business cycles in the trading nations – at the nadir of such cycles demand slumps, at the zenith it is extremely buoyant.

Despite these regular fluctuations, it has been suggested (for example, by Thomson, 1974) that over time, and in another sense, there has been a remarkable stability in the demand for travel, with households, for example, on average making roughly the same *number* of trips during a day albeit for different purposes or by different modes. There may be more leisure travel, but there are fewer work trips and greater use is now made of air transport and the motor-car at the expense of walking. It is suggested that this situation reflects the obvious fact that there is a limit to the time people have available for travel, especially if they are to enjoy the fruits of the activities at the final destinations.

More recent work on travel time budgets indicates that the situation is more complicated than this and that the constancies suggested above should be subjected to a much closer inspection. In the United Kingdom, for example, there is ample empirical evidence (see Gunn, 1981) that average travel times have increased steadily over the past quarter of a century. Explanations are difficult to find but one suggestion is that this is the result of rising incomes and that the constant time budget implied by Thomson only holds for *each* income group. Thus people are moved from low income groups with low travel time budgets to higher income groups with associated higher travel time budgets. Goodwin (1973) has shown that at the aggregate level time expenditure on travel per head increases roughly proportionally to income. Such findings emphasise the importance of time as well as conventional variables in travel demand analysis and, as we see in the following chapter, considerable emphasis is placed upon the role that time costs play in transport decision-making.

Given this rather general, aggregate background it is now relevant to look in much more detail at the actual influences and motivations which affect travel and transport related demand. It seems appropriate to begin by considering the simple demand function.

3.2 What factors influence demand?

It is generally considered that the demand for a commodity (D_a) is influenced by its price (P_a), the prices of other goods $(P_1, P_2 \ldots P_u)$ and the level of income (Y):

$$D_a = f(P_a, P_1, P_2, \ldots P_u, Y). \tag{3.1}$$

While this simple framework holds for transport, as for all other goods and services, there are refinements and detail which need to be highlighted if one is to gain an understanding of the way the transport market operates. The individual terms in the above are, in fact, not simple variables but rather represent complex compounds of several interacting factors. Price, for instance, is not simply the fare paid but must embrace all the other costs involved in obtaining the transport service (of which 'time costs', as we noted above, are generally held the most important), while it may not be total income which influences travel demand by individuals but rather income in excess of some threshold subsistence level. Further there is the need to be very clear on what exactly it is which is being demanded: is it a trip *per se* or is it something more specific than this, for example, a bus trip or a journey over a particular route? Quandt and Baumol (1966) have gone so far as to suggest that it is not transport at all which is being demanded but rather a bundle of transport services. (We look at this idea more fully in the context of forecasting in Chapter 9.)

These types of problems and issues are clearly difficulties which cannot be entirely circumvented in a general discussion of the influences affecting transport demand, but they should be borne in mind as we move on to look in more detail at some of the items contained in the demand function set out as equation 3.1.

The price of the transport service

As has been suggested above, the price of transport embraces considerably more than the simple money costs paid out in fares or haulage fees. In transport modelling and quantitative work these other components of price (i.e. time costs, waiting, insecurity, etc.) may be combined to form a generalised cost index of the type we discuss in Chapter 4, but here we concentrate on money prices and, in particular, on the sensitivity of transport users to the price of transport services.

Generalisations are obviously difficult, especially across all modes of transport, but in many cases it seems clear that price changes within certain limits have relatively little effect on the quantity of travel or transport services demanded. The demand for cargo shipping is, for example, very inelastic, in part because of the lack of close substitutes for shipping services, in part because of the inelastic nature of the demand for the raw materials frequently carried, and in part because of the relatively small importance of freight rates in the final selling price of cargoes.

Studies of urban public transport in a variety of countries also indicate relatively low price elasticities with a direct fare elasticity of around -0.3 being considered normal. Smith and MacIntosh (1974) looking at British municipal bus undertakings, for instance, produce figures ranging from -0.21 to -0.61, but the majority fall at the lower end of the spectrum (Table 3.4 offers some further estimates). McGillivany's (1970) suggestion of a figure of around -0.2 for bus trips in San Francisco and Lave's (1970) finding of a direct fare elasticity of -0.11 for transit trips in Chicago imply the fare elasticity in the United States may be slightly lower than in the UK. In Canada an elasticity of -0.33 is used as a rule of thumb by operators.

The effect of price change on private car transport must be divided between the effect on vehicle ownership and that specifically on vehicle use. Most UK studies of car ownership indicate an elasticity of about -0.3 with respect to vehicle price and -0.1 with respect to petrol price (Mogridge, 1978). American empirical work suggests a rather higher sensitivity (the Chase Econometrics Associates (1974) model, for example, implies a -0.88 purchase price elasticity and a -0.82 fuel price elasticity), but responsiveness is still very low. For car use, the evidence produced by Mogridge indicates an extremely low fuel price elasticity (of the order of -0.1) in the short term which, as we see below, may be attributed to changing patterns of household expenditure between vehicle ownership and use and people's perception of motoring costs. This general order of magnitude is confirmed by Bendtsen (1980) in a series of international comparisons. He finds that petrol price elasticity of demand for car use to be -0.08 in Australia for the period from 1955 to 1976; -0.07 in Britain for 1973/4; -0.08 in Denmark for 1973/4 and -0.12 for 1979/80, and -0.05 in the USA for the period from 1968 to 1975.

If we move to the other extreme of the transport market and look at international airline operations, a similar, though slightly less clear, picture emerges. Table 3.1 presents the results of an investigation of air travel across the North Atlantic conducted by Mutti and Murai (1977). The general impression is of price inelasticity but there is obvious variability between routes. Examinations of internal air traffic within the United States, however, produce much more varied results. Brown and Watkins (1968) and Gronau (1970) show a remarkable degree of consistency by producing price elasticities of -0.85 and -0.75 respectively but Jung and Fujii (1976) came to a somewhat different conclusion, namely, 'The empirical evidence suggests that demand for air travel for distances under 500 miles in the south east and south central portions of the US is price elastic.'

Table 3.1 Demand elasticities for air travel on the North Atlantic 1964–74 by country

Market	Income elasticity	Fare elasticity
Total	1.89	-0.89
United States	2.15	-0.99
United Kingdom	4.38	-0.40
Netherlands	1.77	-0.28
Italy	2.00	-0.72
Germany	2.71	-0.19
France	2.03	-0.14

Source: Mutti and Murai, 1977

The difficulty with all the above statistics is that they are elasticities averaged over several groups. In fact, the price elasticity of transport, as with the price elasticity of other goods, should ideally be set in a specific context. In the case of transport four broad types of classification are important.

(1) *Trip purpose* There is an abundance of evidence that the fare elasticity for certain types of trips is much higher than others. Business travel demand in particular seems to be relatively more insensitive to changes in transport price than other forms of trip. Kraft and Domenich (1970) found that public transport work trips exhibited a fare elasticity of − 0.17 in Boston (USA) compared with − 0.32 for shopping trips. These figures conform closely to those found by London Transport in this country. If we focus on the work that has looked at air traffic, Mutti and Murai (1977) attribute part of the variation they found in fare responsiveness on the North Atlantic to the fact that 'we expect personal travel to be more price elastic than business travel'. Straszheim (1978) subsequently provides confirmation of this view and isolates elasticities for different types of service. In particular he concludes, 'First class fares can be raised and will increase total revenue . . . The demand elasticity for standard economy service is about unity, and highest for peak period travel . . . The demand for discount and promotional fares is highly price elastic . . .' Quite clearly, therefore, it is dangerous to attempt to analyse transport demand without considering the specific type of trip being undertaken.

(2) *The methods of charging* Users of different forms of transport (or, sometimes, different services of the same mode) are often confronted with entirely different methods of payment. Consequently, their perception of the price of a journey may differ from the actual monies expended. Sherman (1967), for example, has suggested that motorists perceive very little of the true overall price of these trips because they base decisions on a limited concept of short-run marginal cost. As Harrison and Quarmby (1969) put it in a pre-decimal summary of the situation, 'Including fuel, oil, maintenance, tyres and mile-dependent depreciation, most private cars show a marginal cost of between 4d and 7d a mile. Various empirical methods indicate 'perceived' costs of between 2d and 4d a mile (in the period 1966-9).' Users of public transport, on the other hand, are usually made much more aware of the costs of their trip-making by the requirement to purchase a ticket, usually prior to beginning their journeys. Nevertheless, given the range of season tickets (which permit bulk-buying of journeys over a specific *route*) and 'travel card'

facilities (which permit bulk-buying of journeys over a specified *network*), the distinction is not a firm one. White's (1981) review of the empirical information available on travel cards, for example, points to a much lower price elasticity for travel card systems than for conventional single ticket cash payment systems.

(3) *The time period under consideration* As with other purchasing decisions, people confronted with a change in transport price may act rather differently in the ultra-short run, the short run and the long run. Immediate reaction in the ultra short term, to a public transport fare rise may be dramatic, with people, almost on principle, making far less use of services, but over a longer period they may soften and their resolve weaken with the result that the longer-run elasticity is much lower than ultra short-term observations would suggest. The ultra short-term elasticity may, therefore, be extremely high but short-lived. This type of situation may be less common than is sometimes thought and, indeed, the reverse response may result in the slightly longer period. In the short term, for example, people may appear relatively unresponsive to a price change either because they do not consider it a permanent change or because technical constraints limit their immediate actions. The demand for private car transport following the dramatic rise in oil prices in the 1970s provides an illustration of this latter type of phenomenon. The situation is well summarised by Mogridge (1978):

> We have seen in the effects of the oil crisis a very clear demonstration that the short-run effects of price are not at all the same as in the long-run. In the short run, people try to continue doing what they were doing before; in the long run they adjust their behaviour. In the short run, the price elasticity of petrol is low, -0.1; in the long run it is taken up by an adjustment in car size.

Table 3.2 presents the findings of US work in this field which reflect the differences in short-term and long-term responses to fuel price changes.

Table 3.2   Petrol consumption elasticities with respect to price

Study	Time period	Short-run elasticity	Long-run elasticity
Houthakker *et al.* (1974)	1963–72	-0.075	-0.24
Kennedy (1974)	1962–72	-0.465	-0.82
Reza and Spiro (1979)	1969–76	-0.210	-0.33

Similarly, when considering the effect of general rises on commuter travel costs, the necessity of having to make journeys to work is likely to result in minimal changes in travel patterns in the short term but over a longer period relocations of either residence or employment may produce a more dramatic effect. This implies that one must take care when assessing elasticity coefficients, and it is useful to remember that cross-sectional studies tend to offer estimates of long-run elasticity while time-series studies reflect short-term responses.

(4) *The absolute level of the price change* Elasticities are generally found to increase the longer the journey under consideration. This should not be seen simply as a function of distance but rather a reflection of the absolute magnitude of, say, a 10 per cent rise on a £5 fare compared with that on a £500 fare. It is also true that longer journeys are made less frequently, and thus people gather information about prices in a different way. Additionally, they often tend to involve leisure rather than business travel (as can be seen in Table 3.3); this suggests that distance may be picking up variations in trip purpose. In the air transport market, for example, DeVany (1974) found that price elasticity rose from -0.97 for a 440 mile trip in the USA to -1.13 for a 830 mile trip. For similar journeys Ippolito (1981) found the respective elasticities to be -0.525 and -1.0.

Table 3.3 Long distance trips in Merseyside/Yorkshire by purpose

Purpose	%
Pleasure	32
Visit friends etc.	25
Sport/entertainment	7
Holiday/forces leave	14
Shopping/personal business	6
Work	14
Other	1

Source: Edwards and Dennis, 1976

Income levels

While there is ample evidence that transport is a normal good in the sense that more is demanded at higher levels of income, this generalisation does not apply to all modes of transport nor to all situations. Income has been demonstrated to exert a positive influence over car ownership decisions (see section 3.6), but this in turn has produced an inverse relationship with public transport use. As incomes have risen and, with them, car ownership has become more widespread, public transport has in many situations proved to be an inferior good. Gwilliam and Mackie (1975) suggest that the long-run elasticity of demand with respect to income is of the order − 0.4 to − 1.0 for urban public transport trip making in the United Kingdom. (Elasticities of this general order of magnitude are supported by Litt (1975) in Canada and by Sohn (1975) using New York data.) Gwilliam and Mackie argue that although car ownership rises with income and hence some trips are diverted from public transport there is still a limited off-setting effect inasmuch as wealthier households make more trips in total.

The income elasticity of demand for many other modes of transport is seen to be relatively high. Table 3.1 has already revealed elasticities in the range 1.77 to 4.38 for North Atlantic air travel, while Taplin (1980) suggests a figure of the order of 2.1 for vacation air trips overseas from Australia. By its nature air travel is a high cost activity (the total costs involved are high even where mileage rates are low) so that income elasticities of this level are to be expected.

As with price, income changes exert somewhat different pressures on transport demand in the long run compared with the short. In general, it may be argued, a fall in income will produce a relatively dramatic fall in the level of demand, but as people readjust their expenditure patterns in the long term the elasticity is likely to be much lower. Looking at the responsiveness of car ownership levels to income changes, British and US studies suggest a short-term income elasticity of between 2.0 and 4.5 while in the long run it appears to fall to around 1.5 (see Button *et al.* (1982) for a survey). However, as with price elasticities, the relationships between long and short-term effects are not completely clear cut. Reza and Spira (1979), for example, produce an estimate of 0.6 for the short-run income elasticity of demand for petrol rising to 1.44 in the long run. If one assumes that petrol consumption is a proxy for trip-making, then one could attempt to justify this in terms of a slow reaction to changing financial circumstances – a reluctance, for example, to accept immediately the consequences of a fall in income. In fact, the situation is likely to be more complex than this since the long run may embrace changes in technology, and possibly locations, that alter the fuel consumption–trip-making relationship. Thus these figures may still be consistent with the initial hypothesis regarding the relative size of short and long-run income elasticities of demand for *travel*.

There is a growing literature on the possibility of a constant travel income budget akin to the travel time budget mentioned in section 3.1 (see Gunn, 1981) with households tending to spend a fixed proportion of their income on transport. Zahavi (1977), for example, when examining data from a wide sample of urban transport users, noticed that the proportion of disposable income spent on cars by car-owning households at any income level appears to be approximately constant at a given moment of time. (UK data suggests a proportion of around $15\frac{1}{2}$ per cent – slightly larger for low incomes – for the period 1971–75.) The evidence for bus transport is less clear, but Mogridge (1978) suggests that while the proportion of disposable household income spent on bus travel seems to rise with income, a constant proportion still emerges if adjustments are made for the number of people in each household. In the longer term there is evidence at the aggregate level that over the past twenty-five years or so there has been a steady increase in the overall proportion of income or disposable income allocated to travel in the UK. (This contrasts to a more or less constant proportion in Canada and the United States.) This may, though, be explained in terms of rising income levels but constant proportional travel budgets within each income group. The general conclusion about the idea that some overall budget mechanism governs individual travel decisions, however, must be that, to date, the evidence available still leaves many questions unanswered and the theory is still largely unproven.

The price of other transport services

The demand for any particular transport service is likely to be influenced by the actions of competitive and complementary suppliers. (Strictly speaking, it is also influenced by prices in all other markets operating in the economy but, with the possible exceptions of the land market, which was discussed in Chapter 2, and electronic communications, the importance of these is less great.) We have already touched upon the importance of motoring costs *vis-à-vis* the demand for public transport services and more is said on this topic later in the chapter. Moreover, there are the cross-price effects between modes of public transport. Table 3.4 presents the results from a number of different studies looking at elasticities of demand (both own fare and cross-fare) for transport in Greater London during the period 1970–75. The variation in results generally reflects the adoption of alternative estimation procedures and time-lag allowances. One of the more interesting points is the almost total insensitivity of the demand for urban car use to the fare levels of both bus and rail public transport modes. This fact, which has been observed in virtually all studies of urban public transport, is the main reason that attempts by city transport authorities to reduce or contain car travel by subsiding public transport fares have, in the main, proved unsuccessful.

Table 3.4   Greater   London   estimated   Monday–Friday   fare elasticities, 1970–75

Study	Elasticity of	With respect to	
		Bus	Rail
Fairhurst and			
Morris (1975)	Bus	−0.60	0.25
	Rail	0.25	−0.40
Glaister (1976)	Bus	−0.56	0.30
	Rail	1.11	−1.00
Collings, Rigby			
and Welsby (1977)	Bus	−0.405	n.a.
Lewis (1978)	Peak road		
	traffic	0.025	0.056

Source: Glaister and Lewis, 1978

Table 3.4 suggests that there is likely to be more switching of demand between public transport modes as a result of one changing its fare structure than between that mode and private transport.

In other transport markets the cross-elasticity of demand may be higher, both between operators of the same mode of transport and between modes themselves. Recently, price reduction in non-conference shipping lines has attracted considerable traffic away from the cartel carriers. Similarly, scheduled airlines have experienced a contraction of demand as reduced rate operators have entered the market.

Evidence on the cross-price elasticity of complementary transport services, such as feeder links to longer distance trunk hauls, is scant. The expansion of the motorway network has, by reducing motorway travel costs, certainly increased the demand for certain feeder roads while at the same time reducing it on competing routes. The exact implications of such network effects are much more difficult to trace out than changes in modal split but, in practical terms, are important features of the transport system.

One of the items missing from the equation 3.1 and not mentioned to date, but which is often included in elementary discussion of demand, is the 'catch-all' variable, tastes. While there may be circumstances when such a term could and, indeed, should be included in the demand function, in general, tastes are more likely to influence the actual *form* of the demand equation. Consequently, a change in tastes may be seen to affect the relationships between demand and the explanatory variables rather than result in some movement along a demand curve following the pattern of an established relationship.

The economic meaning of 'tastes' is seldom made clear, but in practice they seem to embrace all influences on demand not covered by the three previous headings. Over time tastes in transport certainly have changed. Burrell (1972), for instance, has emphasised the increased car orientation of society in private transport while in freight transport the changing structure of the national economy (especially the switch from basic heavy industry to light industry producing high value, low weight products) has shifted the emphasis from price to other aspects of transport service. Both of these changes must to some extent be related to rising standards of living. With more wealth and greater free time there is likely to be an enhanced desire to benefit from the greater freedom and flexibility offered by private transport. A change in location patterns is also possible with larger residential plots away from urban centres now becoming attractive. It is also noticeable from empirical studies that public transport demand is sensitive to changes in service quality, especially to any reduction in the speed or frequency of services. Again this fact reflects the decreased importance attached to the purely monetary dimension. Market research in the West Midlands, for example, revealed that only 27.1 per cent of people felt that keeping fares down would be the greatest improvement to local public transport; the remainder looked for service quality improvements, e.g. 14.6 per cent for greater reliability, 10.4 per cent for higher frequency, 10.4 per cent for more bus shelters, 10.0 per cent for cleaner vehicles, etc. (see Isaac, 1979).

An extensive survey by Lago *et al.* (1981) examined a wide range of international studies concerned with urban public transport service elasticities. The general conclusion that services will generate less than proportional increases in passenger and revenue (i.e. $E_s \langle 1$) would seem to contradict the above findings but this may be misleading. To begin with the survey looks at a number of service quality attributes in isolation rather than a package of service features. It also admits that many of the services sought by potential public transport users are qualitative rather than quantitative and, hence, are not amenable to the types of analysis reviewed. The survey also highlights the fact that service quality is far more important when the initial level of service is poor; the general elasticities found for peak period ridership, for instance, are much lower than those for the off-peak. The evidence presented suggests that service headway is one of the more important service variables; the studies examined indicates an elasticity of the order of -0.42 compared with, for example,

−0.29 for in-vehicle bus travel time.

The available evidence suggests that today low price is also no longer the dominant determinant of freight modal choice. In a survey conducted by the Price Commission (1978), for instance, it was found that only in 52 per cent of cases did consignors elect to use the cheapest road haulage operator available for local trips, 77 per cent for intra-regional trips and 64 per cent for trunk-hauls. Many were so unconcerned about finding the lowest price that competitive quotations were not sought.

What is it that influences demand for a particular haulier in these circumstances? A survey of 5000 members of the old Traders Road Transport Association conducted in 1958 asked what were the six most important factors in their transport choice: while 50 per cent quoted cost, *over* 70 per cent went for speed of delivery and certainty of timing. The answers given to the Price Commission in a more recent survey are reproduced in Table 3.5. The emphasis placed upon vehicle suitability is seen to reflect customer concern about such factors as weather protection, systems for securing loads and compatability of vehicle with product. These are concerns unlikely to have been of paramount importance when heavy industry dominated the economy.

Table 3.5   Service features consignors require from road hauliers

Factor	Local (%)	Intra-regional (%)	Trunk (%)
Vehicle suitability	43	45	69
Quick delivery	29	36	2
Prompt collection	10	12	14
'Good reputation'	15	5	1
Access to handling facilities	8	4	—
Condition of vehicles	—	—	8

Source: Price Commission, 1978

Many industrialists prefer to use their own vehicle fleets rather than engage public hauliers despite considerable cost disadvantages (Sharp, 1971). The reasons for this utilisation of high cost transport are similar to those used by other consignors who select between hauliers (see Table 3.6). Once again it is service quality which dominates the decision process, consignors seeking reliability, control and speed in preference to a low price. Of course, this should not be interpreted to mean that price is of no consequence but rather that its importance has diminished over time as the nature of industrial production has changed.

Table 3.6　Reasons for the maintenance and use of an own account fleet

Factor	Score
Reliability	14.9
Control	13.0
Customer relations	9.4
Speed of delivery	9.2
Flexibility	7.8
Costs v. prices	7.4
Ability of 'own account' to meet timing constraints	6.6
Price is subordinate to service considerations	6.5
Specialised capability	5.5
Speed of response	5.1
Adaptability	3.6
Consistency	3.5
Avoidance of damage or contamination	3.4
Security	2.6
Other (not financial)	1.1
Other (financial)	0.5
	100.0

Source:　Department of Transport, 1979

3.3　The notion of a 'need' for transport

The demand function indicates what people would buy given a particular budget constraint, but it is often argued that allocation of resources on this basis results in inequalities and unfairness because of differences in household income or other circumstances. There are, thus, some advocates of the idea that transport services, or at least some of them, should be allocated according to 'need' rather than effective demand. The concept of need is seldom defined (or at best rather imprecisely so (see Williams, 1974), but seems to be closely concerned with the notion of merit goods – i.e. needs '... considered so meritorious that their satisfaction is provided for through the public budget over and above what is provided for through the market and paid for by private buyers' (Musgrave, 1959). The idea is that just as everyone in a civilised society is entitled to expect a certain standard of education, medical cover, etc., so they are entitled to enjoy a certain minimum standard of transport provision.

One can point to a number of transport policy initiatives which are based upon this idea. The Road Traffic Act 1930, for example, introduced, besides other things, road service licences into the bus industry which embraced the notion of *public need*. The Traffic Commissioners interpreted this to mean the provision of a comprehensive network of services for an area irrespective of the effective demand for specific routes. Licences were granted on this basis and operators cross-subsidised the unremunerative services with revenue from the more profitable ones. More explicit were the social service grants given to the railways under the 1968 Transport Act whereby 222 services were subsidised for social reasons, once again despite deficit effective demand for their services. Additionally, the government has, for many years, provided both capital and operating cost subsidies to assist the shipping and air services to the remoter islands of Scotland. The grants and subsidies given by local authorities, both urban and rural, are also, to a considerable extent, meant to ensure that transport services meet the needs of the local community.

This notion of need rather than effective demand raises two important issues. Firstly, exactly what is the nature of 'need' in reality and secondly, if one accepts that the concept has some operational meaning, how can it be incorporated into economic analysis? We look at these two questions in turn.

The need for adequate transport provision stems from the idea that people should have access to an acceptable range of facilities (Stanley and Farrington, 1981). It is, therefore, essentially a 'normative' concept. Transport is seen as exerting a major influence on the quality of the lives of people and a certain minimum quality should be ensured. The White Paper on *Transport Policy* (Department of Transport, 1977) emphasises this view of mobility: 'The social needs for transport also rank high – the needs of people to have access to their work, shops, recreation and the range of activities on which civilised society depends.' Defining the exact level of mobility in this context is difficult, but it is helpful to look at the groups who, for one reason or another, seem in need of transport services in addition to those that would be forthcoming in the market.

The most obvious group is the poor who cannot afford transport. Transport expenditure forms a substantial part of a household budget and, consequently, those on the lowest income must make fewer trips, shorter trips or trips on inferior modes of transport. A major problem is that as income levels rise, in general, there is a tendency towards higher car ownership leaving only depleted and expensive public transport facilities for those at the lower end of the income distribution. A household with a car tends, for instance, to make on average about 300 fewer bus journeys a year than comparable households without a car. But there are also wider issues, in that this change in the transport sector has implications for population distribution. In particular, higher car ownership in rural areas, and the resultant reduction in the *demand* for local public transport, has put pressure on rural bus and rail services. Between 1970 and 1974 the National Bus Company, which is responsible for most rural stage services in England and Wales, reduced its bus kilometres by 7 per cent. This, in turn, has been one of the causes of rural depopulation. The question then arises as to whether society, in general, needs a balance between urban and rural society.

While inadequate income poses one problem, there are other groups in society that are often felt to need assistance. The old, infirm and children are obvious examples where irrespective of income, effective demand may be felt an inadequate basis upon which to allocate transport resources. The available evidence suggests that only about 10 per cent of households in the aged or disabled category have private transport at hand. Even when a household does own a car (or has one made available through employment agreements) there are still members of it who may be deemed as in need of additional transport. A study of mobility by Hillman *et al.* (1973), for instance, found that 70 per cent of young married women in the outer metropolitan area of London had no car available for their everyday use – even 30 per cent of those qualified to drive were in this position. There are arguments, therefore, that these groups are in need of adequate and inexpensive public transport services (or special transport provision in the case of the disabled) and that the normal market mechanism is inadequate in this respect. The Lincolnshire Structure Plan of 1979 offers a fairly typical example of the views of many local authorities on this point when it is argued that '... it is essential that provision should be made to meet the needs of members of non-car owning households and others without personal access to a private car'.

If one accepts the notion that need is, in certain contexts, the relevant concept rather than effect demand, then, for practical purposes, this idea requires integration into more standard positive economic theory. (It should perhaps be noted that many people do not accept the idea of 'need' as an allocative device but advocate tackling problems of low income or disadvantage at their source through measures such as direct income transfers, but this is an issue outside our present discussion.) Perhaps the simplest method of reconciling the difficulty is to treat the monies paid out by government and other agencies in subsidies to social transport services, as the effective demand of *society* for the services. One can then perceive the situation as analogous to that of conventional consumer theory. Just as effective demand reflects the desire of an individual to purchase a particular transport service so government's response to need reflects society's desire to purchase particular transport services for certain of its members. This certainly seems to be the position adopted in connection with the social service subsidies given to British Rail under the 1968 Transport Act.

3.4 The valuation of travel time savings

The importance of travel time in transport economics should by now be apparent. While the action of travel involves some time costs, it is perhaps more useful to consider travel time in a chapter on demand and benefits rather than costs. This is because travel or transport time savings are normally considered to be a major component of any scheme designed to improve transport efficiency. As we see in Table 3.7 time savings form the major component of inter-urban road investment benefits – a situation also found in most fields of passenger transport. For reasons of comparability with other forms of benefit, a vast amount of energy has gone into devising methods of placing money values on such benefits.

Table 3.7   Benefits from an average road improvement scheme

Benefit	*%*
Accident savings	20
Vehicle operating cost savings	0
Working time savings	
Car	26
Light goods vehicles	11
Heavy goods vehicles	11
Buses	3
Non-work time savings	
Car	23
Buses	6
Total	100

Source: Department of the Environment, 1976, Vol. 2

Two quite distinct methodologies have been developed for time evaluation, the distinction being made between time saved in the course of employment and time saved during non-work travel (including commuter trips when fixed working hours are involved). The distinction is drawn because work time involves lorry drivers, seamen, pilots, etc. not simply in giving up leisure but also in incurring some actual disutility from the work undertaken. Hence, if they could do the same amount of work in less time these people would be able to enjoy more leisure and *also* suffer less disutility (or the employer must pay them more to encourage a continuation of the same work hours with a higher output). Savings in non-work time do not, by definition, reduce the disutility associated with work and, consequently, although more leisure may be enjoyed, they are likely to be valued below work travel-time savings.

The valuation of work travel time (which embraces all journeys made when travellers are earning their living) is made simpler if we accept the traditional economic idea that workers are paid according to the value of their marginal revenue product. On this basis, the amount employers pay workers must be sufficient to compensate them for the marginal time and disutility associated with doing the job. Thus it becomes possible to equate the value of a marginal saving in work travel time with the marginal wage rate (plus related social payments and overheads). An alternative way of arriving at this cost savings approach is by reflecting upon the opportunity costs involved – as Benjamin Franklin once said, 'Remember that time is money.' Time savings at work permit a greater output to be produced within a given time period which, again drawing on the marginal productivity theory of wage determination, will be reflected in the marginal wages paid. Official UK policy is to value work travel time savings as the national average wage for the class of transport user concerned plus the associated costs of social insurance paid by the employer and a premium, added to reflect overheads – a total addition of 31.6 per cent in 1978.

It has been suggested that the cost savings approach outlined above only offers a lower limit to the valuation of work time and that in some circumstances time savings may be of much greater value. Concorde's manufacturers, for instance, argued that the value of business executives' time savings are as much as three times their salaries because supersonic travel reduces the amount of time that overhead capital associated with executive activity is idle. A doubling of salary rate is suggested for similar reasons by British airlines. Such estimates are, however, difficult to substantiate either theoretically or by recourse to empirical investigation.

A major problem with the wage equivalence approach is that it assumes employees consider the disutility of travel during work to be the same as the disutility of other aspects of their work which they may be required to undertake if travel time is reduced. In many instances workers may consider the travel much less arduous than these alternative tasks. This implies that savings in work-time travel should, in such cases, be valued at less than the wage rate plus additions. Also some people may view travel time as highly productive –

many rail and air travellers, for instance, certainly work on their journeys – suggesting that reduced travel time would not significantly alter output. The wage rate ceases to be a useful measure of work travel time savings in such cases.

While labour economics provides a useful foothold to obtain values of work travel time, rather more empiricism is required in the evaluation of non-work travel time. The behavioural approach involves considering trade-off situations which reflect the willingness of travellers to pay in order to save time. In other words, if a person chooses to pay X pence to save Y minutes then he is revealing an implicit value of time equal to at least X/Y pence per minute. Empirical studies attempting to value non-work travel time have looked at a number of different trade-off situations (Harrison and Quarmby (1969) offer a survey), notably when travellers have a choice among:

(1) Route;
(2) Mode of travel;
(3) Speed of travel (by a given mode over a given route);
(4) Location of home and work; and
(5) Destination of travel.

The standard approach in these trade-off studies is to employ a simple equation of the general form:

$$P_1 = \frac{e^y}{1+e^y} \text{ where } y = \alpha_0 + \alpha_1 (t_1 - t_2) + \alpha_2 (c_1 - c_2) \qquad (3.2)$$

where P_1 = probability of choosing mode (route, etc.) 1;
y = choice of mode (route, etc.); takes value of 1 for mode (route, etc) 1 and 0 for mode (route, etc) 2;
e = exponential constant;
t_i = door-to-door travel time by the ith mode (route, etc); $i = 1,2$;
c_i = door-to-door travel cost by the ith mode (route, etc); $i = 1,2$;
α_1, α_2 and α_3 = constants to be estimated.

A value of time is then inferred by looking at changes in the dependent variable which result from a unit change in either the time or the cost difference. Strictly it may be found as the ratio α_1/α_2 in equation 3.2.

Many of the early studies of non-work travel time concentrated on urban commuter trips (see Table 3.8 for a summary of such work) because there was pressure at the time to provide information for cost-benefit analysis of urban transport investment plans. In consequence, mode and route choice evaluation techniques were developed to a high level of mathematical sophistication. Early work by Beesley (1965) specifically employed discriminant analysis to examine the journey to work mode choices of employees at the Ministry of Transport during 1965/6. This technique essentially finds the trade-off value of time that minimises the number of misallocations of commuters to alternative modes. Beesley found that commuter trip time savings were valued at between 30 and 50 per cent of the gross personal income of the commuters. One of the main problems with this pioneering study is that it failed to isolate on-vehicle travel time from the other components of journey time (e.g. waiting and walking time). The defect was subsequently remedied in a larger study of mode choice in Leeds undertaken by Quarmby (1967) which embraced seven variables including walking and waiting time as well as on-vehicle time. The findings indicate that savings in walking and waiting times are valued at between two and three times savings in on-vehicle time and that, on average, time is valued by both bus and car users as between 21 and 25 per cent of the wage rate (see Table 3.8).

Lee and Dalvi (1969) adopted a less direct approach using questionnaires, rather than looking at actual choices, to discover the level of fare increase required before passengers switched from one mode of public transport to an alternative. Interestingly, in Manchester it was found that on-vehicle time, walking time and waiting time were not separately important and travellers did not distinguish among them. Overall it was estimated that non-work travel time was being valued at 15–45 per cent of hourly income.

While most urban studies have tended to focus on mode choice decisions, the evaluation of non-work inter-urban travel time has tended to concentrate rather more on route and speed choice situations – although imperfections in travellers' knowledge of the latter make speed choice trade-offs suspect. Pioneering work on route choice by Claffey *et al.* (1961) looked at choices made between tolled and free roads in the USA and attempted to allow for differing accident rates and levels of driver discomfort when assessing the time–money cost trade-offs. Mathematical weakness limits the value of this specific model but subsequent reworking suggests time differences are unimportant in route choices of this type. Thomas (1967), again using USA data, conducted a study on a similar basis and here time differences did appear significant and he estimates that non-work travel time appeared to be valued at between 40 and 83 per cent of average income. Dawson and Everall (1972), using a further modification and looking at route choices of motorists travelling between

Table 3.8 *Some values of time found in trade-off studies*

Source	Year of data collection	Mode	Value of unit of time saved (per hr/person at 1968 prices)		Value of time as % of hourly income
Commuter and non-work travel time					
Merlin and Barbier (see Hensher and Hotchkiss, 1974)	1961	Public transport/ car		27	—
		Car/public transport		48	—
Quarmby (1967)	1966	Car/bus	min.value	7 }	20–25
			max.value	25 }	
Beesley (1965)	1963	Public transport	min.value	12	
			max.value	19	} 30–50
		Car	min.value	12	
			max.value	25	
Lee and Dalvi (1969)	1966	Car		66	} 15–45
		Public transport		40	
Dawson and Everall (1972)	1969	Car	small	26	—
			medium	53	—
			large	119	—
Hensher and Hotchkiss (1974)	1970	Ferry		17	—
Pure leisure time					
Dawson and Smith (1959)	1957	Car	min.value	50	—
			max.value	68	—
Dawson and Everall (1972)	1969	Car	medium	72	—
			large	75	—
Work time					
Dawson and Everall (1972)	1969	Car	medium	201 }	75
			large	298 }	

Source: Jennings and Sharp, 1976

Rome and Cansnello and between Milan and Modena where autostrada offered alternatives to ordinary trunk roads, found that observed trade-offs indicate that commuting and other non-work travel time was valued at about 75 per cent of the average wage rate.

It is clear from the limited selection of studies cited above that non-work time savings are, indeed, valued below the wage rate, but it is equally clear that the actual values obtained from the behavioural studies are extremely sensitive to the assumptions made and the estimation technique employed. Hensher (1979) goes further and, in particular, points to the rather strong assumptions that are implicit in the not uncommon practice of taking time values obtained from, say, a mode choice study and employing them in route or speed choice situations. He also questions whether enough consideration is given to the composition of time savings beyond the in-vehicle/waiting time split and, in particular, to preferences between constant journey speed (with a lower average) and faster, variable speeds (with a higher average).

In Britain the Department of Transport and its predecessors have since the 1960s recommended standard values of time for transport analysis purposes (see Table 3.9). The use of standard figures is to encourage uniformity in investment appraisal. While the work–travel time figures are open to only minor criticisms (and even quite major errors here would seem unlikely to distort decisions – see Department of Transport, 1978), the use of standard non-work travel time values has met with more serious criticism.

Table 3.9   Official UK values of time for transport investment appraisal purposes

	Pence per hour	
Time category	*1975*	*1976*
Working time		
Car driver	331	379
Car passenger	287	332
Rail passenger	357	407
Bus passenger	168	196
Underground passenger	313	360
Heavy goods vehicle occupant	155	178
Light goods vehicle occupant	139	158
Bus driver	166	191
Bus conductor	158	182
Leisure time		
In-vehicle time	35	36
Walking and waiting time	70	72

Source: Department of the Environment, 1976 and Department of Transport, 1978

Empirically, non-work travel time values have been shown to be correlated with income level (see Table 3.8), but the official approach until recently has been to use an *average* value across all income levels. The argument supporting this 'equity' value is that if time values were directly varied with income this would tend to bias project selection towards projects favouring the higher income groups. In evaluation, the travel time savings of such groups would automatically be weighted more heavily than those of the less well-off. The Leitch Committee, however, rejected this line of argument because it is not consistent with the way other aspects of transport investment are evaluated. Since the overall distributional effects of transport investment may be treated more directly in the appraisal process (see Chapter 9), the notion of 'equity' values was rejected in favour of income-based time evaluations.

Even if generally acceptable values of travel time could be obtained there are still difficulties associated with using them. One of the major problems is that some projects can result in a small number of large time savings while others produce a multitude of extremely small savings. The problem becomes one of deciding whether sixty one-minute savings are as valuable as (or more valuable than) one saving of an hour's duration. It could be argued that travellers, especially over longer routes, tend not to perceive small time savings or cannot utilise such time savings (see Tipping, 1968). If this is so it would tend to make urban transport schemes appear less attractive *vis-à-vis* inter-urban ones because the main benefits of urban improvements have been small time savings spread over thousands of commuters. One suggestion is that a zero value should be adopted for small travel time savings with a positive value only being employed once a threshold level of saving has been reached (say ten minutes). This ignores the fact that small time savings may, in some circumstances, be combined with existing periods of free or idle time to permit substantial increases in output or in leisure enjoyment. Further, if there are non-linearities in the value of travel time this would imply that widely used trade-off methods of time evaluation based upon *average* time savings must be giving biased estimates of the value of travel time. The debate over the handling of small travel time savings is unlikely to be resolved easily.

Transport studies in less developed countries tend to adopt the convention that while work travel time savings should be given a monetary value based upon the cost-savings approach (although the wage rate is generally modified to allow for imperfections in the local labour market), savings in non-work travel time – especially in rural areas – are given a zero value (Howe, 1976). The justification for this is that the prime objective of improving transport infrastructure in the third world is to assist in economic growth and thus the emphasis should be exclusively concentrated on economically productive schemes – leisure time is not seen as 'productive'. Thomas (1979) has pointed to a serious anomaly, however, when this argument is carried into practice. While non-work travel time savings in rural areas are ignored, savings in vehicle operating costs for such travel is not. Not only is this inconsistent but it also has important distributional implications because the main beneficiaries of low operating costs are almost invariably high income car owners.

3.5 The demand for car ownership

Car ownership in Great Britain has risen considerably since the First World War with only brief halts during periods of major military conflict and occasional decelerations in the trend during periods of macroeconomic depression (see Table 3.10). This upward trend is not unique to Britain but is also to be found in all other countries irrespective of their state of economic development or the nature of their political institutions. The upward trend in car ownership is the result of both the considerable benefits which accompany car availability (notably improved access and greater flexibility of travel) and the long-term increases in income enjoyed by virtually all countries since the Second World War. The 'demonstration effect' has tended to accelerate the process in less developed countries as attempts are made to emulate the consumption patterns of more affluent states.

Table 3.10   Car ownership growth in Great Britain

Year	Cars and vans (thousands)	Cars and vans per capita
1930	1 056	0.0237
1935	1 477	0.0324
1940	1 423	0.0303
1945	1 487	0.0311
1950	2 258	0.0459
1955	3 526	0.0712
1960	5 526	0.1085
1965	8 917	0.1692
1970	11 515	0.2137
1975	13 747	0.2529
1976[a]	14 047	0.2585
1977[a]	13 993	0.2585
1978[a]	14 070	0.2590

[a] Not strictly comparable because of changes in data collection

Source: Department of Transport, *Transport Statistics, Great Britain, 1968–78*, London, HMSO, 1979

Considerable effort has been focused on exploring both the rate of increase in vehicle ownership and reasons why this should differ between countries and between areas within a single country. Information on the underlying demand functions is sought in Great Britain for a variety of reasons. Car manufacturers need to know the nature of changing demands for new vehicles, both within the country and within their export markets, and to be able to forecast likely changes in the type of vehicles which are wanted. While work in this area often sheds some useful light on the workings of the car market, it is only of limited use to transport economists (see Button, Pearman and Fowkes, 1982).

Central government is more interested in the aggregate number of vehicles in the country, mainly for road planning purposes, but also, to a lesser extent, to assist the Treasury in its fiscal duties. The theory underlying much of the early forecasting work in this area is closely akin to the management theory of a 'product life' cycle, where a product has a predetermined sales pattern almost independent of traditional economic forces, although taste and costs are not altogether absent from the model. The logistic curve fitting model developed by the Transport and Road Research Laboratory (TRRL), in its basic form, treats per capita vehicle ownership as a function of time with the ownership level following a symmetric, sigmoid growth path through time until an eventual saturation level is approached (Tanner, 1978). Broadly, it is argued that long-term growth in ownership follows a predictable diffusion process. Initially, high production costs and unfamiliarity will keep sales low, but after a period, if the product is successful, economies of scale on the supply side coupled with a 'Veblenesque effect' on the demand side would result in the take-off of a comparatively rapid diffusion process. Finally, there is a tailing-off as the market becomes saturated and everyone wishing to own a car does so.

The TRRL extrapolative approach provided relatively good forecasts in the 1960s, but it has tended to be less reliable in more recent years (see Table 3.11) and to suffer from a tendency towards over-prediction. While some of the difficulties may be associated with problems of estimating key parameters such as the ultimate saturation level, or with the correct configuration of the growth curve – in later work a power function replaced the logistic – at least one school of thought rejects the underlying extrapolative philosophy as inadequate (Bates *et al.*, 1978). In particular, it is argued, car ownership forecasting should be based upon explicit economic variables such as income and vehicle prices rather than 'proxy' variables such as time. The TRRL forecasting framework has attempted to meet this

Table 3.11   Comparison of actual car ownership and TRRL forecasts

Year of publication	Base year for calculation	Forecast annual growth in cars per capita 1975 ÷ Actual annual growth in cars per capita 1975	Forecast car pool 1975 ÷ Actual car pool 1975
1962	1960	1.14	1.13
1965	1964	1.57	1.57
1967	1966	1.67	1.68
1969	1968	1.84	1.84
1970	1969	1.66	1.66
1972	1971	1.62	1.58

Source: Button *et al.*, 1980

criticism by incorporating economic variables, but both a time trend is still retained and the income and vehicle operating cost elasticities are not estimated internally within the model but derived from 'external' sources. The demand model developed by Bates and others, as part of a larger Regional Highway Traffic Model (RHTM), in contrast is based entirely upon 'causal' variables and all the relevant elasticities are estimated directly within the forecasting model.

At the national level the RHTM relates car ownership per household (expressed mathematically in logit form) to household income. The data used is not the time series registration statistics employed by the TRRL but rather a series of cross-sectional sets of statistics obtained from annual Family Expenditure Surveys and other sources. For forecasting purposes it is necessary to be able to predict reliably the level and distribution of future income. Additionally, it is recognised that changes in motoring costs will influence ownership levels, so rather than deflate changes in money income over time by changes in retail prices to obtain a real income prediction, money income is deflated by an index of anticipated motoring cost changes to give a projection of 'car purchasing income'. Simply, it is assumed that a £1 rise in income will have the same positive effect on car ownership as a £1 fall in car prices. The approach also concentrates on the probability of households having a certain level of vehicle ownership rather than, as with the TRRL model, on forecasting the national average ownership level; this conforms more closely to other recent trends in transport demand forecasting (see Chapter 8). At present the TRRL and RHTM approaches to forecasting car ownership are used in parallel, and official forecasts tend to be based

Table 3.12   Cars per hundred population in United Kingdom regions

Area	1966	1976	1978[a]
UK	18	26	26
North	15	21	21
Yorkshire and Humberside	15	23	22
East Midlands	18	26	25
East Anglia	21	30	30
South-east	21	29	29
South-west	20	30	30
West Midlands	20	26	27
North-west	15	23	23
England	18	26	27
Wales	18	26	25
Scotland	14	20	20
Northern Ireland	16	21	23

[a] Not strictly comparable because of changes in the data base
Source: Central Statistical Office, *Regional Statistics*, London, HMSO, 1979

upon compromise projections with quite wide ranges of possible ownership levels being forecast within upper and lower limits.

Differences in the geographical demand for car ownership interest transport planners both because they need to be able to forecast future demand for links in the local road network and because, where ownership is low, social commitments may require that alternative public transport is provided. At the national level there are quite marked differences in ownership levels, as we see in Table 3.12. The nation can broadly be divided into three regions: the South-west, South-east and East Anglia have a high propensity for car ownership, the West Midlands, Wales and East Midlands form a middle grouping, while the North-west, Yorkshire and Humberside, the North and Scotland have the lowest incidence of car ownership. This general trend towards lower car ownership levels as one moves north has been observed in many studies of the car market but no really satisfactory explanation of the phenomenon exists. It has been observed, however, that if the regions are broken down by their constituent counties then those with low car ownership tend to incorporate substantial urban concentrations and many have a major industrial component in their economies (Button, 1980). This association of urban concentration with low car ownership is also found at the local level and in Table 3.13, which looks at the situation in West Yorkshire, a clear trichotomy emerges among household car ownership levels in urban, suburban and rural areas even after allowing for variations in income levels.

Table 3.13 Household car ownership in West Yorkshire

Area	Household income							
	Less than £1041	£1041–2080	£2081–3120	£3121–4160	£4161–5200	£5201–6240	£6241–7800	More than £7800
Urban	0.07	0.25	0.55	0.68	0.84	0.95	1.16	1.47
Dormitory	0.15	0.53	0.80	1.03	1.41	1.65	1.50	2.07
Small town and rural	0.07	0.34	0.69	0.91	1.03	1.38	1.48	1.83

Source: Button *et al.*, 1982

It seems likely that these spatial variations at the local level may, once allowance has been made for differing income and demographic factors, be explained in terms of the quality of local transport services. Good, uncongested roads combined with poor public transport increases the demand, *ceteris paribus*, for private car ownership. Regional econometric studies of car ownership have attempted to reflect this cost of transport effect by incorporating variables such as residential density in their models (it being argued that a densely populated area is normally well served by public transport while motoring is adversely affected by the higher levels of traffic congestion). More sophisticated local models have shown the frequency of public transport services to influence car ownership rates (Fairhurst, 1975). In West Yorkshire it has been found that car ownership rises as the generalised cost of public transport trips increases (Button *et al.*, 1982). If these studies are correct then there is some evidence that the long-term growth in car ownership may be contained by improving public transport services although from a policy point of view the overall cost of such actions needs to be fully assessed.

3.6 Further reading and references
Readers interested in the influence of different variables on transport demand should refer to the specific references in the text; these generally extend the analysis presented here by outlining various methods of estimating elasticities etc. Discussion of 'need' is usually rather unprecise but Stanley and Farrington (1981) offer a useful and more detailed assessment of measurement problems. The literature on time savings is vast but Jennings and Sharp (1976) is not only a very clear summary of the main issues but also extends the debate beyond evaluation techniques to consider the use made of time values. Hensher (1979) offers a much more rigorous critique, focus-

ing specifically on the inappropriate use that is made of values obtained by empirical means. A detailed account of the development of national car ownership forecasts is provided by Tanner (1978) although the treatment of disaggregate modelling techniques is rather thin. Button *et al.* (1982) provides a more comprehensive overview and critique, with a specific emphasis on the economic content of car ownership forecasting. It also contains a considerable list of further, technical references.

References

Bates, J.J., Gunn, H. F. and Roberts, M. (1978), *A disaggregate Model of Household Car Ownership*, Department of the Environment and Transport Research Report 20, London, HMSO.

Beesley, M.E. (1965), 'The value of time·spent in travelling: some new evidence', *Economica*, Vol. 32, pp. 174–85.

Bendtsen, P.H. (1980), 'The influence of price of petrol and of cars on the amount of automobile traffic', *International Journal of Transport Economics*, Vol. 7, pp. 207–13.

Brown, S. and Watkins, W. (1968), 'The demand for air travel: a regression study of time-series and cross-sectional data in the US domestic market', *Highway Research Record*, no. 213, pp. 21–34.

Burrell, J. (1972), 'Recent developments in car ownership forecasting' in *Urban Traffic Model Research*, London, Planning and Transport Research and Computation PTRC.

Button, K.J. (1980), 'The geographical distribution of car ownership in Great Britain – some recent trends', *Annals of Regional Science*, Vol. 14, pp. 23–38.

Button, K.J., Fowkes A.S. and Pearman, A.D. (1980), 'Disaggregate and aggregate car ownership forecasting methods in Great Britain', *Transportation Research* (Series A), Vol. 14, pp. 263–73.

Button, K.J., Pearman, A.D. and Fowkes, A.S. (1982), *Car Ownership Modelling and Forecasting*, Farnborough, Gower Press.

Chase Econometrics Associates (1974), *The Effect of Tax and Regulatory Alternatives on Car Sales and Gasoline Consumption*, NTIS Report No. PB–234622.

Claffey, P.J., St Clair, C. and Weider, N. (1961), 'Characteristics of passenger car travel on toll roads and comparable free roads', *Highway Research Bulletin*, no. 306.

Collings, J.J., Rigby, D. and Welsby, J.K. (1977), 'Passenger response to bus fares', *Directorate General Economics and Resources Report*, Vol. 24, Department of the Environment.

Dawson, R.F.F and Everall, P.F. (1972), 'The value of motorists' time: a study in Italy', *Transport and Road Research Laboratory Report*, LR. 426.

Dawson, R.F.F. and Smith, N.D.S. (1959), 'Evaluating the time of private motorists by studying their behavior', *Road Research Laboratory Research Note 3474*.

Department of the Environment (1976), *Transport Policy – A Consultative Document* (2 vols.), London, HMSO.

Department of Transport (1977), *Transport Policy*, Cmnd 6836, London, HMSO.

Department of Transport (1978), *Report of the Advisory Committee on Trunk Road Assessment* (Leitch Committee), London, HMSO.

Department of Transport (1979), *Road Haulage Operators Licensing (Report of the Independent Committee of Enquiry into Road Haulage Operators' Licensing)*, London, HMSO.

DeVany, A.S. (1974), 'The revealed value of time in air travel', *Review of Economics and Statistics*, Vol. 56, pp. 77–82.

Edwards, S.L. and Dennis, S.J. (1976), 'Long distance day tripping in Great Britain', *Journal of Transport Economics and Policy*, Vol. 10, pp. 237–56.

Fairhurst, H.M. (1975), 'The influence of public transport on car ownership in London', *Journal of Transport Economics and Policy*, Vol. 9, pp. 193–208.

Fairhurst, M.H. and Morris, P.J. (1975), 'Variations in the demand for bus and rail travel up to 1974', *London Transport Executive Report* R210.

Glaister, S. (1976), 'Variations in the demand for bus and rail travel in London 1970 to 1975', mimeo, London School of Economics.

Glaister, S. and Lewis, D. (1978), 'An integrated fares policy for transport in London', *Journal of Public Economics*, Vol. 9, pp. 341–55.

Goodwin, P. (1973), 'Time, distance and cost of travel by different modes', *Proceedings of the 5th University Transport Study Group Annual Conference.*

Gronau, R. (1970), *The Value of Time in Passenger Transportation: The Demand for Air Travel,* New York, Columbia University Press.

Gunn, H.F. (1981), 'Travel budgets – a review of evidence and modelling implications', *Transportation Research* A., Vol. 15, pp. 7–23.

Gwilliam, K.M. and Mackie, P.J. (1975), *Economics and Transport Policy*, London, Allen & Unwin.

Harrison, A.J. and Quarmby, D.A. (1969), 'The value of time in transport planning: a review', in *Report of the Sixth Round Table on Transport Economics*, European Conference of Ministers of Transport, Paris.

Hensher, D.A. (1979), 'Formulating an urban passenger transport policy: a re-appraisal of some elements', *Australian Economic papers,* Vol. 18, pp. 119–30.

Hensher, D.A. and Hitchkiss, W.E. (1974), 'Choice of mode and the value of travel time savings for the journey to work', *Economic Record,* Vol. 50, pp. 94–112.

Hillman, M., Henderson, I. and Whalley, A. (1973), *Personal Mobility and Transport Policy*, PEP Broadsheet 542, London.

Houthakker, H.S., Verleger, P.K. and Sheenan, D.P. (1974), 'Dynamic demand analysis for gasoline and residential electricity', *American Journal of Agricultural Economics*, Vol. 56, pp. 412–18.

Howe, J.D.G.F. (1976), 'Valuing time savings in developing countries', *Journal of Transport Economics and Policy*, Vol. 10, pp. 113–25.

Ippolito, R.A. (1981), 'Estimating airline demand with quality of service variables', *Journal of Transport Economics and Policy*, Vol. 15, pp. 7–15.

Isaac, J.K. (1979), 'Price and quality in road passenger transport', *Journal of the Chartered Institute of Transport*, Vol. 38, pp. 359–61.

Jennings, A. and Sharp, C.H. (1976), 'The value of travel time savings and transport investment appraisal', in I.G. Heggie (ed.), *Modal Choice and the Value of Travel Time*, Oxford, Oxford University Press.

Jung, J.M. and Fujii, E.T. (1976), 'The price elasticity of demand for air travel – some new evidence', *Journal of Transport Economics and Policy*, Vol. 10, pp. 257–62.

Kennedy, M. (1974), 'An economic model of the world oil market', *Bell Journal of Economics and Management Science*, Vol. 5, pp. 540–77.

Kraft, G. and Domenich, T.A. (1970), *Free Transit*, Lexington, D.C. Heath.

Lago, A.M., Mayworm, P. and McEnroe, J.M. (1981), 'Transit service elasticities – evidence from demonstration and demand models', *Journal of Transport Economics and Policy*, Vol. 15, pp. 99–119.

Lave, C.A. (1970), 'The demand for urban mass transportation', *Review of Economics and Statistics,* Vol. 52, pp. 320–23.

Lee, N. and Dalvi, M.Q. (1969), 'Variations in the value of travel time', *Manchester School*, Vol. 37, pp. 213–36.

Lewis, D.L. (1978), 'Public policy and road traffic levels: a rejoinder', *Journal of Transport Economics and Policy*, Vol. 12, pp. 98–102.

Litt, R.M. (1975), *A Cross-Sectional Study of the Demand for Urban Transit in Canada,* Department of Economics, University of Western Ontario.

McGillivany, R.G. (1970), 'Demand and choice models of modal split', *Journal of Transport Economics and Policy*, Vol. 4, pp. 192–207.

Mogridge, M.J.H. (1978), 'The effect of the oil crisis on the growth in the ownership and use of cars', *Transportation*, Vol. 7, pp. 45–65.

Musgrave, R.A. (1959), *The Theory of Public Finance*, New York, McGraw-Hill.

Mutti, J. and Murai, Y. (1977), 'Airline travel on the North Atlantic, *Journal of Transport Economics and Policy*, Vol. 11, pp. 45–53.

Price Commission (1978), *The Road Haulage Industry*, House of Commons Paper HC 698, London, HMSO.

Quandt, R.E. and Baumol, W.J. (1966), 'The demand for abstract transport modes, theory and measurement', *Journal of Regional Science,* Vol. 6, pp. 13–26.

Quarmby, D.A. (1967), 'Choice of travel mode for the journey to work: some findings', *Journal of Transport Economics and Policy*, Vol. 1, pp. 273–314.

Reza, A.M. and Spiro, M.H. (1979), 'The demand for passenger car transport services and for gasoline', *Journal of Transport Economics and Policy*, Vol. 13, pp. 304–19.

Sharp, C. (1971), 'The optimum allocation of freight traffic', *Journal of Transport Economics and Policy*, Vol. 5, pp. 344–56.

Sherman, R. (1967), 'A private ownership bias in transit choice', *American Economic Review*, Vol. 77, pp. 1211–17.

Smith, M.G. and McIntosh, P.T. (1974), 'Fares elasticity: interpretation and estimation', in *Symposium on Public Transport Fare Structure*, Transport and Road Research Laboratory Report, SR37UC, Crossthorne.

Sohn, C.M. (1975), *The Demand for Mass Transportation in New York City*, Ph.D. thesis, Department of Economics, State University of New York.

Stanley, P.A. and Farrington, J.H. (1981), 'The need for rural public transport: a constraints-based case study', *Tijdschrift voor Economische en Sociale Geografie*, Vol. 72, pp. 62–80.

Straszheim, M.R. (1978), 'Airline demand functions on the North Atlantic and their pricing implications', *Journal of Transport Economics and Policy*, Vol. 12, pp. 179–95.

Tanner, J.C. (1978), 'Long-term forecasting of vehicle ownership and road traffic', *Journal of the Royal Statistical Society* (Series A), Vol. 141, pp. 14–63.

Taplin, J.H.E. (1980), 'A coherence approach to estimates of price elasticities in the vacation travel market', *Journal of Transport Economics and Policy*, Vol. 14, pp. 19–35.

Thomas, S. (1979), 'Non-working time savings in developing countries', *Journal of Transport Economics and Policy*, Vol. 13, pp. 335–7.

Thomas, T.C. (1967), *The Value of Time for Passenger Cars: an Experimental Study of Commuters' Values*, Washington, US Bureau of Public Roads.

Thomson, J.M. (1974), *Modern Transport Economics*, Harmondsworth, Penguin.

Tipping, D. (1968), 'Time savings in transport studies', *Economic Journal*, Vol. 78, pp. 843–54.

White, P.R. (1981), '"Travelcard" tickets in urban public transport', *Journal of Transport Economics and Policy*, Vol. 15, pp. 17–34.

Williams, A. (1974), '"Need" as a demand concept (with special reference to health)', in A.J. Culyer (ed.), *Economic Policies and Social Goals*, London, Martin Robertson.

Zahavi, Y. (1977), 'Equilibrium between travel, demand, system supply and urban structure', in E.J. Visser (ed.), *Transport Decisions in an Age of Uncertainty*, The Hague, Martinus Nijhoff.

4. The Direct Costs of Transport

4.1 The supply of transport

Elementary economic theory tells us that, in most circumstances, supply is a positive function of price. The actual amount of transport offered at any price level will, however, be heavily influenced by the costs involved. This, and the following chapter, look at the various costs associated with supplying transport services and, in particular, at the relationships between the resources required to provide these services and the types of output finally 'consumed' by travellers and freight consignors. This chapter is specifically concerned with the production functions perceived by the providers of transport, which relate the various factor inputs to the final services offered, and with the financial costs of these factor inputs.

The chapter differs from the following one in that it only deals with *direct costs* as borne by the supplying agency. These are normally, but not always, financial costs which are incurred as the result of purchasing factor services in the market (i.e. the wages of labour, the interest on capital, the price of fuel, etc.). There is one very important exception, however, namely the actual cost of the travellers' or consignors' own inputs. Transport is special (but not unique) in that the actual person being transported has to contribute his own time inputs and, when private motor transport is involved, his personal energies, skills and expertise. The opportunity costs of this time and the utilisation of acquired skills will, therefore, directly enter the production function for trip-making. The external costs we move on to consider in the following chapter, although representing genuine resource costs, do *not* directly influence the decisions of transport suppliers in their provision of transport services. In brief, therefore, this chapter is exclusively concerned with the perceived or reaction costs which influence the supply of transport services. It should be pointed out, however, that the separation of direct and external costs is something of an expositional device and that in practice this distinction is becoming increasingly blurred as official policies attempt to make transport agencies fully cognizant of the *full* resource implications of their actions.

The importance of the distinction between those costs that enter the supplier's production function and those that do not is clearly reflected in an example drawn from Hicks (1975) concerning freight transhipment facilities. The objective of transhipment or consignment consolidation is to reduce costs by transhipping goods at some point between their origin and destination so that greater vehicle utilisation is achieved. The Post Office provides the classic example where large consignments of letters destined for a single city are collected together at a single sorting office and subsequently dispatched for final delivery in smaller consignments. (Other examples of transhipment include the operators of bakeries – such as Rank-Hovis MacDougal – and cargo handling firms.) Transhipment may be from one type of vehicle to a different mode (e.g. rail to road) or between different vehicles of the same mode. By being able to use large purpose built vehicles for the trunk haul stage of the operation but small delivery vans for the final distribution to customers the transport undertaking reduces his line-haul and delivery costs. Because the

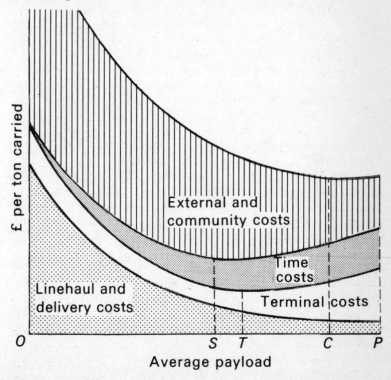

Figure 4.1   Freight consolidation costs (represented cumulatively)

degree of transhipment is closely related to average payload – greater consolidation inevitably increasing the average payload – we can see in Figure 4.1 that line-haul costs will fall with consolidation until the maximum physical or legal average payload (P) is reached. If only haulage costs were to be considered P would represent the optimal payload, but there are also the resources costs involved with consolidation itself – the provision of depots, handling staff, administrative costs, etc. These terminal costs are likely to rise with the level of transhipment. Consequently, the transport operator when considering transhipment and looking at his costs will feel the optimal level of consolidation would imply an average payload of T in the diagram.

So far we have only looked at the terminal and movement costs confronting the transporter; however, the final customer awaiting delivery will also have costs which vary with transhipment levels. The greater the amount of consolidation, and the higher the final average payload, the fewer the number of deliveries that will be needed. Longer frequencies between deliveries push up the costs of stock holding for customers and the overall level of inventories held. Thus the time costs of increased consolidation rise with average payload suggesting that overall, final recipients of goods would prefer a level of consolidation consistent with an average payload of S in Figure 4.1. There is a clear distinction, therefore, between the *direct* costs influencing the transporter's optimum and those affecting the final customer. Additionally, there are also wider *external costs* influencing those not directly concerned with transport operations; these include those affected by vehicle noise or fumes or who have their own travel disrupted by freight vehicles. Generally, increased consolidation and higher payloads will reduce these costs, because fewer trips are needed to transport the same volume of goods and consolidation generally means less environmentally intrusive vehicles can be used in sensitive areas. Hence, from society's point of view, the optimal level of consolidation in the diagram is when *all* costs are minimised, i.e. at point C.

In this chapter, and in the freight context, we would only be concerned with the first two categories of cost although where a transport undertaking is operating 'own account' services, carrying its own goods, the time element also becomes relevant. In the passenger transport context since, by definition, one is operating an 'own account' service (even when using public transport) the time element is relevant. The introduction of externalities into the overall production function is left to the following chapter.

4.2 Fixed and variable costs

Direct costs can be divided in a number of ways but two are particularly relevant to transport, namely distinctions according to variability over time and distinctions among the parties responsible for elements of cost. The first of these distinctions is discussed in this section. In the long run, or so the introductory texts tell us, all costs are variable, but the long run is itself an imprecise concept (even a tautology) and the ability to vary costs over time differs among modes of transport. The long run in the context of a seaport is, for instance, very different from that in road haulage or the bus industry. Port infrastructure is extremely long-lived, specific, indivisible and extremely expensive. It is, in reality, impossible to consider the standard question associated with long-run costs – namely, 'what is the cheapest way of providing a given capacity in the long run?' – when talking of time horizons twenty, thirty or even fifty years hence. Road haulage is different, capital costs are lower, physical durability less, and there is always the prospect of varying the use, within limits, of the vehicle fleet. Lorries are, unlike ports, mobile

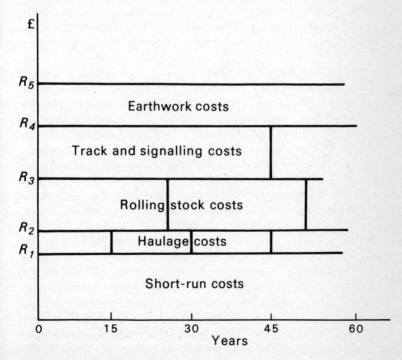

Figure 4.2   Railway costs

both among a range of potential employments and among a range of locations.

The nature of many costs, therefore, means that they may be considered fixed in the short term: there are temporal indivisibilities. The period under consideration will, as we have seen, differ among transport sectors, but it will also differ within a single transport undertaking. Railway operators offer a useful illustration of this. A railway service involves using a large number of factor services, many of these being highly specific and each with its own physical life-span. When it comes to considering line closures the essential questions revolve around deciding exactly which costs are fixed. Figure 4.2 offers a general illustration of the main cost items associated with a rail service together with an appropriate, although not exact, indication of the physical life of existing equipment. In the very short period, since all other items have already been purchased (i.e. they are fixed), the only savings the railways can make are in very variable costs, notably those attributable to labour, fuel and maintenance. However, if the railways are earning sufficient income to cover these costs (i.e. $0R_1$ or above in the diagram) then there is no justification for closing the line. After a period of about fifteen years, however, locomotives become due for replacement. Consequently locomotive costs become variable over a fifteen year horizon and the managers of BR must decide whether revenues justify replacement. Is fifteen years, therefore, the long run? The answer is probably no because other factors have still longer lives, rolling stock lasting for twenty-five years and track and signalling for forty years. (Earthworks have an effective infinite life and once constructed do not enter into further decision-making processes.) Further decisions regarding closure must, therefore, be made after twenty-five and forty years even if the line earns sufficient revenue to cover its locomotive replacement needs. Consequently, the long run for BR, in this context, is anything up to forty years with, in the interim, a series of successive short-run cost calculations having to be made.

It should be quite apparent that the distinction between fixed and variable costs is a pragmatic device requiring a degree of judgement and common sense on the part of the decision-maker. In the short term – whatever that may be – some costs are clearly fixed resulting in a falling short-run average cost of use until capacity is reached. Figure 4.3, for instance, may be seen to illustrate the average cost of increased use of a ship ($SRAC_1$) which falls steeply until capacity is fully utilised. A second ship may then, if demand is sufficient, be brought into operation exhibiting a short-run average cost curve of $SRAC_2$. The fixed capacity constraint for each ship typifies that found in

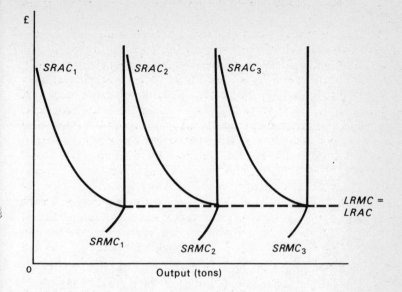

Figure 4.3 The long and short-run costs of shipping

most modes of transport and tends to differ from the smooth, stereotype, symmetrical U-shaped SRAC curves often associated with manufacturing industry. The long-run curve is, following elementary economics, formed by the envelope of the short-run average cost curves.

In many sectors of the economy the long-run average cost curve is not horizontal, as in our illustration, but is often found to be downward sloping as a result of economies of scale. (The ability to replicate makes it unlikely that the textbook U-shaped LRAC curves exist unless there are inefficiencies in the industry.) These economies may potentially take a variety of forms in transport (e.g. in vehicle size, in fleet size, and in the provision of infrastructure) and may be thought to vary according to the type of transport involved and the mode of operation being undertaken. We can look at each of the main possibilities for scale economies in transport in turn.

Economies from larger vehicle size
The classic example of this is in shipping where capacity (in terms of volume) increases much faster than surface area but this is also a feature of most other modes of freight transport. Thermal processes (such as engine size) also generally exhibit scale economies in all

forms of transport and crew numbers do not increase proportion-
ately with the size of mobile plant. Table 4.1 gives some indication of
economies of scale in bulk carriers, but similar economies are also
found in oil tankers. Such scale economies are not unique to shipping, but they are perhaps more pronounced in that mode.

Table 4.1   Economies of scale in bulk carriers

Ship size (thousand dwt)	15	25	41	61	120	200
Index of size	100	167	267	432	793	1318
Capital cost index	100	140	197	291	457	641
Operating cost index (excluding fuel)	100	121	134	155	201	275
Seagoing fuel consumption index	100	155	230	353	578	843
Crew size	31	38	38	38	38	38

Source: Goss and Jones, 1971

Evidence produced in the early 1970s by Edwards and Bayliss
(1971), and depicted in Figure 4.4, suggest that there may be limits to
the cost advantages of using extremely large road haulage vehicles.
Diseconomies of scale appear to begin setting in after about 11
tonnes carrying capacity has been reached. More recent evidence
from the Armitage inquiry into the environmental impact of heavy
lorries (Department of Transport, 1980), however, indicates that
there are still economies of scale to be enjoyed by using vehicles in
excess of the 32.5 tonnes gross maximum weight permitted in 1980
(see Table 4.2).

*Table 4.2   Estimated savings by increasing maximum lorry weight
above 32.5 tonnes*

35 tonnes, 4 axles	5–7%
38 tonnes, 5 axles	5–9%
40 tonnes, 5 axles	7–14%
42 tonnes, 5 axles	9–13%
44 tonnes, 6 axles	11–13%

Source: Department of Transport, 1980

While economies of scale clearly do exist in utilising larger units of
mobile plant – at least up to some point – it should be noted that it is
often impossible to take advantage of them even when demand for
transport services is high. In many cases the associated infrastructure
cannot handle the larger vehicles (ports and airports pose specific

problems in this context) while in others the consignments of traffic are small and can be more efficiently handled in smaller vehicles (see, for example, Jansson and Shneerson, 1978). Returning to our maritime example, large ships on liner routes often incur heavy costs as frequent landings and embarkings of individual consignments require rearrangements of the entire cargo. As Thomson (1974) has pointed out, 'Although transport is the instrument whereby *other* industries achieve economies of scale, its very nature often prevents the achievement of economies of scale within itself' (emphasis original).

Economies of scale in infrastructure provision
Transport demand is not spread evenly over space but tends to be concentrated on links between particular trip-generating and trip-attracting points, e.g. journey to work trips are concentrated along links between residential and industrial estates; holiday air transport demand is highest between the main cities in the United Kingdom and popular recreational resorts in Spain, Greece, etc. Thus, there is a tendency in transport, as we saw in Chapter 3, for demand to be

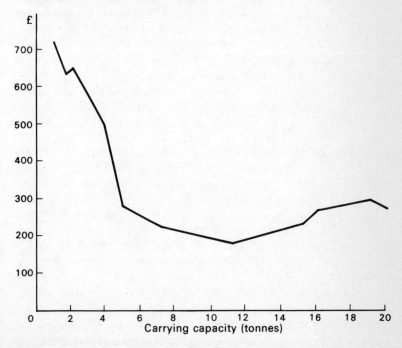

Figure 4.4   Cost variability and lorry size

concentrated on certain portions of the network and *ipso facto*, certain parts of the static infrastructure. Technically this concentration of traffic is possible because of substantial scale economies in infrastructure provision.

Table 4.3   Economies of large port operations

	Vancouver	Seattle
Traffic (1973)	88 000	377 000
No. of berths	3	11
Wharfage	23.63	33.75
Handling and through port charge	81.27	40.00
Vessel service and facility charge	0	26.60
Tailgate loading	22.28	0
Total of port charges per container	127.18	95.35

Source: Heaver, 1975

An examination of the costs associated with handling container traffic in an average port (Vancouver) and a large port (Seattle) in Table 4.3 (which assumes the charges paid by container traffic reflect port costs) reveals the economies enjoyed from scale. It seems in port operations that a fourfold increase in size reduces costs by approximately one-quarter. Similarly, with internal transport, Tanner (1968) quotes the cost of four-lane motorways as being on average 78 per cent of those with six lanes. However, it should be said that evidence of scale economies in road provision is not altogether conclusive. The findings of Keeler and Small (1977), looking at fifty-seven freeway segments in the San Francisco area, favour constant returns while Walters (1968), again employing US sources, finds evidence 'that there are increasing costs of (road) construction in urban areas'. The difficulty here, as with other forms of infrastructure costing, is to isolate comparable construction costs from those costs associated with specific locations. In terms of railways, the move from a single to a double-track system involves roughly a quadrupling of capacity by eliminating conflict between directions; that to quadruple track should more than double capacity by permitting segregation by speed. The estimated costs of these options (at 1967 prices) are seen in Table 4.4 and clearly they rise much less rapidly than the increase in potential capacities.

Economies from large fleet size
Larger fleets of vehicles may offer economies in maintenance, standardisation (or, in some cases, the availability of a mixed vehicle

Table 4.4 Annual costs per mile of rail track (1967 prices)

| | Nos. of Tracks | | |
	1	2	4
Interest	3 020	4 260	7 900
Revenue of track and structure	1 400–2 840	1 896–3 442	3 422–4 474
Signalling	2 600	4 030	8 060
Total	£7 020–8 460	£10 190–11 730	£19 380–20 430

Source: Foster and Joy, 1967

fleet to meet variable demand), easier crew scheduling, etc., although administrative problems and remoteness of decision-maker from customer may temper these advantages. Evidence on the existence of fleet economies of scale, however, is far from conclusive for all modes of transport and indeed there seems to be a gradual emergence of constant returns for many modes with limited scale economies in specialised forms of transport.

Table 4.5, which looks at different scales of urban bus operations, suggests that large bus fleets offer only diseconomies although differing operating conditions may distort the picture – the smaller operators, for instance, tend to run their services outside the larger cities. Statistical analysis by Lee and Steedman (1970), looking at the accounts of forty-four municipal bus undertakings for 1966/7, suggests the notion of constant returns to scale, a situation agreeing with Williams's (1981) study of eleven American publicly owned operations. Wabe and Coles's (1975) examination of sixty-six operators, however, 'provides evidence that diseconomies of scale exist in the

Table 4.5 Productivity of UK urban bus operators

Operator	Staff per bus	Thousand bus miles per employee	Receipts per employee (£ thousand)	No. of buses
London Transport	5.1	57	2.3	6201
Other big cities	3.7	73	2.8	1712[a]
Other local authorities				
largest	4.0	71	2.7	540[a]
smallest	1.5	79	2.2	12[a]
Private operators	1.3	161	2.8	5[a]

All figures for 1973 except private operators (for 1972)
[a] Average bus company
Source: Button, 1977

provision of bus services'. Koshal's (1970) work in India offers international support for the notion of constant returns in bus operations. Walters's (1968) work in road haulage produced the same
result, although the large number of owner drivers working in this
sector makes exact costing difficult. In aviation the Edwards
Committee (Board of Trade, 1969) found evidence of scale economies when there was fleet standardisation but generally concluded
that the optimal size of fleet depends upon the task in hand. The difficulty with empirical work in this field, and in shipping, is the diversity of the market conditions which are encountered and the support
which is often forthcoming from government to finance 'the nation's
flag carrier'.

A further indication of constant returns to fleet size is the diversity
of the scale of operators in most sectors of transport: large companies often compete directly against one or two vehicle firms. Road
haulage is possibly the most extreme example, as we see in Table 4.6,
but throughout the whole of transport – except for areas directly
regulated by government – one finds large and small firms competing
with each other. Differential managerial skills may permit some
firms to grow larger than others but this does not imply technical
economies of scale exist.

Table 4.6   Public road hauliers by size of fleet, 1977

Fleet size	Nos. of operators	Nos. of vehicles in fleets
1	25 100	25 100
2–5	14 300	44 400
6–20	5 500	53 700
21–100	1 400	49 500
over 100	100	16 300
Total	46 400	189 000

Source: Department of Transport, 1979

The variable costs of transport – those related to the rate of output
– are generally considered to be dominated by labour and fuel items
because these are thought highly flexible in the short term. Since
infrastructure costs are relatively fixed, it is the cost of the mobile
plant which is normally treated as marginal. Tables 4.7, 4.8 and 4.9
give some indication of the relative importance of these items in
overall airline, road haulage and bus operating costs. It should perhaps be pointed out that even in the long term the costs of mobile
plant are, in aggregate, likely to exceed those of infrastructure, but
individual vehicle costs, in many cases, are relatively small. The costs

Table 4.7   IATA – scheduled international airline service

Cost item	%
Flight deck crew	8.5
Fuel and oil	20.6
Insurance and depreciation	8.1
Maintenance and overhaul	11.1
Landing fees and *en route* charges	5.1
Station and ground operators	12.4
Cabin attendants and passenger services	10.7
Ticketing, sales and promotion	17.9
Others	5.6
Total	100.0

Source: Hammarskjold, 1976

of aircraft operations represent a sector with very high costs per unit of mobile plant while road haulage is a sector where the total operational costs per vehicle are low. The importance of both direct and indirect labour costs and fuel costs, however, is apparent at both ends of the spectrum.

The tables each represent broad averages across many different types of operation but variable costs differ not simply with level of vehicle usage but also with the type of transport operation undertaken. Vehicles, for example, have an optimal speed above or below which fuel costs tend to rise steeply; consequently operations involving continually stopping and starting will, *ceteris paribus*, increase

Table 4.8   Expenditure by British public road hauliers (% of total costs in 1965)

Cost item	%
Fuel	16.5
Spares	4.4
Tyres	3.8
Other materials	0.7
Maintenance (inc. wages) and vehicle hire	8.9
Drivers' and attendants' wages	33.3
Licences and insurance (vehicles)	6.2
Depreciation (vehicle) and HP interest	10.2
Building depreciation and overheads, rates	7.7
Other staff wages	8.3
Total	100.0

Source: Edwards and Bayliss, 1971

Table 4.9   Cost structure of British bus fleets, 1969/70

Expenditure Item	London Transport Executive (%)	Local authorities[a] (%)	Other operators (%)
Wages and road staff	53.2	51.2	47.4
Fuel	6.1	7.8	9.3
Repairs and maintenance[b]	3.9	5.1	6.6
Depreciation of vehicles	2.2	1.7	7.1
Redemption of debt	—	2.3	—
Insurance of vehicles	—	0.7	1.0
Wages of other staff	29.6	24.2	19.7
Others[c]	5.0	6.8	8.9

Source: Department of the Environment, 1972
     [a] Excludes PTA fleets (not shown in this table)
     [b] Includes tyres, spare parts and lubricating oil
     [c] Excluding interest payments, capital expenditure and income and profit taxes

variable costs (Gyenes, 1980). Maintenance costs can also vary considerably with the type of terrain over which journeys are made. To some extent these variations may be offset by employing specialised vehicles whose variable cost profiles conform most closely to the type of operation undertaken. In the airline context there exists a whole range of different aircraft designed to meet the needs of different operational patterns – airbuses for short haul, large volume traffic, wide-bodied jumbos for long range operations, etc. Table 4.10 gives some indication of the running and standing costs of different forms of operation in the UK road haulage sector. While these figures are not strictly variable and fixed costs, they do convey a general impression of how costs vary, even within sectors, with the type of transport operation performed.

The cost profiles also vary with the type of firm controlling the operations. Wallis (1980), in his study of urban bus operations in major Australian cities, for example, suggests that private operators enjoy lower costs in certain areas than their publicly owned counterparts, notably through:

• greater flexibility and efficiency in use of labour;
• relatively small proportions of maintenance and administrative costs;
• lower basic rates of pay; and
• lower wage/salary on-costs (taxes, pensions, etc.)

While in part cost variations may be explained in terms of either the

Table 4.10 Road haulage running and standing costs per mile, 1977 (pence)

Cost	Fleet size	Bulk tankers	Tipping	Smalls and parcels	Long distance	Other general	Other sectors	All sectors
Running }	100+	20	—	12	15	21	14	18
Standing }		27	—	30	18	31	42	28
Running }	21–100	17	13	12	15	16	16	15
Standing }		22	19	28	16	22	26	21
Running }	1–20	19	15	12	13	12	16	14
Standing }		31	12	19	19	14	25	18

Source: Price Commission, 1978

size of the operator or the type of operation undertaken, cost differences may also reflect alternative operational objectives. There is ample evidence that large national airlines often employ high-cost modern equipment to enhance their image. But even at the level of local public transport, similar indications of X-inefficiency exists. Teal *et al.* (1981), for example, cite instances of local authorities preferring to operate their own paratransport system rather than make use of established private operators despite demonstrably higher costs.

Labour costs, although flexible, are usually much less variable than fuel costs. This is not simply because of imperfections in the labour market (e.g. fixed working hours, union agreements on redundancies, training costs, etc.) which often make it difficult to increase or reduce the size of the labour force – even in the sense of dividing up public transport crews to conform with daily peaks in travel demand – but also because of the nature of many types of transport operation. Once a particular form of transport operation has been decided upon, and capital invested, there are high labour costs associated with maintaining and servicing this equipment irrespective of the traffic carried. Further, once an undertaking is committed to a scheduled service, labour becomes a fixed cost in providing this service.

One of the major problems in this latter context is the technologically unprogressive nature of many forms of transport operations which makes it difficult to substitute one factor input for another as their relative prices change. In the case of the mercantile marine it has proved possible to substitute fixed for variable factors (notably capital for labour) as labour costs have risen but this is much less easy in areas such as public transport provision. It is difficult to see how the basic operations of taxi-cabs, for example, could be retained with a substantial reduction in labour input. Attempts to reduce labour costs in the urban public transport sphere by introducing one-man operated vehicles has had some limited effect on costs (Brown and Nash (1972) estimated a 13.7 per cent cost saving and Lee and Steedman (1970) a cost reduction of about 20 per cent), but this should be seen as a once-for-all step rather than the prospect of continual factor substitution.

4.3 Specific, joint and common costs

The second method of dividing out costs, according to the groups of services produced, involves allocating responsibility for costs to specific users or consignors. While the fixed/variable cost dichotomy poses problems about the relevant time period to consider, cost responsibility raises issues of the traceability of costs. Some costs are very specific and can, therefore, be allocated quite easily – the steve-dore costs of loading and unloading a particular cargo onto and off a ship is a case in point. In other cases a degree of averaging may be necessary but, nevertheless, costs can generally be traced to specific groups of classes of user. But there are also a whole range of other costs that may be either 'joint' or 'common' to a number of users and are difficult to trace directly to any specific group. It is sometimes said that fixed costs may generally be treated as joint or common while variable costs may be treated as specific but this is too simpl-istic. Many variable costs are, in practice, joint (e.g. the fuel costs in-curred in moving a train in one direction and bringing it back are joint to both movements) or common (e.g. the basic maintenance costs of retaining a freight and passenger rail link) while certain fixed costs are clearly specific (e.g. the capital costs of freight wagons have no connection with passenger demand).

Strictly, joint costs exist when the provision of a specific service necessarily entails the output of some other service. Jointness is a technical feature and exists at all points in time, i.e. both before as well as after any investment decisions are made. Return trips (or 'back-hauls'), where the supply of transport services in one direction automatically implies the provision of a return service, are the classic examples in transport economics. The fact that true joint products are produced in *fixed* proportions means there can be no variability in costs making it logically impossible to specify the cost of, say, an outward journey when only the overall cost of the round trip is known. Joint costs are, consequently, non-traceable. This further implies that joint costs can only be escaped jointly, with services in both directions being withdrawn together.

In a market situation joint costs pose few problems in practice (Mohring, 1976). If there is a competitive road haulage service offer-ing a round trip between A and B and back again each week using M trucks then equilibrium rates would soon emerge for each service (i.e. from A to B and from B to A). Although there are specific deliv-ery, terminal, pick-up costs, etc., little difference exists between the costs of running the lorries fully loaded or empty and hence prices would be primarily influenced by the differences in the demand in each direction. In the short term the combined revenues from the A to B and the B to A services may not be sufficient to cover joint costs but in such a situation the number of trucks offered would soon fall below M, increasing the price of trips in *both* direc-tions until joint costs are recovered. Excess revenue above joint costs would have the opposite effect. The key point is that differences exist in the demands for the out and return services and that different prices should be charged for each in equilibrium. Consequently, knowledge of the relevant demand elasticities together with that of joint cost permits the problems of traceability to be avoided. We return to consider this problem in more detail in our discussion of pricing in Chapter 6.

Common costs are similar to joint costs, in that they are incurred as the result of providing services to a range of users, but differ in that the use of resources to provide one service does not *unavoidably* result in the production of a different one. The classic example of common costs in transport is the provision of track facilities. A road may be used in common by lorries and cars but the withdrawal of rights for hauliers still leaves costs to be borne by motorists. With several classes of user it is often possible to trace certain components of cost to those responsible but there is still usually a large proportion which is untraceable. We now turn to look at some attempts that have been made in the United Kingdom to allocate common track costs across different categories of traffic.

4.4 Problems of common cost allocation – the road and rail track cases

The allocation of common track costs among users poses particular practical problems in transport and deserves specific attention. The road network in the UK is the responsibility of local and central government. Users, since the effective abolition of the Road Fund in 1937 and its legal death in 1955, make no direct, hypothecated payments to use the network – save for a small number of tolled bridges – but do pay considerable sums to government each year in the form of fuel tax, value added tax, car tax and vehicle excise duty. When deciding upon the desirability of making a road journey, potential users are to some extent influenced by these taxes. Attempts have, therefore, been made, on the grounds of economic efficiency, to allocate accurately the public costs of road provision (both the construction and maintenance of the track) to users. The EEC, for example, now wishes members to ensure that all road users pay at least their allocated short run marginal costs of track provision and that the full long-term cost is recovered in total (Jennings, 1976).

Although there are problems of deciding exactly what constitutes the total cost of road track provision in any period – e.g. should the maintenance costs be estimated in the same way as depreciation in nationalised industries or simply considered as they are incurred (Ministry of Transport, 1968) and what exactly constitutes the capital cost of any one year? (Jenning, 1979) – national comparisons of

Table 4.11   Road taxation and road expenditure as percentages of state revenue, 1977

Country	Road taxation	Road expenditure	Ratio of expenditure to taxation
Belgium	7.9[a]	6.9[a]	0.945
Denmark	8.1	4.8	0.593
France	13.9	7.4	0.532
West Germany	8.8	7.4	0.841
Italy	26.6[b]	10.0[b]	0.376
Netherlands	6.8	1.9	0.279
Great Britain	6.5	2.4	0.369
EEC	10.2	5.6	0.549
Japan	3.8	5.4[b]	1.421
USA	5.3[b]	5.1	0.962

[a] 1975   [b] 1976

Source: British Road Federation, *Basic Road Statistics*, 1979

annual expenditures against tax revenue (Table 4.11) suggest that all EEC governments recover from road users more than is spent on road provision. It may be felt that the UK ratio is low and should be brought into line with other states but this is only justified if the overall economic, demographic and geographic features of the countries are the same and other countries are themselves behaving optimally. There is also certainly no reason why, as some have advocated, the ratio should approximate to unity. Part of the revenue raised from road users must be considered as a 'pure' tax in the same way that there are taxes on other expenditures. Also there are social costs associated with road transport (see Chapter 5) and motoring taxes may, in part, be seen as a method, albeit a very imperfect one, of making road users aware of such costs. Additionally if prices in other sectors of the economy deviate from costs, there are sound economic reasons for this to be also the policy on roads (see Chapter 6).

While there is no sound reason why expenditure should match revenue in aggregate, it may still be desirable for each class of road vehicle to more or less cover its allocated track costs – this is the view, for example, of the EEC. Allocation of track costs to vehicle categories is, therefore, still important. The difficulty is that roads provide a common service to a variety of modes of transport (cyclists, motor cars, light vans, heavy lorries, buses, etc.) and the exact apportionment of marginal costs is, therefore, far from easy. The method of allocation favoured by the Department of Transport is based upon a refined version of an approach pioneered in the *Road Track Costs* study (Ministry of Transport, 1968) which crudely attempts to allocate long-run marginal costs (LRMCs) to different classes of road users. Broadly, capital and current maintenance costs are separated and allocated along the lines of Figure 4.5.

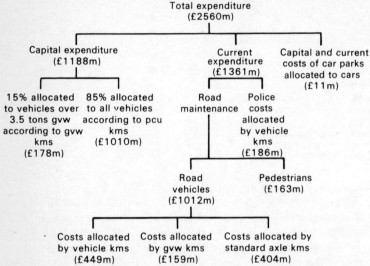

Figure 4.5   The Department of Transport method of allocating public road costs for 1980/81

Of total capital expenditure in any one year, 15 per cent is allocated directly to heavy goods vehicles according to the use they make of roads on the grounds that they necessitate higher design standards. The remaining 85 per cent is allocated out on passenger car unit (*pcu*) kilometres (*pcu* being an estimate of the amount of road required to accommodate a vehicle expressed in terms of car equivalents) on the argument that capital expenditure is determined by changes required in the physical capacity of the network. Current maintenance expenditures are allocated according to a series of *ad hoc* calculations that attempt to relate the various component items (such as resurfacing, grass cutting, lighting, road markings, traffic signs, drainage, etc.) to different vehicle characteristics, namely their size, number of standard axles (high axle loadings doing considerable damage to road surfaces) and the use made of roads. The criteria used to decide how costs are affected by the vehicle characteristics are based upon 'expert advice from traffic engineers and research scientists'. Special items such as policing and car parks are treated separately.

Table 4.12   Ratio of road user taxation revenue to road expenditure estimates by class of vehicle in the United Kingdom

Vehicle category	1965/66	1970/71	1975/76	1978/79	1980/81
Car and taxis					
Non-business	2.1:1	2.0:1	2.0:1	2.2:1	2.4:1
Business			1.5:1	2.0:1	2.4:1
Buses and coaches	1.4:1	1.4:1	0.8:1	1.4:1	1.5:1
Light vans	3.3:1	2.2:1	1.9:1	2.8:1	3.4:1
Goods vehicles					
Not over 3.5. tonnes gvw	1.8:1	1.5:1	0.8:1	2.0:1	2.9:1
Over 3.5 tonnes gvw			1.5:1	1.1:1	1.0:1
Total	2.1:1	1.9:1	1.5:1	1.8:1	1.9:1

Source: Department of Transport, 'The allocation of road track costs (1980/81)'

Table 4.12 compares the cost allocations with revenues for different broad categories of road user. Substantial variations emerge which vary in their magnitude over time. A similar picture is seen within vehicle classes, and in Table 4.13 we see that while many sizes of heavy goods vehicle pay tax considerably in excess of the public road costs attributable to them, others, mainly large vehicles with a small number of axles, do not. This may be particularly undesirable if these large vehicles are also responsible for generating a high level of external costs.

The Department of Transport's method of cost attribution has recently come under some criticism. At one level, Button (1979) has suggested that the detailed allocation within the Department's framework is biased against heavy goods vehicles because of (i) the excessive emphasis on vehicle weight in the allocation of capital costs when much of the network's design is determined by vehicle speed; (ii) the implied assumption in the calculation that the network is of optimal size; (iii) the rather dubious nature of *pcu*s as a measure of road capacity; and (iv) the relevance of the 'standard axle' measure used in the calculations. In particular, there is evidence that there may be an element of double counting when estimating heavy goods vehicle costs. Cars are accredited with a small allocation of road maintenance costs, but this is only possible because of the high engineering standards of roads required to carry heavy goods traffic. Hence, heavy goods vehicles are allocated both the additional costs of high design standards and the bulk of maintenance costs whereas with lower design specifications, suitable for cars only, cars would be allocated much higher maintenance costs (Bhatt *et al.*, 1979).

Table 4.13   Road taxation revenue to public road costs for selected heavy goods vehicle sizes 1980/81

| Vehicle type | Gvw (tonnes) | | Road user taxation revenue/track cost allocation |
	Over	Not over	
Rigid			
2 axles	3.5	5.0	2.60:1
	10.0	11.0	1.80:1
	14.0	15.0	1.28:1
	16.0	17.0	1.01:1
3 axles	16.0	17.0	1.98:1
	22.0	23.0	1.34:1
	24.0	25.0	0.96:1
4 axles	24.0	25.0	1.36:1
	28.0	29.0	1.14:1
	30.0	31.0	0.90:1
Articulated			
3 axles	3.5	12.0	2.97:1
	20.0	21.0	1.52:1
	22.0	23.0	1.32:1
	24.0	25.0	1.02:1
4 axles	—	25.0	1.52:1
	28.0	29.0	1.43:1
	30.0	31.0	1.04:1
	32.0	33.0	0.82:1
5 axles	—	33.0[a]	1.31:1
	—	33.0[b]	1.06:1

[a] tri-axle tractor
[b] tri-axle semi-trailer

Source: Derived from Department of Transport, 'The allocation of road track costs (1980/81) United Kingdom'

At a more fundamental level, Nash (1979) suggests that the traditional road track cost approach is really asking the wrong question and that track cost allocation should be along altogether different lines. He suggests the way ahead is to adopt a sequential approach where greater emphasis is placed upon differing demand elasticities among road users. Specifically he advises:

(1) Forecast traffic growth rates by vehicle type using alternative assumptions about future taxation levels and structures.
(2) Estimate the full costs of catering for different traffic growth rates.
(3) Identify the level and structure of taxes at which the revenue obtained from an incremental slice of traffic matches incre-

mental costs both for traffic as a whole and for individual traffic types.

(4) To the extent that the resulting taxes fall short of government revenue requirements, raise taxes on vehicle classes along second best lines (i.e. according to demand elasticities).

Such calculations obviously place greater demands on informational sources but they do offer a rather more realistic basis for track cost allocation and pricing consistent with principles adopted elsewhere in the transport sector.

Railway track allocation is done in a slightly different context because the railways, unlike the roads case, are responsible for providing *both* track and rolling stock. The necessity for devising a method of allocation stems not simply from designs for internal efficiency but also to permit the allocation of common fixed costs between those services that are operated on commercial criteria (e.g. freight) and those that are operated on social criteria (e.g. rural services) and are given central government subsidies. In urban areas local authority responsibility for transport co-ordination also requires reliable data on the *total* marginal costs of all competing modes.

One of the difficulties with railway operations is that common costs (which must include signalling, termini, etc. in addition to track) form a very substantial part of total cost (about 40 per cent in 1977). Normal commercial practice would be to use a 'cost-plus' method of pricing so that each customer would pay a rate covering his specific costs plus contribution to overheads. Provided this results in all costs being recovered in aggregate the problem of common cost allocation is not a serious issue. Unfortunately, for the reasons mentioned above, plus the difficulty of devising a sufficiently sensitive price discrimination regime given the diversity of services offered (see Chapter 6), the railways have found it important to be able to allocate their track costs.

A major difficulty in this area is that the railway's 'jargon' does not conform to conventional economic definitions. The railways talk of 'direct costs' and 'indirect costs' but the former (which embraces haulage costs, maintenance, marshalling, booking, insurance, collection and delivery by road) is clearly different from the economic notion of short-run escapable costs (and may or may not exceed them). As the Select Committee on Nationalised Industries (1960) said, 'The direct costs ascertained by traffic costing methods are not the same thing as short run marginal costs. Nor do they correspond with the savings that would flow immediately from the discontinuance of a small part of railway activities.' Equally, indirect costs, as defined by the railways (i.e. track, signalling and general administration) are not sufficiently fixed costs which are common to all traffic. While certain costs (e.g. those of earthworks) are invariant with traffic it is often possible to allocate track and signalling costs to particular services according to causation. The type and density of traffic determine whether a single track route is operated with no signalling or a multi-track, multiple-aspect signalling system is provided. Joy (1964) showed how these costs can vary with the quality of service – an express Category A service on double track with twelve trains a day cost £8250 per mile per annum in track costs (at 1961 prices); a less frequent, Category B service, £7250; heavily used non-express Category C services, £6250; and slow, Category D services, £3500. It is possible with poorer quality services to have more basic signalling and lower track maintenance standards. Further there are quite significant differences associated with the costs of track used exclusively for passenger services and that used only for freight. The Beeching Report (British Railways Board, 1963) found that a single track maintained to passenger standards costs at least £3500 per mile per annum but if it were only required to conform to freight standards it would cost £2000 per mile per annum, and it has been argued this could be reduced further (Joy, 1973).

The 1968 Transport Act and the introduction of social service subsidies for specific routes in 1969 (withdrawn in 1974 in favour of a block 'Public Service Obligation' grant) necessitated a much more detailed and uniform method of cost allocation which could be applied to specific services – the system required 'identification and costing of those services and facilities whose cost should properly be borne or aided by the community' (Ministry of Transport, 1966). The common costs were allocated according to the 'Cooper Brothers' formula (which it should be noted was essentially an average, rather than marginal, cost type of framework) which endorsed the idea of allocating track costs on the basis of gross ton miles and signalling costs on the basis of train miles. With homogeneous traffic flows evenly spread this is reasonable but with mixed traffic and peaks in use the allocation technique is unlikely to match causation with costs.

An exception to the Cooper Brothers' standard approach is the 'Method 2' allocation for heavily trafficked suburban lines and certain rural routes carrying little freight. Here the track costs are all attributed to the socially desirable passenger services since they determine the capacity of the route. (In 1970 it was modified slightly to allow for wear and tear associated with the minority services.)

Here the costs of track are clearly avoidable if the social service is withdrawn, but this argument may also apply almost as strongly to other social services not covered by 'Method 2' because many tend to 'lean on' each other rather than on other types of service. Hence, withdrawal of social services may permit termini costs of a common station used by them all to be saved.

British Rail moved in the late 1970s to a system of 'contribution accounting' which entails breaking down revenue and costs into some 700 major sub-sectors (or 'profit centres'). These profit centres – which are composed of single traffic flows, groups of flows or specific passenger services – are defined so that resources allocated to them can be specifically identified with a minimum of controversy. Even so not all common costs can be so allocated and thus British Rail accounts reveal the surplus of revenue over directly attributed expenses which are a 'contribution' to the indirect costs. The sum of all avoidable cost recovered may not cover *all* business costs, however, and a 'basic facility cost' is likely to remain. British Rail argue, though, that this approach, given the high proportion of indirect costs, 'ensures a high level of certainty in profit assessment' (see Gwilliam (1980) for further comment).

The problems of allocating costs common to several services is, therefore, seen to be a difficult one. Economic principles advocate the notion of seeking avoidable costs associated with specific users and then allocating these accordingly. The problem is in defining the base from which to begin the series of allocations – in the case of roads are they mainly designed for cars with lorries imposing additional costs or are they there to provide a quality of service with the faster car traffic necessitating higher engineering standards? We have seen that it is possible to allocate many items on an avoidable cost basis although practical application may necessitate a high degree of averaging.

4.5 Transport user costs – the notion of generalised costs

From the traveller's point of view, or that of a consignor of freight, a multiplicity of factors influence decisions. In particular, travellers take notice of the time it takes to make a trip and the money costs involved and, frequently, also the quality of the service offered. Consignors are concerned not simply with the financial costs of carriage but also the speed, reliability and time-tabling of the service. The demand for transport is not, therefore, simply dependent upon financial costs but rather on the overall opportunity costs involved. Transport is not unique in this, but it does differ from other services in that money costs may only form a relatively small part of overall costs. In terms of decision-making, the money cost of a trip may have minimal influence over whether it is undertaken or the transport mode preferred; a fact which may explain the considerable use of private motor cars even when 'cheaper' alternative modes are available (Sherman, 1967).

In analysing transport demand or when forecasting future consumer response it is sometimes possible to assess responses to the individual components of overall cost, but in many situations it has proved useful to have a composite measure. This may be true in situations where multi-dimensional cost functions are unwieldly or when a simple uni-dimensional measure, by focusing attention on general trends in cost, permits a clearer understanding of changes in the demand for transport services. As a pragmatic device to reduce the wide range of costs which influence travel to proportions comprehensible to policy-makers and, also, to offer a useful and manageable input to forecasting activities, a single index expressing 'generalised cost' has evolved. The idea, if not the title, can be traced back to work in the USA by Warner (1962) but much subsequent refinement stems from UK research.

The generalised cost of a trip is expressed as a single, usually monetary, measure combining, generally in linear form, most of the important but disparate costs which form the overall opportunity costs of the trip. On occasions a generalised time cost measure may replace the financial index (Goodwin, 1974). The characteristic of generalised cost is, therefore, that it reduces all cost items to a single index and this index may then be used in the same way as simple money costs are in standard economic analysis.

Simply, generalised costs can be defined as

$$G = g(C_1, C_2, C_3, \ldots C_n) \tag{4.1}$$

where G is generalised cost and $C_1, C_2, \ldots$ are the various time, money and other costs of travel. This permits the demand for trips to be expressed as a function of a single variable (i.e. $Q_D = f(G)$). While in simple indices, generalised cost is formed as a linear combination of time and money (or distance) costs in most applied analysis the time and money components are divided into a number of elements (e.g. walking time, waiting time, on-vehicle time, etc.). This results in an expression of the general form:

$$G = \sum_i M_i + \sum_j t_j T_j \tag{4.2}$$

where the M_i are the actual money costs of a journey (e.g. fare or petrol costs), T_j are the time costs (e.g. on-vehicle time, waiting time, etc.), and t_j are the monetary values of the various time components (these were discussed in detail in Chapter 3).

A specific form of the generalised cost function was used in the South-east Lancashire, North-east Cheshire (SELNEC) transport study conducted in the late 1960s (Wilson *et al.*, 1969). The generalised cost index used in the combined trip distribution–modal split element of the analysis (see Chapter 8) was of the form:

$$G_{ij}^K = a_1\, t_{ij}^K + a_2\, e_{ij}^K + a_3\, d_{ij}^K + p_j^K + \zeta^K \tag{4.3}$$

where G_{ij}^K is the generalised cost of travel by mode K between points i and j;

t_{ij}^K is the travel time from i to j by mode K (in minutes);

e_{ij}^K is the excess time (e.g. waiting time for public transport) for the journey from i to j (in minutes);

d_{ij}^K is the distance from i to j which acts as a surrogate for the variable money costs of trips (which are assumed proportional to distance;

p_j^K is the terminal cost (e.g. parking charges) at j (in pence);

ζ^K is a modal penalty reflecting the discomfort and lesser convenience associated with public transport journeys; and

a_1, a_2 and a_3 are parameters which, since p_j^K and ζ^K have unit coefficients, value other cost items in monetary terms.

4.6 Perceived or resource costs?

Economics is concerned both with costs which influence behaviour in the short term and with those which affect long-term decisions. In the short term, people may well only perceive a limited range of costs or not fully appreciate the full magnitude of some cost items. Nevertheless, it is this set of costs which influences their immediate actions. The problem of perception is generally associated with the external costs which travellers generate by ignoring their actions (see Chapter 5) but here we are concerned with the misperception of the costs they bear themselves.

People misperceive the costs of their journeys (or if moving goods) for a number of reasons:

(1) The money or time cost may be so small that it is not worth taking into account (Sharp and Jennings, 1973).

(2) Certain variable costs may be regarded wrongly as fixed costs; included here would be the tendency for car users only to take account of petrol costs of journeys and ignore depreciation of

the vehicle and its maintenance (Quarmby, 1967).

(3) Users may be unaware of the connection between a particular action and the costs to which it gives rise, e.g. a fast driver may be unaware of the additional fuel costs he incurs.

(4) Habit can make regular trip-makers unaware of changing cost conditions over time even if they were fully cognizant of the full resource costs of their actions at some earlier point in time. This is more likely to be a problem encountered by car users than public transport travellers who face regular ticket purchases (Bannister, 1978).

While the final three reasons for misperception result from poor or inadequate information, the first represents a departure from the conventional economic idea of maximising behaviour. While this latter subject poses interesting theoretical questions, reasons (2)–(4) are likely to be of greater quantitative importance for transport economists. Lack of appropriate information is likely to result in different travel behaviour to that anticipated in full information situations. For forecasting purposes, therefore, it is important to have measures of future likely perceived costs because this is what potential travellers will base their behaviour on.

Whereas perceived generalised costs offer the rational basis for forecasting and for travel behaviour analysis, it is actual resource costs which are appropriate for investment decision-taking. Where people accurately perceive the costs of their travel there is no difference between the perceived and resource generalised cost. Where there is misperception, however, resource costs, being the full opportunity cost of trip-making, will exceed the perceived costs and this may result in over-investment in transport facilities if adjustments are not made. (Of course, we are still ignoring external costs of pollution etc. but these complicate rather than change the argument.)

The social welfare gains associated with an investment should be assessed by comparing the resource costs with the benefits generated – the difficulty is that the actual traffic levels using the facility depend upon perceived costs. In Figure 4.6 we have a linear demand curve for use of a road with an initial perceived generalised cost of usage equal to p^1. A widening of the road speeds traffic causing the perceived generalised cost to fall to p^2. If, however, the actual resource costs of trip-making along the road are f^1 and f^2 for the respective pre and post investment situations, then there will be 'deadweight' welfare 'losses' generated at both the t^1 and t^2 traffic levels. (At the pre-investment traffic flow, t^1, this loss is equal to area c and at the post-investment flow, t^2, it is h.) If no account is taken of this, however, the apparent consumer surplus gain from the road widening is equal to $(d+e+f+g)$. In fact, since the genuine resource costs are measured by f^1 and f^2, the investment will result in a net benefit of $(b+c+d+e-h)$. The area $(b+e+d)$ represents a straight resource cost saving under the demand curve by reducing the resource costs of travel, while $(c-h)$ reflects the change in deadweight welfare loss between the two traffic flow situations.

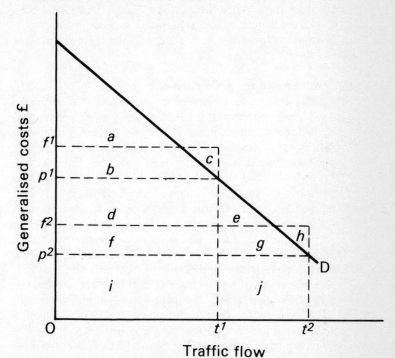

Figure 4.6　Welfare gains from a cost reduction with misperceived transport costs

Neuberger (1971) has generalised this calculation to take account of the effects of policies which alter costs and travel patterns over a network of roads and offers the general formula:

$$\sum_i \sum_j \sum_K \tfrac{1}{2}[(t^1_{ijK} + t^2_{ijK})\,(p^1_{ijK} - p^2_{ijK})]$$

$$- \sum_i \sum_j \sum_K [t^2_{ijK}\,(f^2_{ijK} - p^2_{ijK}) - t^1_{ijK}\,(f^1_{ijK} - p^1_{ijK})] \qquad (4.4)$$

where p_{ijK} is the perceived cost of travelling by mode K between origin i and destination j;

f_{ijK} is the full resource cost of travelling by mode K between origin i and destination j;

t_{ijK} is the number of trips by mode K between i and j.

When there is just one mode and one route this reduces to the diagramatic representation. In many instances, particularly when mode K is public transport, $f_{ijK} = p_{ijK}$ causing the second term in the equation to equal zero. When this occurs we have the 'rule of half' measure of welfare benefit which is discussed in detail in Chapter 9. The second term may, therefore, be treated as the correction factor for misperception.

4.7 Some criticisms of the generalised cost concept
The adoption of a single index idea of transport costs has permitted significant advances in transport forecasting and project appraisal to be made. This does not mean, however, that the concept is not without its critics nor that other advances have not been made by those choosing to ignore its existence. There are three broad lines of criticism which can be levelled against generalised cost. The first of these concerns the inherent constraints implicit in aggregation of different elements of cost, in particular the aggregating of the various cost components into a unique index restricts the separate elasticities of demand with respect to *each* individual cost component (Grey, 1978). One has an elasticity with respect to generalised cost – the generalised elasticity (Oldfield, 1974) – but cannot, for example, assess the specific effect of a reduction in travel time costs. The composite nature of the generalised cost means any component element is but a small part of the overall index, and hence a substantial change in, for example, on-vehicle travel time will only represent a small change in generalised cost. The real effect of any transport change is, in practice, only likely to affect certain elements of the index but it is this effect which concerns decision-makers. When considering road pricing or subsidised public transport the urban transport authority is little concerned with the generalised cost elasticity.

Secondly, there is concern about the long-term stability of money as the numerator. Because income rises over time, it is argued, the utility of money will fall relative to other items, especially time which is fixed in quantity. McIntosh and Quarmby (1972) have, therefore, argued that time should be used as the basis of measurement and the operational concept should be generalised time costs. Additionally, time is equally distributed (in the sense that everyone has twenty-four hours in a day) which circumvents some of the difficulties of using money values of travel cost components. Moreover since time values are normally dependent upon income (see section 3.4), the employment of money indices of generalised costs is often thought to bias decisions in favour of the wealthy. Further, Wagon and Wilson (1971) have pointed to intuitively unrealistic results obtained from forecasting exercises using monetary, rather than time, values – specifically that average journey lengths are predicted to fall with time. The validity of this as a genuine failing of money generalised costs, as opposed to weaknesses in the forecasting framework in which the measure was used, is unclear.

Thirdly, even if the basic notion of generalised cost is accepted there are critics who oppose the use of a 'universal' index for application throughout the country. The introduction of standard values of time for transport studies in the UK together with the general adoption of the McIntosh and Quarmby (1972) formula – i.e. $G = m$ (money costs) $+ t$ [(in-vehicle time) $+ 2$ (walking $+$ waiting $+$ transfer time)]–represented a move towards such a standard index. A major difficulty is that there is little firm evidence to support the universality of any weighting scheme employed or any agreed general value for time. Although the use of official time valuations and formulae ensure consistency in *approach*, they may lead to inconsistencies in *results* if the overall index is only accurate in certain sets of circumstances. At present there seems little firm evidence that either the McIntosh and Quarmby formulation or the official time values apply in all circumstances. Grey (1978) has, therefore, advocated the calibration of separate functions for each study conducted with coefficients calculated directly from local data.

Generalised cost is, despite these criticisms, a useful tool in helping us to understand, in broad terms, how variations in travel cost can influence travel behaviour. Above all, it is an extremely useful pedagogic aid which can help policy-makers articulate their ideas and plans to a more general audience. It also serves as a pragmatic device for assisting in certain types of modelling and decision-making where otherwise, as Searle (1978) points out, no information would be forthcoming at all. In this context the index is likely to be an imperfect instrument but, when used with sufficient circumspection, it can yield useful insights into the possible effects of alternative transport policies.

4.8 Further reading and references
Walters (1965) provides a useful theoretical examination of the more technical issues involved in separating short from long-run transport costs; it is also non-mathematical in its approach. Joy's (1973) study of the recent history of British Rail offers a unique examination of

the difficulties in apportioning costs as seen through the eyes of a former chief economist on the railways board. *The Road Track Cost Report* (Ministry of Transport, 1968) still provides interesting reading for those interested in the practical problems of finding a workable method of allocating track cost to users. Grey's (1978) paper on generalised costs offers both a more detailed description of the theory behind the concept and an account of its uses besides being a carefully argued, stimulating and clearly presented criticism of generalised cost as a tool in transport economics. The references it contains permit the history of the concept to be traced and provides the opportunity to discover case study material on its application.

References

Bannister, D. (1978), 'The influence of habit formation on modal choice – a heuristic model', *Transportation*, Vol. 7, pp. 19–33.

Bhatt, K., Neels, K. and Beesley, M. (1979), 'Review of road expenditures and payments by vehicle class. 1956–1975', *Transportation Research Record* 680, pp. 26–34.

Board of Trade (1969), *British Air Transport in the Seventies*, Cmnd 4018, London, HMSO.

British Railways Board (1963), *The Reshaping of British Railways*, London, HMSO.

Brown, R.H. and Nash, C.A. (1972), 'Cost savings from one-man operations of buses', *Journal of Transport Economics and Policy*, Vol. 6, pp. 281–4.

Button, K.J. (1977), *The Economics of Urban Transport*, Farnborough, Saxon House.

Button, K.J. (1979), 'Heavy goods vehicle taxation in the United Kingdom', *Transportation*, Vol. 8, pp. 389–408.

Department of the Environment (1972), *Passenger Transport in Great Britain 1970*, London, HMSO.

Department of Transport (1979), *Road Haulage Operators' Licensing (Report of the Independent Committee of Enquiry into Road Haulage Operators Licensing)*, London, HMSO.

Department of Transport (1980), *Report of the Inquiry into Lorries, People and the Environment*, London, HMSO.

Edwards, S.L. and Bayliss, B.T. (1971), *Operating Costs in Road Freight Transport*, London, Department of the Environment.

Foster, C.D. and Joy, S. (1967), 'Railway track costs in Britain', in *Development of Railway Traffic Engineering*, London, Institute of Civil Engineers.

Goodwin, P.B. (1974), 'Generalised time and the problem of equity in transport studies', *Transportation*, Vol. 3, pp. 1–24.

Goss, R.O. and Jones, C.D. (1971), *The Economics of Size in Dry Bulk Carriers*, London, Government Economic Service Occasional Paper 2.

Grey, A. (1978), 'The generalised cost dilemma', *Transportation*, Vol. 7, pp. 261–80.

Gwilliam, K.M. (1980), 'Rail transport', in P.S. Johnson (ed.), *The Structure of British Industry*, London, Granada.

Gyenes, L. (1980), 'Assessing the effect of traffic congestion on motor vehicle fuel consumption', *Transport and Road Research Laboratory Report 613*.

Hammarskjold K. (1976), *The State of the Air Transport Industry*, Montreal, IATA.

Heaver, T.D. (1975), *The Routing of Canadian Container Traffic Through Vancouver and Seattle* , Vancouver, WESTMAC.

Hicks, S.K. (1975), 'Urban goods movement: a political economist's viewpoint', in K.W. Ogden and S.K. Hicks (eds.), *Goods Movement and Goods Vehicles in Urban Areas*, Melbourne, Commonwealth Bureau of Roads.

Jansson, J.O. and Shneerson, D. (1978), 'Economics of scale of general cargo ships', *Review of Economics and Statistics*, Vol. 45, pp. 287–93.

Jennings, A. (1976), 'Infrastructure pricing and the EEC Common Transport Policy', *Journal of Transport Economics and Policy*, Vol. 10, pp. 177–95.

Jennings, A. (1979), 'Determining a global sum for taxation of road users', *Journal of Transport Economics and Policy*, Vol. 13, pp. 68–78.

Joy, S. (1964), 'British Railways track costs', *Journal of Industrial Economics*, Vol. 13, pp. 74–89.

Joy, S. (1973), *The Train that Ran Away*, London, Ian Allan.

Keeler, T.E. and Small, K.A. (1977), 'Optimal peak-load pricing investment and service levels on urban express-ways', *Journal of Political Economy*, Vol. 85, pp. 1–25.

Koshal, R.K. (1970), 'Economies of scale in bus transport II: some Indian experience', *Journal of Transport Economics and Policy,* Vol. 4, pp. 29–36.

Lee, N. and Steedman, I.W. (1970), 'Economies of scale in bus transport I: some British municipal results', *Journal of Transport Economics and Policy*, Vol. 4, pp. 15–28.

McIntosh, P.T. and Quarmby, D.A. (1972), 'Generalised costs and the estimation of movement costs and benefits in transport planning', *Highway Research Record*, no. 383, pp. 11–23.

Ministry of Transport (1966), *Transport Policy*, Cmnd 3057, London, HMSO.

Ministry of Transport (1968), *Road Track Costs*, London, HMSO.

Mohring, H. (1976), *Transportation Economics*, Cambridge, Mass., Ballinger.

Nash, C.A. (1979), 'The track costs issue – a comment', *Journal of Transport Economics and Policy*, Vol. 14, pp. 113–16.

Neuberger, H.L.I. (1971), 'Perceived costs', *Environment and Planning*, Vol. 3, pp. 369–76.

Oldfield, R. (1974), 'Elasticities of demand for travel', *Transport and Road Research Laboratory, Supplementary Report 116 UC*.

Price Commission (1978), *The Road Haulage Industry*, House of Commons Paper HC 698. London, HMSO.

Quarmby, D.A. (1967), 'Choice of travel mode on the journey to work', *Journal of Transport Economics and Policy*, Vol. 1, pp. 273–314.

Searle, G. (1978), 'Comment – generalised cost: fool's gold or useful currency?', *Transportation,* Vol. 7, pp. 297–9.

Select Committee on Nationalised Industries (1960), *Report: British Railways*, London, HMSO.

Sharp, C.H. and Jennings, A. (1973), 'The value of small quantities of time and transport investment appraisal', in *Papers and Proceedings of the 5th Conference of the Universities Transport Study Group.*

Sherman, R. (1967), 'A private ownership bias in transit choice', *American Economic Review*, Vol. 77, pp. 1211–17.

Tanner, J.C. (1968), 'An economic comparison of motorways with 2 or 3 lanes in each direction', *Road and Research Laboratory Report*, LR.203.

Teal, R.F., Marks, J.V. and Goodhue, R. (1980), 'Subsidised shared-ride taxi service', *Paper Presented to the Transportation Research Board.*

Thomson, J.M. (1974), *Modern Transport Economics*, Harmondsworth, Penguin.

Wabe, J.S. and Coles, O.B. (1975), 'The peak and off-peak demand for bus transport: a cross-sectional analysis of British municipal operations', *Applied Economics*, Vol. 7, pp. 25–30.

Wagon, D.J. and Wilson, A.G. (1971), 'The mathematical model', *Technical Working Paper 5, SELNEC Transport Study*, Manchester.

Wallis, I.P. (1980), 'Private bus operations in urban areas – their economics and role', *Traffic Engineering and Control*, Vol, 22, pp. 605–10.

Walters, A.A. (1965), 'The long and the short of transport', *Bulletin of the Oxford Institute of Economics and Statistics*, Vol. 27, pp. 97–101.

Walters, A.A. (1968), *The Economics of Road User Charges*, Baltimore, John Hopkins Press.

Warner, S.L. (1962), *Stochastic Choice of Mode in Urban Travel: A Study in Binary Choice*, Evanston, Northwestern University.

Williams, M. (1981), 'The economic justification for local bus transport subsidies', *International Journal of Transport Economics*, Vol. 8, pp. 79–88.

Wilson, A.G., Hawkins, H.F., Hill, G.J. and Wagon, D.J. (1969), 'Calibration and testing of the SELNEC transport model', *Regional Studies*, Vol. 3, pp. 337–50.

5. Pollution and Congestion – the External Costs of Transport

5.1 What is an externality?

Chapter 4 was concerned with showing the types of financial costs confronting transport users. It is quite clear from our everyday experience, however, that there are other costs associated with transport that are not directly borne by those generating them. Air travellers impose noise costs on those living below aircraft flight paths, road travellers inflict dirt and vibration on those living adjacent to major trunk routes while, at the same time, impeding the progress of pedestrians in towns. Maritime transports frequently pollute bathing beaches with their oil discharges. These are external costs generated by transport users and inflicted on the non-travelling public. Formally, externalities exist when the activities of one group (either consumers or producers) affect the welfare of another group without any payment or compensation being made. They may be thought of as relationships other than those between a buyer and a seller, and do not normally fall within the 'measuring rod of money'. There are also external benefits as well as costs although these are generally thought less important in the transport sector. The fact that wide streets, for example, act as fire breaks, in addition to serving as transport arteries, may be thought of as an external benefit associated with urban motorways.

A vast theoretical literature has grown up over the last fifty years refining the rather complicated concept of external costs. While much of the detail of this work has a greater or lesser importance in a transport context there are two major distinctions which need to be highlighted.

The distinction between pecuniary and technological externalities
The formal difference between these two categories of externality is that when the latter effects occur in production (or consumption) they must appear in the production (or utility) function while this is not the case with pecuniary externalities. Pecuniary effects occur when, say, a firm's costs are affected by price changes induced by

other firms' actions in buying and selling factors of production. An example can help to clarify this. A new motorway may block or destroy a pleasant view formerly enjoyed by the resident of an area. The fact that this directly enters the resident's utility function means it is a technological externality. If this new motorway also takes business away from a local garage and transfers it to a motorway service station, then the reduced income suffered by the garage proprietor is a pecuniary externality since the effect is indirect, namely through changes in the prices charged by the two undertakings.

The distinction is a fine one, particularly since in practice both forms of externality usually occur simultaneously, but it is an important one. Technological externalities are real resource costs which strictly should be taken into account in decision-making if optimal efficiency is to be ensured. Pecuniary externalities do not involve resource costs in an aggregate sense but they do normally have important distributional implications (e.g. in our motorway example the service station gains while the garage loses). The fact that there may be pecuniary externalities associated with a project does not reduce the *total* net benefit but rather reveals that there are adjustments in the economy which influence who is to enjoy the gains and who is to suffer the costs. The distinction between technological and pecuniary externalities is, therefore, extremely important in the appraisal of public sector transport investment where one is concerned with the incidence of the costs and benefits in addition to their overall level (see Chapter 8).

The distinction between pollution and congestion

Conventional welfare economics distinguishes between a variety of externality categories according to the different types of agent involved. Rothenberg (1970) offers a simple dichotomy which is possibly of more use in the transport context than some of the more complicated categorisations. He distinguishes between two forms of what he calls 'generic congestion'. The underlying idea is that externalities result from attempts by different agents to share a common service which is not provided in discrete units earmarked for each (i.e. it has 'public good' characteristics). The presence of other users already affects the quality of service which is rendered to each. Generic congestion may be divided into:

Pure pollution 'The essence of pollution ... is that there are some other users who do abuse the medium – the polluters – while others are relatively passive victims of such abuse – the public – Jet planes make the noise, housewives are forced to submit to it'.

Pure congestion 'If highway traffic is the classic example of congestion, then the central inter-personal distributive fact about it is that all users are using the medium (the public good) in much the same way, each is damaging service quality for both others and himself, and the ratio of self: other damage is approximately the same for all users . . . The whole user group loses homogeneously by their self-imposed interaction.'

The remainder of this chapter focuses in turn on these two types of externality and on the extent to which they can be associated with transport activities. Initially, we look at the pure pollution generated by the movement of goods and the journeys of people and then turn to consider the economics of traffic congestion.

5.2 Transport and the environment

Transport pollutes the environment in many ways. Mechanised transport generates noise, vibrations, toxic fumes, dirt and fears for safety, and often results in community severance, planning blight and disruption, loss of privacy and a need for people and industry to relocate. Specific attention has been paid to the damage that heavy road freight traffic can do to the environment of urban areas (Button and Pearman, 1981) and to the environmental effect of major new transport investments such as airports. In the former case concern may be explained by the large number of individuals affected while in the latter it is the magnitude of the effect upon a relatively small group.

Many environmentalist groups argue for substantial reductions or total elimination of these adverse environmental effects but this ignores the cost associated with removing such nuisances. While some people suffer from the environmental intrusion associated with transport, others clearly benefit from being able to travel more freely or move goods more cheaply. In almost all cases environmental improvements would reduce the net benefits enjoyed by transport users. Economists tend, therefore, to think in terms of optimising the level of pollution rather than 'purifying' the environment entirely.

If we look at Figure 5.1 we see plotted on the vertical axis the money value of the costs and benefits of reducing the noxious fumes emitted by motor cars and, on the horizontal, the environmental improvements that accompany a reduction in such fumes. The marginal costs of reducing the emissions are likely to rise quite steeply. While more sophisticated filters may be fitted and fuel subjected to more extensive refining, both become increasingly costly to apply as the toxicity of the exhaust is reduced. Additionally, they reduce the efficiency of vehicles and may, in the case of improved refining, impose higher levels of pollution on those living around refineries. The marginal benefits of 'cleaner' road vehicles, in contrast, are likely to fall with successive improvements. The public is likely to be relatively less conscious of lower levels of emission and be aware that many of the seriously toxic materials (e.g. lead) are likely to be amongst the first to be removed in the clean-up programme. Consequently, the marginal cost and revenue curves associated with improved emission quality are likely to be of the form seen in Figure 5.1. There is quite clearly an optimal level of improvement (i.e. OE_1) beyond which the marginal costs of further emission reductions exceed the marginal benefits. If the clean-up programme reduced emissions to the point where further reductions would yield no additional benefit (i.e. exhaust fumes would be considered 'pure' – although this may not mean zero toxicity if individuals' perceptions are faulty), then the situation is not optimal. Improvements beyond OE_1 to OE_2, in fact, result in a net welfare loss equal to the shaded area *ABC* in the diagram.

Consequently, when talking about the excessive environmental harm caused by various forms of transport it is important to

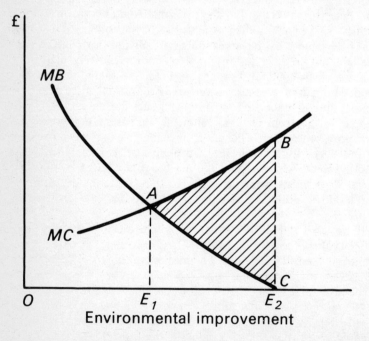

Figure 5.1   *The costs and benefits of environmental improvement*

remember that this is an exess above the *optimal* level of pollution *not* above zero pollution or some perceived 'pure' environment. We return to this topic and methods of attaining the optimum in Chapter 7.

5.3 The magnitude of the environmental problem

Figure 5.1 presents hypothetical marginal cost and benefit curves associated with reducing motor vehicle exhaust emissions. In order to make practical use of these concepts it is first necessary both to measure physically the levels of pollution and then to put a monetary value on the units of pollution generated. This section looks at the measurement problem and considers ways in which pollution can usefully be evaluated. Also some attempt is made to assess the economic importance of various forms of transport-associated environmental effects. These topics embrace many complex issues and have been subjected to major research efforts. The coverage presented here is, by necessity, limited and a much fuller account of work in this field is contained in Sharp and Jennings (1976).

Noise

The Wilson Committee (Office of the Ministry of Science, 1963) reported that in 1961 the London Noise Survey found that the sound of traffic affected more people than any other form of noise – 36 per cent of people in Inner London were disturbed by road traffic, 9 per cent by aircraft noise and 5 per cent by railway operations. This needs to be put in the context of a further survey conducted by Market and Opinion Research in 1972 which found that 12 per cent of respondents thought that excessive noise was one of the three or four most serious problems in Britain. One of the major difficulties in measuring noise in an economically useful manner is that noise differs in a variety of ways (e.g. in its type, loudness, frequency, duration, timing, etc.) and also affects people differently (e.g. some people are annoyed by particular but relatively weak sounds while others are quite happy in an extremely noisy situation and some claim to gain positive enjoyment from the near deafening music generated by modern pop groups). There is also the problem of background noise. As industrialisation and urbanisation has advanced, so the general noise level has increased and, with it, society's general acceptance of a relatively high level of background noise.

The first major problem, therefore, is that noise nuisance depends upon both the intensity and the frequency of the noise. The *'A'* weighted decibel scale (*dB(A)*) attempts to allow for this by offering a measure based on a weighted average of decibel readings where the weights reflect the level of unpleasantness caused by different frequencies and the decibels reflect the actual intensity of the noise. (While this measure is used in most transport related work, a slightly different set of weights is employed in the perceived noise scale (*PNdB*) used in the measurement of aircraft noise). The *dB(A)* scale is logarithmic and Table 5.1 gives some example of *dB(A)* measured peak noise of different forms of transport relative to other sources of noise.

Table 5.1   The relative noise generated by different forms of transport

Noise source	dB(A)
Jet aircraft on the ground	130
Noise under the flight path of a supersonic aircraft within 5 miles of take-off	125
Pop group	110–125
Noise under the flight path of heavy jet within 5 miles of take-off	115
Riveting machine in sheet metal shop	115
House near airport	100
Heavy lorry	88–92
Train	90–92
Sports car	80–82
Large car	77–83
Major road with heavy traffic	63–75
Residential road with local traffic only	56–65
Quiet bedroom	30
Sound proofed broadcasting studio	20

Source: Sharp and Jennings, 1976

The *dB(A)* scale is sometimes prefixed by a term such as L_{10} which means that it relates to a specific proportion of time (i.e. L_{10} refers to the 10 per cent peak noise level). On some occasions decibel measures have been combined with other indicators of noise annoyance in a composite index. The Noise and Numbers Index (NNI) developed for the economic appraisal of the Third London Airport, for example, combined the average peak level of noise at an airport (measured in *PNdBs*) with an indicator of the daily number of aircraft heard. The logarithmic nature of the NNI means that a one unit increase in the index represents a greater increase in noise nuisance, the higher the existing level of the index.

A scale against which noise nuisances may be measured does not, in itself, offer an economist trying to optimise noise emitted by transport much assistance – he needs to be able to place a monetary value on the noise so that the opportunity costs of different policies may be assessed. There are several ways in which noise has been evaluated.

The Commission on the Third London Airport (1971) considered changes in property values with higher noise levels. A number of surveys were conducted at the existing Heathrow and Gatwick airports seeking both the actual sale prices of properties at different distances from the airports and estate agents' estimates. The latter were used in the final analysis and the findings are seen in Table 5.2.

Table 5.2   The effects of airport noise on house prices

Class of property	Percentage reduction in house prices by noise level (NNI)		
	35–40	45–55	Over 55
Heathrow			
Low price			
(Average £3 000)	0	2.9	5.0
Medium price			
(Average £6 000)	2.6	6.3	10.5
High price			
(Average £10 000)	3.3	13.3	22.5
Gatwick			
Low price			
(Average £3 000)	4.5	10.3	—
Medium price			
(Average £6 000)	9.4	16.5	—
High price			
(Average £10 000)	16.4	29.0	—

Source: Commission on the Third London Airport, 1971

While the Third London Airport method is useful it does present some difficulties. In particular, house prices vary for many different reasons and not simply because of the noise levels inflicted upon them. In the example seen in Table 5.2, for instance, house prices around Gatwick tend for a variety of reasons to be higher than Heathrow which explains the greater fall in house values with respect to noise levels in the former. There have been attempts to devise more detailed house price indices, but these are still far from satisfactory. This does not in itself invalidate the house valuation technique but it does suggest that values obtained by employing it should

be used with circumspection and, more specifically, that a value for
noise nuisance derived using it in one area may be inappropriate for
transport studies elsewhere without adjustment.

An alternative method of evaluation is to discover how much
sufferers are prepared to pay for a specified reduction in the level of
noise nuisance. That is, one looks at exclusion facilities. Direct
questioning is seldom helpful either because individuals have little
perception of, say, what a *5dB(A)* improvement implies or because
respondents may speculate on possible private gains by misrepresent-
ing their preferences. Instead of direct questioning one can observe
how much people are actually prepared to pay for a given noise
reduction. Starkie and Johnson (1975), for example, attempted to
assess how much people are prepared to pay to double glaze their
houses. Such an approach, however, can only offer very general
evaluations of noise annoyance. On the one hand, double glazing
offers benefits other than simple noise reduction (notably lower
heating bills) implying that noise evaluations derived in this manner
yield at best a maximum estimate. On the other hand, the exclusion
is only partial (in that it does not extend outside the house or apply
when windows or external doors are open) and thus even the maximum estimate obtained is only for a very limited form of noise
nuisance removal.

Atmospheric pollution
Atmospheric pollution is generated by all forms of mechanised
transport. Even electric railways require energy which is usually pro-

*Table 5.3   Estimated discharge of air pollution in the USA in 1971
(million tons)*

Source	Carbon Monoxide	Particu- lants	Oxides of Sulphur	Hydro- carbons	Oxides of nitrogen	Total
Transport	77.5	1.0	1.0	14.7	11.2	105.4
Fuel combustion in stationary sources	1.0	6.5	26.3	0.3	10.2	44.3
Industrial production	11.4	13.6	5.1	5.6	0.2	35.9
Solid residual disposal	3.8	0.7	0.1	1.0	0.2	5.8
Miscellaneous	6.5	5.2	0.1	5.0	0.2	17.0
Total	100.2	27.0	32.6	26.6	22.0	208.4

Source: Council on Environmental Quality, 1973

duced at coal, nuclear or oil-fired power stations. Air pollution is a portmanteau term for emission of a whole series of pollutants, which are generated in different quantities and different proportions by the different transport modes. In the United States it has been estimated that the transport industry is responsible for about half of the 200 million tons of gaseous residuals discharged into the atmosphere annually, with the motor car being the main culprit. The internal combustion engine is the largest single source of hydrocarbons and oxides of nitrogen which combine to form smog. A listing of the different agents responsible for air pollution in the United States is given in Table 5.3 together with a breakdown of the chemicals emitted.

In addition to the multi-dimensional nature of pollution there is the problem of deciding upon the exact toxicity of each agent. The danger to health caused by lead particles released by petrol-driven vehicles in the United Kingdom has, for example, been subjected to considerable debate in recent years. Perception of atmospheric pollution is also imperfect, and there is a problem that people often associate visible or particularly odorous fumes with toxicity which is not always the case. (Diesel fumes, for instance, are often regarded as more objectionable than petrol fumes but are, in fact, less dangerous.) Attempts to measure air pollution have, in general, tended to take the form of objective estimates of the constituent chemical components of *direct* exhaust emissions. Table 5.4 offers the results of one such study.

Table 5.4   Emission of air pollutants in passenger transport

Pollutant	Emissions per passenger mile in milligrams			
	Cars and taxis	Diesel train	Road diesel	Electric train
Carbon monoxide	28 420	775	630	—
Hydrocarbons	1 440	155	130	—
Aldehydes	45	25	20	—
Oxides of nitrogen	990	465	380	Trace
Oxides of sulphur	110	710	250	—
Lead	40	—	—	—

Source: British Rail, 1976

While these data offer useful insights they are only of very limited use to the transport economist. The neglect of the indirect pollution associated with petrol, diesel and electricity processing and generation has already been mentioned. Additionally, these figures are too general to form the basis of any policy discussion. The level of pollution for any particular mode of transport varies with individual vehicles and – a feature of considerable importance in policy formulation – with operating conditions. A reduction in the average speed of a diesel lorry, for example, from 25 to 15 mph increases carbon monoxide emission by 47 per cent and hydrocarbon emissions by 56 per cent. Similarly, the different cycles of movement (accelerating, cruising, decelerating, and idling) have associated with them separate emission profiles – see Table 5.5. Also the rate of dispersal of the pollution is important. In open countryside, with significant air movement, the fumes are soon dispersed but in many cities, with walls of buildings flanking transport arteries, there is a tendency for pollution levels to build up. Local atmospheric conditions may also play a role in transforming normally harmless emissions into major pollutants. The photo chemical smog initially associated with Los Angeles, but now experienced in many large cities with similar climates, is the result of the sun's action on nitrogen oxides and unburned hydrocarbons emitted from petrol engines.

Table 5.5   Gaseous emissions at various stages in the transport cycle (milligrams)

Pollutant	*Running conditions*							
	Idling		*Accelerating*		*Cruising*		*Decelerating*	
	Petrol	*Diesel*	*Petrol*	*Diesel*	*Petrol*	*Diesel*	*Petrol*	*Diesel*
Carbon monoxide	69 000	Trace	29 000	1 000	27 000	Trace	39 000	Trace
Hydrocarbons	5 300	400	1 600	200	1 000	100	1 000	300
Oxides of nitrogen	30	60	1 020	350	650	240	20	30
Aldehydes	30	10	20	20	10	10	290	30

Source: Sherwood and Bowers, 1970

The techniques for evaluating air pollution nuisance are still very primitive. The approach that is most commonly proposed in theory is to measure the number of lost days of production attributable to pollution induced illness, and to multiply this by the value of an average day's output. To date, such techniques have been little used because of both the practical problems of attribution and the rather limited nature of the approach – in particular, this method of evaluation ignores the discomfort and displeasure generated by air pollution that does not result in perceptible ill health or death. It also takes no account of the worries and fears people may have about the *possibility* of adverse consequences.

Accidents

Movement is by nature dangerous. Those actually involved in transport are clearly facing the possibility of accident but there are also dangers for bystanders, especially pedestrians. Nor are the costs of physical damage, both to people and property, the only considerations, there are also the fears of possible death or injury that may reduce the general welfare enjoyed by people living near airports or major roads. Difficulties in measuring this latter component of accident cost has resulted in emphasis being directed almost exclusively at the more tangible elements. Table 5.6 gives details of accident rates associated with various modes of road transport. It is apparent that different vehicle and road types are responsible for different accident rates although other parameters may be important at the micro level (e.g. time of day, weather conditions, age of driver, etc.).

Table 5.6   Accident involvement rates in Great Britain, 1977

Vehicle type	Involvements per 100 million vehicle kms				
	Motorway	Other non built-up areas	All non built-up areas	Built-up areas	All roads
Cars and Taxis					
Fatal	1.0	3.1	2.8	2.6	2.7
Serious	7.0	25.0	22.0	40.0	31.0
Slight	18.0	46.0	41.0	146.0	95.0
All severities	27.0	74.0	65.0	188.0	128.0
Goods vehicles (under 30 cwt unladen)					
Fatal	1.4	2.6	2.4	3.1	2.8
Serious	9.0	22.0	20.0	36.0	29.0
Slight	21.0	42.0	39.0	131.0	88.0
All severities	31.0	67.0	61.0	171.0	119.0
Goods vehicles (over 30 cwt unladen)					
Fatal	2.7	5.2	4.4	5.9	4.9
Serious	9.0	25.0	20.0	36.0	25.0
Slight	19.0	42.0	35.0	106.0	58.0
All severities	31.0	72.0	59.0	148.0	88.0

Source: Department of Transport, 1979

While these objective statistics give an indication of the dangers of various modes of transport this may not correspond to people's perception of accident risk. Air travel is, for example, in terms of danger one of the safest means of transport (there were only 297 deaths and 93 injuries on scheduled UK airlines between 1968 and 1978 compared with 77 799 deaths and 3 740 286 injuries on the roads over the same period) but people tend to be more nervous about flying than about travelling by car. The reason is that people's perception functions are not linear, and that, while car accidents are more frequent, the spectacular and disastrous nature of aircraft accidents tends to capture the imagination.

One method of evaluating the costs of accidents is to consider the costs of treatment (both to humans and property) and the loss of welfare incurred by the injured parties. Some allowance for the sorrow and concern experienced by relations and friends of those involved is also sometimes included. Deaths pose particular problems in terms of direct welfare costs. Two methods have been employed to evaluate the saving of life. The *ex post* (gross output) method considers the production loss as a result of a death. The difficulty with this is that one could actually place a positive value on the death of a retired or severely disabled person if they were going to be net consumers rather than producers over the remainder of their anticipated lives. The alternative *ex ante* (net output) approach looks at the social benefit of saving a life including the welfare of the person whose life has been spared. The method, therefore, focuses more on the extra total consumption of goods and services possible by avoiding the death. This latter approach underlies the methodology employed by the Department of Transport when undertaking road investment appraisal in the United Kingdom. Table 5.7 shows the

Table 5.7   Road accident cost by road type

Type of cost	Motorway	Rural	Urban	Weighted average
Cost per accident (£)				
Fatal	52 000	47 600	41 900	44 000
Serious	3 810	3 800	2 750	3 060
Slight	870	810	450	520
Average cost of injury accident	4 120	4 240	1 810	2 360
Average cost of damage only accident	310	270	220	230

Source: Department of the Environment, 1976

official estimates of road accident costs in 1976; periodic revisions are conducted to allow for inflation.

A limitation of the *ex ante* approach is that it attempts to place a financial value on accidents rather than on the *fear* of being involved in an accident. Jones-Lee (1976) has developed a theory of choice under uncertainty as a basis for evaluating the fear of death by traffic accident. The approach is to 'ask' individuals to make trade-offs between reduced risk and wealth. This may be done either by questionnaires posing hypothetical situations (e.g. Jones-Lee used choice of travel by airlines with different safety records and fares) or by direct observation of actual trade-off situations (e.g. Ghosh, Lees and Seal (1975) used motorway speeds). A more recent, but not fully developed, theoretical advance is the idea that reduced risk of death also reduces anxiety and that the two components – i.e. life and anxiety – need to be separated to obtain accurate estimates of the cost of a death (Mooney, 1977).

Visual intrusion

Transport infrastructure and mobile plant is frequently visually intrusive and often far from aesthetically pleasing. The problem is measuring the effect. Some attempts have been made to assess the intrusion of motorways on the landscape by looking at the percentage of the skyline obscured (e.g. Clamp, 1976), but this approach only considers one dimension of a multi-faceted problem. In particular, transport infrastructure must be viewed in the context of its surroundings – a new motorway located in a formerly unspoilt countryside is likely to be viewed differently from one that blots out an unsightly waste tip. Design is also important. Also it should be remembered that vehicles are as intrusive as infrastructure and large lorries or buses are, for example, often totally out of place in unspoilt villages or 'historic towns'. Whether it is the actual size of vehicles which is alarming or simply the level of traffic flow is difficult to disentangle (see Rosman, 1976).

Vibrations

Low flying commercial aircraft, heavy goods vehicles and railway wagons create vibrations which can affect buildings. Again *useful* measures are elusive. While it is known, for example, that ground-borne vibration is related to axle loads, it has proved impossible to relate this effectively to any measure of structural damage. The evidence suggests, however, that the physical damage caused may be less than is sometimes claimed. Improved engineering techniques have reduced the damage caused by road transport and much of the damage formerly thought 'caused' by heavy lorries is more likely to have simply been 'triggered' by them. As Whiffen and Leonard (1971) point out, 'Attention can be drawn to vibration by the rattling of doors, windows, lids of ornaments, mirrors, etc. . . . The association of these audible and visible signs with the possibility of damage to the building results in exaggerated complaints about vibration, even though, in fact, there may be no risk of damage.'

Vibrations may still be a cost in an economic sense, however, even if there is no structural damage to buildings. Martin (1978) found that 8 per cent of the population are considerably bothered by vibrations from road traffic, but his suggestion that this could be measured cardinally by looking at the spectra of emitted low frequency noise has yet to be attempted.

Community severance
Roads, railways, canals and other transport arteries often present major physical (and sometimes psychological) barriers to human contact. An urban motorway can cut a local community in two, inhibiting the retention of long established social ties and, on occasions, making it difficult for people to benefit from recreational and employment opportunities on the other side of the barrier. Although it may be possible to obtain estimates of pedestrian delays and re-assignments resulting from the impedence, suppressed trips are much harder to identify. Quantification of community severance is not, therefore, an immediate prospect. As the *Jefferson Report* (Department of Transport, 1977) stated, '. . . the overall conclusion is that no acceptable way is seen of extending the assessment of severance beyond an individual examination of some of the perceived effects except, perhaps, by means of subjective statements in appropriate cases'.

5.4 Introduction to traffic congestion
The demand for transport is not constant over time. In large cities there are regular peaks in commuter travel while on holiday routes, both within the country and to overseas destinations, there are seasonal peaks in demand. Transport infrastructure, although flexible in the long run, has a finite capacity at any given period of time. One cannot, for example, expand and contract the size of an airport terminal to meet seasonal fluctuations in demand. When users of a particular facility begin to interfere with other users because the capacity of the infrastructure is limited, then congestion occurs. Of course, some degree of congestion is almost unavoidable if facilities are not to stand idle most of the time, but the question is just how

much congestion is desirable. Since people accept some level of congestion but resent 'excessive' congestion, because of the time and inconvenience costs imposed, there is some implied notion of an optimal level of congestion. To be able to formalise this it is first necessary to understand a little more about the nature and underlying economic causes of congestion.

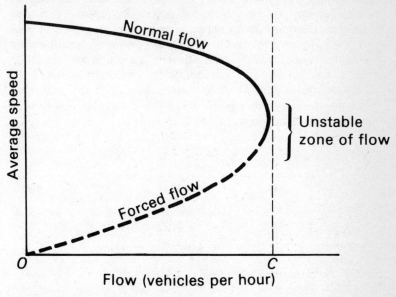

Figure 5.2   The speed-flow relationship

Road traffic congestion poses some of the greatest problems and also offers a useful basis of analysis. The economic costs of road congestion can be calculated using the engineering concept of the speed–flow relationship. If we take a straight one-way street and consider traffic flows along it over a period of time at different speed levels then the relationship between speed and flow would appear as in Figure 5.2. Flow is dependent upon both the number of vehicles entering a road and the speed of traffic. Hence, at low volumes of traffic, when vehicle impedence is zero, high speeds are possible, constrained only by the capability of the vehicle and legal speed limits, but as the number of vehicles trying to enter the road increases so they interact with existing traffic and slow one another down. As more traffic enters the road, speed falls but, up to a point, flow will continue to rise because the effect of additional vehicle number outweighs the reduction in average speed. This is the

normal flow situation. At the point where increased traffic volume
ceases to offset the reduced speed the road's 'capacity' is reached at
the maximum flow. (This is the road's *engineering* capacity and
differs from the economic capacity which is defined as that flow at
which the costs of extending the capacity are outweighed by the
benefits of doing so.) Absence of perfect information means that
motorists often continue to try and enter the road beyond this
volume causing further drops in speed and resulting in the
speed–flow relationship turning back on itself. These levels of flow
are known as forced flows. There is often a degree of 'learning from
experience' which can improve the quality of decision-making and in
practice, without any intervention, flows would settle around the
zone of instability during rush hour periods. A cross-sectional study
of the main urban centres (see Table 5.8) suggests that this zone of
instability occurs at speeds of about 18 km/ph.

Table 5.8   Traffic speeds in selected cities

City	Year	Population (million)	City centre traffic speed (kmph)	
			Peak hour	Off peak
New York	1970	13.3	16	26
Detroit	1970	4.0	17.7	—
Salt Lake City	1970	0.9	27	—
London	1971	7.4	20.6	20.3
Birmingham	1965	1.1	22.1	—
Leeds	1965	0.5	18	—
Paris	1970	6.4	16.9	—
Athens	1971	2.7	15.5	24
Copenhagen	1967	1.7	14.5	—
Stockholm	1969	1.3	18	—
Calcutta	1971	7.5	11–16	19
Singapore	1972	2.2	21	—

Source: Adapted from Thomson, 1977

The actual form of the speed–flow relationship and the engineering capacity of any individual road will depend upon a number of
factors. Clearly, the physical characteristics of the road (its width,
the number of lanes, etc.) is of central importance – these may be
seen as the long-term influences. Short-term factors include the form
of traffic management and control schemes in operation (traffic
lights, roundabouts, etc.). Finally, the type and age of vehicles combined with their distribution may influence capacity.

A fairly typical set of speed–flow relationships which illustrate these points are, for example, offered by Neutze (1963) in his study of Sydney's arterial road system. Information obtained from over 400 locations on main roads in the city was used in the exercise, the results of which are seen in Figure 5.3. As one might expect, the capacity of six-lane roads exceeds that of either two or four-lane roads, although at most traffic densities the speed is slightly higher on the two rather than the four-lane roads. The explanation for this is that traffic management policies slow down flows of the four-lane roads because road-side parking is permitted and thus the capacity of curb-side lanes is severely restricted, and they also tend to pass through more densely populated areas with more restrictive traffic management controls.

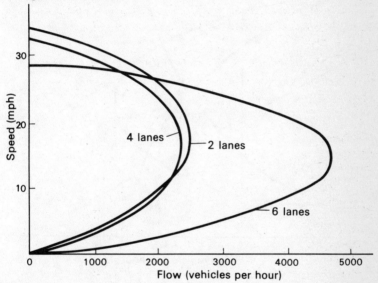

Figure 5.3 Speed-flow relationships on different road types in Sydney

5.5 The economic costs of congestion

While the speed–flow relationship is useful in explaining the physical effects of congestion, it does not give any indication of the economic costs. Generalised costs (see Chapter 4) provide the vital link between physical traffic flows and cost. Broadly, faster travel in urban areas means cheaper travel in terms of generalised costs – vehicles are used more effectively and travel times are reduced. The *AC* curve in Figure 5.4 represents the average generalised cost of trip making at different levels of traffic flow. It is a *reverse* mapping of the speed–flow curve seen in Figure 5.2 with the positively sloped portion corresponding to the negatively sloped section of the speed-flow curve – this stems from the inverse relationship between speed and generalised cost. The backward bending AC curve yields two separate MC curves with the shapes indicated – i.e. the positively sloped MC_1 curve is derived from the positively sloped portion of the AC curve and the negatively sloped curve (MC_2) from the negatively sloped portion.

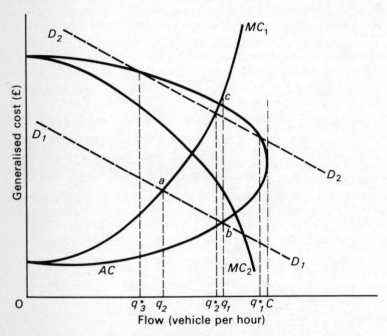

Figure 5.4   Optimal traffic flows

A further interpretation can be placed on the AC and MC curves. The curves reflect the average and marginal generalised costs associated with different flows – they show all the time and money costs borne by road users when trip-making. In this sense they may be seen as representing 'social costs' in the limited sense that they are the costs to the *society of road users*. However, any individual user entering the road will only consider the costs he personally bears. He will, in most circumstances, either be unaware of or unwilling to consider the external, congestion, costs he imposes on the other road users. Consequently, the individual motorist will only consider the average costs experienced by road users and take no account of the congestive impact of his trip on other vehicles. It is frequently argued that the *MC* curve, therefore, relates to the marginal *social* cost for the *new trip-maker and existing road users* of an addition to the traffic flow while the *AC* curve is equivalent to the marginal *private* cost curve – i.e. the additional cost borne and perceived by the *new trip-maker* alone. The difference between the *AC* and *MC* curves at any traffic flow reflects the economic costs of congestion at that flow.

The fact that potential trip-makers tend to respond to private costs and ignore external considerations (unless they are particularly altruistic) means that road users treat the *AC* curve as the decision-making measure of cost. If the demand for use of the road is D_1 in Figure 5.4, the resultant flow will without any intervention be q_1. From a social point of view this is excessive because the q_1th motorist is only enjoying a benefit of q_1b but imposing costs of q_1c. The socially optimal flow is where $MC_1 = D_1$, i.e. a flow of q_2. The additional traffic beyond this level to q_1 can be seen to be generating costs of (q_2acq_1) but only enjoying a benefit of (q_2abq_1) – a 'dead weight' welfare loss of (abc) is apparent. A traffic flow lower than q_2 is also sub-optimal because the potential consumer surplus gains from trip-making are not being fully exploited.

An interesting situation arises if demand is somewhat higher, say at level D_2 in the diagram. Here D_2 intersects the negatively sloped section of the *AC* curve and does so at two levels of flow (q^*_1 and q^*_3). The actual flow in this situation, and without intervention, will again be above the optimum flow. The flow will exceed q^*_3 – where D_2 intersects *AC* – because as demand rises traffic will continue to enter the road (i.e. moving around and up the positive *AC* curve) until flow q^*_1 is reached but there will be no further movement around the backward bend because private costs to motorists will exceed the extra benefit they will derive. The social optimum flow, however, is when demand is cut from below by the MC_2 curve – marginal cost here being seen as reflecting both the costs of additional traffic flow to the marginal user *and* the costs he imposes on other road users. This suggests an optimal traffic flow of q^*_2 (where $q^*_3 \langle q^*_1 \rangle q^{*2}$). In other words, while the negatively sloped MC_2 curve is mathematically possible it is of no economic significance in the analysis quite simply because there will always be an intersection with the positively sloped section which yeilds a higher social benefit.

5.6 Types of traffic congestion
The basic theory of traffic congestion set out above is derived from standard economic theories of cost. In more general terms, if we let

TC be the total costs of providing a road which has *N* trips being made along it per unit of time then we may define:

$$TC = N. \, C\,(N,K) + f\,(K) \qquad (5.1)$$

where *C* is the cost of one trip to a vehicle driver and f(*K*) is the cost per time period of providing *K* units of road capacity. The short-run marginal cost is then derived as:

$$\frac{\delta(TC)}{\delta N} = C(N,K) + \frac{N\delta C}{\delta N}. \qquad (5.2)$$

The *N*th vehicle, thus, incurs a cost to itself of C(*N,K*) – which is the average cost of making a trip – while also slowing all other road users by a total amount costing $N(\delta C/\delta N)$ (see Mohring and Boyd, 1971).

In practice, as we would expect from our discussion of the speed–flow relationship, the total cost function varies with the details of the transport system under consideration. Vickrey (1969) distinguishes five separate types of congestion relevant in this context. While these are couched in terms of road congestion, they are equally applicable to most other modes of transport – one can quite simply substitute airlane or waterway for roads. The types of congestion are:

(1) *Simple interaction* This occurs at comparatively low levels of traffic flow where the number of mobile units is small. Delays are minimal and usually result from slow and careful driving on the part of users who wish to avoid accidents. Total delay tends to vary as the square of the volume of traffic, so that each additional motorist causes a delay to *each other* road user roughly equal to that which he himself suffers. This is essentially the type of congestion we have been concerned with above.

(2) *Multiple interaction* This occurs at higher levels of traffic flow where, although the road capacity is not reached, an additional vehicle causes considerably more impedence to each other vehicle than with simple interaction. Empirical evidence suggests that for every minute the marginal user is delayed, other vehicles each suffer a delay of three to five minutes.

(3) *Bottleneck situations* These occur when a particular stretch of a road (or other piece of transport infrastructure) is of more limited capacity than either the preceding or subsequent links

in the network. If the flow is below that of the capacity of the bottleneck then either simple or multiple interaction may occur, but once the capacity is reached, and in particular if this is sustained for any length of time, then queues develop. An exceptionally high level of congestion is then likely to arise.

(4) *Triggerneck situations* When a bottleneck situation results in queues of traffic, these may impede the general flow of traffic even for those not wishing to use the section of road with limited capacity. At the extreme, congestion may become so severe that the traffic comes to a complete standstill and can only flow again after some vehicles have backed up.

(5) *Network and control congestion* The efforts of traffic engineers and managers (by the introduction of different traffic control devices) may reduce congestion costs at certain times of the day or, for example, in the case of bus lanes, for specific types of traffic but increase them at other times or for other modes. This results from the general bluntness of most traffic control schemes which may help solve major problems but do, at times, create other, albeit usually less significant, difficulties. This type of congestion was not fully appreciated in the United Kingdom until the mid 1970s and had earlier led to excessively high estimates of urban congestion costs. Previously it was assumed that congestion tended to be of the simple or multiple interactive kind but as the discussion paper on *Transport Policy* (Department of the Environment, 1976) says, 'Once account is taken of the limitations placed upon urban traffic speeds by factors such as the incidence of traffic lights and the multi-purpose nature of urban road networks, traffic speeds associated with even very low levels of congestion can be expected to be quite low – almost certainly below 20 mph in central areas.'

In addition to these five types of traffic congestion which can arise when the infrastructure is fixed, Vickrey also points to the more general problem of transport congestion in the economy as a whole. In the context of urban areas, roads in the United States take up 30% or more of the land area of city centres, while in Western Europe the figure is between 15% and 20% and in third world countries about 10%. The question then becomes one of whether in the *long term* the general welfare of urban society is being excessively reduced by too much transport infrastructure congesting city centres. The acceptance of this view makes it rather difficult to define meaningfully optimal levels of transport provision in the traditional welfare sense.

5.7 The economic value of congestion

Congestion, or to be more exact excessive congestion, has been shown to imply a 'dead-weight' welfare loss and to reduce the economic efficiency of any transport system. In recent years there has been some debate, however, about whether this welfare loss is compensated by other beneficial effects of congestion which are not immediately apparent in the standard, static, marginal cost type of analysis. These arguments tend to follow three broad lines, those focusing on issues centring on the distributional effect of congestion on different groups in society, those concerned with more straightforward efficiency problems and those which take other forms of cost into account.

The main costs imposed by traffic congestion are usually found to be time costs (although there may also be fuel and other components of generalised costs to be considered). Queuing up for the use of a transport facility and slowing down in its consumption takes up the user's time. Measures to reduce the demand, increase the supply, or the introduction of market prices to optimise congestion (all of which are discussed later in the book) impose some form of either financial or welfare loss which, although on very simple efficiency criteria they must be lower than the congestion costs saved, still have to be borne by someone. Those who favour the retention of a high level of congestion as a method of allocating scarce transport facilities (e.g. Richardson, 1974 and Sharp, 1966) argue that, since in the short term time is evenly distributed to everyone – i.e. there are twenty-four hours in every person's day – it is a more equitable method of allocation than many alternative techniques. If a traveller really wants to make a journey he would be willing (and able) to wait, whereas if a high, congestion deterring, charge is levied his financial budget constraint may make it impossible to make the trip. While there seem to be some grounds for this type of argument if one accepts that transport is unique in requiring a substantial time input for its consumption (a proposition that is far from self-evident), in the longer term the wider distributional issue is probably more effectively tackled by direct income redistributional measures. There seems no reason, in the general case, for singling out transport rather than a number of other economic activities for this special treatment. In addition, even when goods have in the past been provided free of charge, there is empirical evidence that, despite the equal distribution of time, it is the rich who tend to obtain them and, *ipso facto*, a disproportionate share of the benefit (Barzel, 1974).

Moving to the second mitigating argument in favour of allocation by congestion we turn to efficiency considerations. Congestion is seen by some as a complementary method of allocating certain types of facility, supplementing rather than competing with other, usually monetary price, mechanisms (Smolensky *et al.*, 1971). The dead-weight loss associated with congestion may in some situations, it is claimed, be outweighed by other forms of welfare benefit. In some instances people, for example those on aircraft stacking at congested airports, may use time spent in queuing productively while, in others, the deadweight loss associated with sub-optimally excessive congestion may be exceeded by the administrative or other costs of achieving optimal utilisation of the transport facility. As we see in Chapter 7 this has been one argument used against the introduction of sophisticated metering devices for urban road pricing. More generally, it is argued that, since transport users are far from homogeneous, different groups of users will value time differently and hence a system with both time allocated and financially allocated facilities could well be optimal. If analogies are made with other forms of economic activity from retailing to car manufacturing then both money and time are used for allocation. For example, one can get fast, personal service at a small local store but prices are likely to be higher than at a large, possibly distant, supermarket where queuing is normal at checkouts. This sort of approach is in general use for some forms of transport, with many countries, for instance, having fast, tolled motorways running parallel to slow, free trunk roads. At the urban level in San Juan there are express buses which operate over the same route as other local buses, stopping at the same points, but charging a higher fare. The higher price reduces the number of customers and makes it a much more rapid service. (This is a particularly interesting example because the facilities would be identical if price differences had not been introduced.) Also one can often choose between expensive, readily available air services or cheap stand-by and 'Skytrain' facilities which often involve queuing or waiting for a flight. With a given distribution of income, this increased choice necessarily increases welfare which may, in turn, offset any, or at least part of, the dead-weight loss incurred on congested parts of the system. Essentially there is product differentiation taking place in response to variations in the opportunity cost of time among consumers.

The difficulty with this argument is that in many cases physical factors make it impossible to provide different types of transport service. In other cases, economies of scale are sufficient to make the provision of alternatives excessively wasteful. One approach, favoured by theoreticians, may be to decide upon the optimal flow, and only let that flow on to the road or facility at any one time leaving a queue of potential users waiting. The optimal flow in this sense being such that the length of the queue of traffic wishing to use the road would make the opportunity time cost of waiting equal to the money price at which the traffic flow is optimal. It is difficult to see how this could be put into practice on urban roads although it may be appropriate for making optimal use of facilities such as bridges or ferries where queuing is practicable. The information costs of estimating optimal queue lengths may also prove an insurmountable practical problem.

Finally, a high level of congestion may itself be optimal (even with the dead-weight losses it imposes and where neither of the former lines of argument are applicable) when other forms of cost are also considered. It may be, for example, that the transaction costs of moving from an over-congested to an optimally congested situation exceed the conventionally defined benefits of eliminating a dead-weight loss. The transition costs involved in removing an externality such as excessive congestion are of three broad types: the cost per unit of reducing the externality, initial lump sum costs of organisation, and information/enforcement costs of carrying the action through (Dahlman, 1979). To remove excessive congestion would, in virtually all cases, involve costs in one or more of these categories and it could well be that in many cases such transaction costs could be very high. A related point is that the actual reduction of congestion to the optimal level *for transport users* may mean spreading other forms of external cost (generally noise and air pollution) to a much wider group of non-users in the community. Raising landing fees at over-used major airports, for example, is likely to divert traffic elsewhere and place environmental costs on people living near other, formerly underutilised airports. Congestion may in these circumstances, where the demand for transport concentrates the incidence of environmental costs on a relatively small group in the community, be felt to offer a more acceptable use of transport infrastructure than if congestion is reduced but this results in demand being spread geographically. This is more likely if the initial congestion is concentrated in relatively insensitive areas, but its reduction would increase the environmental nuisance experienced in residential or other sensitive locations.

5.8 Further reading and references
Kneese (1977) offers a detailed examination of environmental economics and, although it is not specifically aimed at transport econ-

omists, much of the material is still highly relevant. A more specific examination of the environmental implications of transport activities is contained in Sharp and Jennings (1976). This is less analytical in approach but does contain many interesting insights in addition to a vast amount of information (mainly in tabular form). The evaluation of life has been subjected to considerable research in recent years and the resultant literature is voluminous. Perhaps the most accessible further reading in this area that also offers some rigorous questioning of conventional methodology is Jones-Lee (1976). Although the field has moved on slightly since 1976, the book contains a good review of the main theories in the area as well as original research findings. Congestion is an equally well researched topic with an extensive literature. Else (1981) provides some novel ideas but Walters (1961) is a classic paper which the careful reader may feel stands up well to recent attacks. The Armitage Report (Department of Transport, 1980) provides a useful and informative case study of the environmental costs associated with heavy lorries.

References

Barzel, Y. (1974), 'A theory of rationing by waiting', *Journal of Law and Economics*, Vol. 17, pp. 73–95.

British Rail (1976), *Environmental and Social Impact Study*, London, British Railways Board.

Button, K.J. and Pearman, A.D. (1981), *The Economics of Urban Freight Transport*, London, Macmillan.

Clamp, P.E. (1976), 'Evaluation of the impact of roads on the visual amenity of rural areas', *Department of the Environment Research Report* 7.

Commission on the Third London Airport (1971), *Report,* London, HMSO.

Council on Environmental Quality (1973), *Environmental Quality – 1973*, Washington, CEQ.

Dahlman, C.J. (1979), 'The problem of externalities', *Journal of Law and Economics,* Vol. 22, pp. 141–62.

Department of the Environment (1976), *Transport Policy: A Consultation Document (2 vols.)*, London, HMSO.

Department of Transport (1977), *Route Location with Regard to Environmental Issues*, London, HMSO.

Department of Transport (1979), *Road Haulage Operators' Licensing (Report of the Independent Committee of Enquiry into Road Haulage Operators' Licensing)*, London, HMSO.

Department of Transport (1980), *Report of the Inquiry into Lorries, People and the Environment*, London, HMSO.

Else, P.K. (1981), 'A reformation of the theory of optimal taxation', *Journal of Transport Economics and Policy*, Vol. 15, pp. 217–32.

Ghosh, D., Lees, D. and Seal, W. (1975), 'Optimal motorway speed and some values of time and life', *Manchester School*, Vol. 43, pp. 134–43.

Jones-Lee, M.W. (1976), *The Value of Life on Economic Analysis*, London, Martin Robertson.

Kneese, A.V. (1977), *Economics and the Environment*, Harmondsworth, Penguin.

Martin, D.J. (1978), 'Low frequency traffic noise and building vibration', *Transport and Road Research Laboratory Supplementary Report*, SR.429.

Mohring, H. and Boyd, J.H. (1971), 'Analysing "externalities": "direct interaction" versus "asset utilisation" frameworks', *Economica*, Vol. 38, pp. 347–61.

Mooney, G.H. (1977), *The Valuation of Human Life*, London, Macmillan.

Neutze, G.M. (1963), 'The external diseconomies of growth in traffic', *Economic Record*, Vol. 39, pp. 332–45.

Office of the Ministry of Science (1963), *Noise: Final Report of the Committee on the Problem of Noise*, Cmnd 2056, London, HMSO.

Richardson, H.W. (1974), 'A note on the distributional effects of road pricing', *Journal of Transport Economics and Policy*, Vol. 8, pp. 82–5.

Rosman, P.F. (1976), 'Alternative sizes of lorry: two investigations into public preferences', *Transport and Road Research Laboratory Special Report*, SR.210.

Rothenberg, J. (1970), 'The economics of congestion and pollution: an integrated view', *American Economic Review, Papers and Proceedings*, Vol. 60, pp. 114–21.

Sharp, C.H. (1966), 'Congestion and welfare: an examination of the case for a congestion tax', *Economic Journal*, Vol. 76, pp. 806–17.

Sharp, C.H. and Jennings, A. (1976), *Transport and the Environment*, Leicester, Leicester University Press.

Sherwood, P. and Bowers, P. (1970), 'Air pollution from road traffic', *Road Research Laboratory Report*, LR.352.

Smolensky, E., Tideman, T.N. and Nichols, D. (1971), 'The economic uses of congestion', *Papers of the Regional Science Associations*, Vol. 26, pp. 37–52.

Starkie, D.N.M. and Johnson, D.M. (1975), *The Economic Value of Peace and Quiet*, London, Saxon House.

Thomson, J.M. (1977), *Great Cities and their Traffic*, London, Gollancz.

Vickrey, W. (1969), 'Congestion theory and transport investment', *American Economic Review (Papers and Proceedings)*, Vol. 59, pp. 251–60.

Walters, A.A. (1961), 'The theory and measurement of private and social costs of highway congestion', *Economica*, Vol. 19, pp. 676–9.

Whiffen, A.C. and Leonard, D.P. (1971), 'A survey of traffic induced vibrations', *Road Research Laboratory Report*, LR.418.

6. The Pricing of Transport Services

6.1 The principles of pricing

Pricing is a method of resource allocation; there is no such thing as the 'right' price but rather there are optimal pricing strategies which permit specified goals to be obtained. The optimal price, for example, to achieve profit maximisation may differ from that needed to maximise welfare or ensure the highest sales revenue. In some cases there is no attempt to devise a price to maximise or minimise anything but rather prices are set that permit lower level objectives (e.g. security, minimum market share, etc.) to be attained. Further, prices may be set to achieve certain objectives for the transport supplier in terms of *his* welfare (this is normally the case of private enterprise transport undertakings) while in other fields prices may be set to improve the welfare of *consumers* (as has been the case with some publicly owned transport undertakings). The distinction here is a fine one and many undertakings consider that the employment of the pricing mechanisms to achieve their objectives is automatically to the benefit of customers. One of the major problems in discussing pricing policies in practice is to decide what exactly the objective is. A good example is port pricing where there has been a blurring between the 'European' doctrine of setting prices to facilitate the economic growth of the port's hinterland and the 'Anglo–Saxon' approach which attempts to ensure that ports cover their costs and, where possible, make a profit irrespective of the effects on the wider local economy (see Bennathan and Walters, 1979).

This chapter looks at the appropriate pricing policies to adopt for transport undertakings with a variety of objectives and confronted by different market conditions. While the latter sections focus on criteria concerned with maximising the social benefits of transport, this section briefly reviews the prices likely to exist in situations where transport suppliers are interested in purely commercial criteria (defined here as the pursuit of their own self-interest).

Profit maximisation is the traditional motivation of private enterprise undertakings. The actual price level in this case depends upon the degree of competition in the market. Where competition is considerable then no single supplier has any control over price and must charge that determined by the interaction of supply and demand in the market as a whole (Adam Smith's 'invisible hand'). Within this perfectly competitive environment, it is impossible for any supplier to make super-normal profits in the long term because of the incentives such profits would have on new suppliers entering the market and increasing aggregate supply. Elementary economics tells us that in the long run price will be equated with the marginal (and average) costs of each supplier (see Lipsey, 1979).

In contrast, a true monopoly supplier has no fear of new entrants increasing the aggregate supply of transport services and has the freedom *either* to set the price *or* to stipulate the level of service he is prepared to offer. The effective constraint on the monopolist is the countervailing power of demand which prevents the joint determination of both output and price. However, given the absence of competition and the degree of freedom enjoyed by the monopolist, it is almost certain that a profit-maximising price will result in charges above marginal and average cost (the only exception being the most unlikely situation of perfectly elastic *market* demand curve). This is one reason why governments have tended to regulate the railways, ports and other transport undertakings with monopoly characteristics.

This simple description of textbook situations does, however, hide certain peculiarities which may arise in some transport markets. Since the actual unit of supply, the vehicle, is mobile it is possible for the transport market to appear to be essentially competitive but the individual suppliers to price as if they were monopolists or, at least, exercised some monopoly power. The unregulated urban taxi-cab

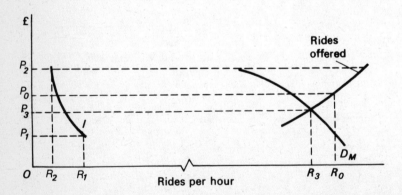

Figure 6.1   Taxi-cab fare determination

market is an example of this (see Shreiber, 1975). In Figure 6.1 D_M is the market demand for taxi-cab 'rides' per hour in a market supplied solely by cruising taxi-cabs. The cost of taxi cruising activities is almost constant irrespective of whether a fare is carried or not and to stay in business the cab operator must charge fares which permit such costs to be recovered. In the diagram, I is the iso-revenue curve for a single operator which allows the recovery of costs at different fare-ridership levels. It is constrained to a minimum fare (P_1) by the physical impossibility of carrying more than R_1 passengers an hour. Also, it is unlikely that a fare above P_2 ever would be feasible – potential users would simply not accept it. For the market as a whole, therefore, fares must exceed P_1 if taxi-cab services are to be offered but this should not be seen as the true long-term floor level of fares. Because potential customers are seldom positioned exactly where empty cabs are cruising, there must be an excess of rides offered *above* total demand if sufficient rides are to be supplied. This lack of synchronisation means that the 'rides offered curve' in Figure 6.1 is not a true supply curve since it is dependent upon demand conditions. At higher fares, the rides offered will increase but even at the intersection with the total demand curve (with R_3 rides offered) there will still be unsatisfied demand (Shreiber, 1977), i.e. the amount of taxi rides *taken* is less than the amount demanded. This is because the taxis may not be at the same location as potential customers. Only if cabs were always exactly where they were wanted would demand always be satisfied. The demand will, in normal circumstances, only be fully satisfied at a price above the intersection – say P_0 – because at this and higher prices the ratio between the amount of rides demanded and the amount offered will correspond to the *rate of occupancy*. This is so because the amount demanded is then assumed equal to the number of rides taken, and there are no frustrated passengers who give up waiting because they are unable to obtain a ride. The fare level may be set at any point above P_0 but below P_2; hence the apparently perfect taxi-cab market does not have a unique price. However, there are reasons to suspect that the final price will be nearer P_2 than P_0 thus permitting the earning of supernormal profit by the cab operators. It also means that those who still wish to pay the fare and use taxi-cab services will have a good service provided for them – the rides offered being *well* in excess of those demanded – although the short waiting time and abundance of capacity is likely to be wasteful in resource utilisation. The tendency towards high fares is caused by the relatively inelastic demand for the services of any individual taxi. Unlike normal perfect markets, individual suppliers are not normally confronted with perfectly elastic demand schedules for their services but when hailed by a potential customer are virtual monopolists able to charge a high fare for their services. People seldom turn away a cab upon hearing the fare to hail another one – the low probability of a lower cab fare does not justify it. Once fares are at the higher level there is, therefore, no incentive for individual cabs to cut their fares because to customers they all appear alike and no additional business is attracted (i.e. revenue for any cab acting differently will inevitably fall).

Of course, the cab market is somewhat more complicated than the simple model suggests (there are, for instance, cab ranks, and it may be possible to differentiate cabs by colouring schemes etc.), but the fear that cabs could exploit local monopoly power of the type described and keep fares sub-optimally high is one reason why authorities in most major cities control fare levels. While this may be justified it is hard to see why at the same time most cities (and London is a notable exception to this) regulate the number of taxi-cabs operating within their domain; if fares are deemed optimal at P_0 then rides offered will automatically adjust to R_0 and there is no need for official regulation of capacity which can seriously distort the market (see, for instance, Beesley 1973).

While it is possible that the simple picture of perfectly competitive price determination is often complicated in the transport sector, it is equally true that the basic model of monopoly also on occasions needs modification. There are few if any natural monopolies in transport, there are normally competitive modes even if the one in question tends to be monopolistic in character. Also users of transport services often have the alternative of either changing their method of production (in the case of freight transport) or pattern of consumption (with passenger modes) so that transport is itself competitive with different forms of human activity. In some cases where these countervailing forces are weak or the introduction of competition would mean wasteful duplication of services, government may institutionalise a monopoly but by controlling price and other commercial aspects of its operations prevent the exploitation of customers. British policy with regard to the railways tended to favour this general approach until 1947 when rather more direct control was introduced through nationalisation.

The fear of potential competition tends to regulate the activities of essentially monopoly transport suppliers even when government intervention is minimal. The pricing policies pursued by liner conferences, when shippers combine to monopolise scheduled services between major ports, offers an illustration of this. Some discussion of detailed pricing of consignments by conferences is contained in section 6.4; here we focus on the general principles. Sturmey (1975) argues that conferences do not price to maximise immediate profits but rather to maximise the present value of the flow of revenue from the market. The emphasis on revenue reflects the concern with market size while that on the present value shows that long term objectives dominate short run considerations. If, in Figure 6.2, the intention was to maximise profit in each market then price would be set, assuming the conference enjoyed a short-term monopoly position, at P_M with a monthly output of Q_M. If sales revenue maximisation (subject to cost recovery) is the objective then price P_R is charged. In practice, however, Sturmey argues that conference rates will be below P_M because the high short-term profits would encourage competition to enter the market; they are also unlikely to equal P_R because the conference looks beyond the immediate period

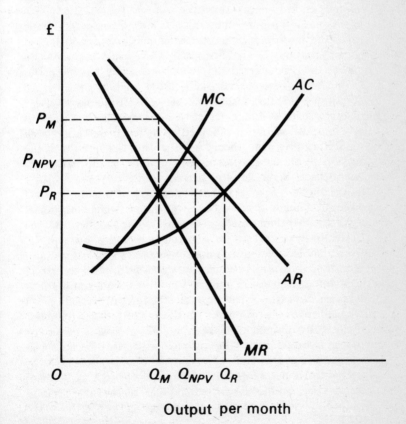

Figure 6.2   Pricing of conference services

although there is no *a priori* method of telling whether they will be above or below this level. The conference is likely to base its pricing policy on a relatively long time horizon – hypothesised by Sturmey to be the period over which the scale of productive enterprise is unchanged, but long enough to allow for additional capital equipment, which duplicates existing equipment, to be installed – although not long enough for all factors to be considered truly variable. The net revenue over this period, discounted to yield its current worth (see Chapter 8.2), is then seen as the key variable to maximise. The conference rate is, therefore, likely to be, say, at P_{NPV} in Figure 6.2 at which the maximum present value is obtained without attracting new entrants.

6.2   Marginal cost pricing

As was pointed out in the previous section, the pricing policy adopted by any transport undertaking depends upon its basic objectives. The traditional, classical economic assumption is that firms price so that profits are maximised. More recent variations on the theory of the firm suggests that many undertakings adopt prices that maximise sales revenues (Baumol, 1962) when in an expansive phase, or simply price to ensure that certain satisfactory levels of profit, security, market domination, etc. are achieved (Simon, 1959) when a defensive stance is adopted. Whatever the underlying operational objective, the theory of the firm assumes that the supplier is intent on maximising *his own* welfare, be this defined in terms of profits or higher level objectives.

Welfare economics takes a rather wider view of pricing, looking upon price as a method of resource allocation which maximises social welfare rather than simply the welfare of the supplier. In some cases, since the good or service is actually provided by a public agency, this may be equated with maximising the suppliers' welfare. In other instances, controls or incentives may be applied to private companies so that their pricing policy is modified to maximise social rather than private welfare. This may take the form of restrictions on pricing flexibility, or the taxing and subsidising of firms so that their prices are socially optimal. Social optimality has a wide variety of meanings but in broad terms it means maximising the joint net social surplus (i.e. the total revenue (TR) plus consumers' surplus (CS) generated by an undertaking minus the total cost (TC)). We can, therefore, define the objective of public policy as the maximisation of

$$SW = TR + CS - TC \qquad (6.1)$$

where TC represents total, usually including social, costs.

Maximisation of equation 6.1 and rearrangement yields:

$$\frac{d}{dQ}(TR + CS) = \frac{d}{dQ}(TC) \qquad (6.2)$$

where the right-hand side of the expression is marginal social cost. On the left-hand side, $(TR + CS)$ is the area under the demand curve which, by denoting demand as $D = P(Q)$, we can re-express as

$$(TR + CS) = \int_0^Q P(Q)dQ,$$

and differentiation of this with respect to output yields

$$\frac{d}{dQ}(TR + CS) = \frac{d}{dQ}\int_0^Q P(Q)dQ = P(Q). \qquad (6.3)$$

In other words, social welfare is maximised when price is equated to marginal social cost (i.e. from 6.2 and 6.3 when $P = MSC$). Traditional theory tells us that such a condition prevails in the long term when perfect competition exists despite the fact that each firm is attempting to maximise its own profits. The ability to exercise any degree of monopoly power, however, permits a firm to price above marginal cost so that it can achieve additional profit at the expense of reduced output and at costs to the consumers. The price charged by a profit maximising monopolist will force some potential consumers to forgo consumption despite their willingness to pay for the costs of their activities. Indeed, it was the fear of monopoly exploitation that led to controls being imposed on railway pricing in the late nineteenth century and has led to the United States controlling rate fixing by shipping conferences operating from its ports.

While it has been shown that social welfare is maximised by adopting marginal cost pricing, the exact definition of the appropriate marginal cost has been left vague. More specifically, there is the question of whether long-run ($LRMC$) or short-run marginal cost ($SRMC$) pricing is the more appropriate (short-run being when there is a fixed capacity which can be modified only in the long run). $SRMC$ pricing has the advantage that it ensures existing capacity is used optimally but does not take account of capital and other fixed cost items. Wiseman (1957) was particularly concerned with this problem since, he argued, that the shorter the time period under consideration, the lower will appear the $SRMC$ and, *ipso facto*, the price charged users. This concern is misguided, however, because if there is fixed capacity, as is almost always the case with transport in the short term, a premium should be added to *SRMC* as an effective rationing device to contain excessive demand. Price is, after all, an allocative device.

Figure 6.3 shows the demand for a passenger railway service with capacity Q_1. The marginal cost of carrying each additional passenger is constant until the capacity of the system is reached where upon the *SRMC* becomes infinite. If a price of P_1 is charged then demand will exceed capacity by $Q_d' - Q_1$. In these circumstances, where demand will exceed absolute capacity using *SRMC* pricing policy, a mark-up to price level P_1' is appropriate to ration the available seats. The extra revenue thus generated in excess of *LRMC* provides an indication that it would be beneficial for the capacity of the railway service to be expanded. The optimal scale of service will, in fact, be offering capacity Q_2 where the price charged travellers is equated with *LRMC* (and the up-turn of $SRMC_2$ curve). We see, therefore, that the long-run optimum is where $P = LRMC = SRMC$. In some cases, (for

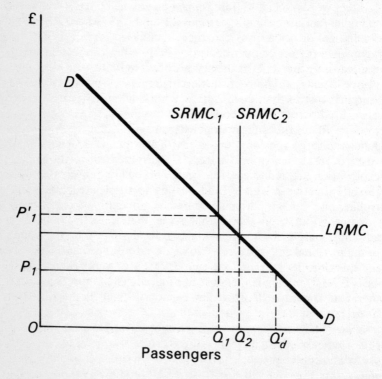

Figure 6.3   Short-run and long-run marginal cost pricing

example, airports or motorway systems) indivisibilities may make it impossible to provide exactly the optimal capacity Q_2 and a choice must then be made between a sub-optimally small system or a sub-optimally large one. Under such conditions decisions must be based upon weighing the full costs and benefits of the alternatives against one another.

6.3 Difficulties of 'second best' situations

The preceding analysis contained a number of implicit, as well as the stated, explicit assumptions. In particular, it assumed that all other prices in the economy are set equal to marginal cost. A variety of factors – some economic, others political or institutional – mean that in reality all other prices in the economy are not equal to marginal cost. The problem, again couched in terms of the railway example, then becomes one of deciding whether marginal cost pricing is, in these circumstances, appropriate in the railway context.

Under some circumstances the problem may not be serious and, from a purely pragmatic stance, it may be more efficient to charge marginal cost prices than to bear the costs of working out any optimal adjustments. In other cases, deviations from marginal cost principles elsewhere in the economy may be so remote that they have minimal influence on the demand for transport. Under such conditions, and assuming the distortions cannot be removed, Davis and Whinston (1967) demonstrate that piecemeal optimisation within separate sectors of the economy using marginal cost pricing is optimal. Mishan (1962) suggests that since in many cases people spend a fixed amount of their income upon transport, there is, therefore, only a very low cross-elasticity of demand between transport as a whole and other goods consumed in the economy. This situation means that the issue can be reduced to optimising the allocation of traffic between *forms of transport*, on a piecemeal basis, rather than have to consider the allocation of expenditure between a certain form of transport and *all* other goods. If, in our example, all competing forms of transport apply marginal cost pricing principles then these should also be adopted by the railway service. Such a philosophy underlay much of the thinking behind the notion of 'controlled competition' which formed the basis of the 1968 Transport Act.

While Mishan's empirical approach has a certain practical common-sense appeal for some forms of transport – such as inter-urban passenger transport – it has less applicability in the freight sector or in the context of international travel. Freight costs have a considerable bearing upon both final prices charged for products and the location of the manufacturing industry; these are the main reasons for the attempts to develop a Common Transport Policy within the EEC. If all other inputs to industry are priced above marginal cost because, say, of the monopoly power of suppliers, but transport is priced at marginal cost, then this could lead to an over-development, from the national efficiency point of view, of transport-intensive industry. (Although it is possible that the relatively 'cheap' transport could break the monopoly power of the suppliers of other inputs forcing them, in the long run, to price at marginal cost.) International air and sea transport has the complication that, except in certain well-defined areas, many nations consciously subsidise their 'flag bearers', enabling them to charge rates below $LRMC$ and, on occasions, even below $SRMC$. Any single operator charging fares based on marginal cost in this situation would find himself unable to attract the optimal volume of traffic, and thus some deviation from the marginal cost principle may be necessary.

More formally, following Turvey (1971), let us assume there is a UK shipping line X, which is currently charging P_X and supplying capacity of Q_X in Figure 6.4a – where D_X is the Marshallian demand curve for the line's services assuming the marginal utility of income is constant. Competition is provided by an overseas line Y charging P_Y and supplying capacity Q_Y in Figure 6.4b. If X raises its rates by ΔP_X this will reduce customers' 'willingness to pay' by $\frac{(P_X + \Delta P_X)\Delta Q_X}{2}$. The rise in price introduced by X will cause the demand for Y's services to rise (from D_Y^1 to D_Y^2) leading to a change in 'willingness to pay' of $\frac{(P_Y + \Delta P_Y)\Delta Q_Y}{2}$. The total change in social welfare (ΔSW) is thus

$$\Delta SW = \left[\frac{(P_X + \Delta P_X)}{2} \Delta Q_X \right] + \left[\frac{(P_Y + \Delta P_Y)}{2} \Delta Q_Y \right], \tag{6.4}$$

but this ignores a parallel change in total social costs (ΔTSW) which can be represented as

$$\Delta TSW = MC_X \Delta Q_X + MC_Y \Delta Q_Y \tag{6.5}$$

where MC_X, MC_Y represent the respective marginal costs. Subtracting the change in social cost from that in social welfare and maximising we find, in re-arranged form:

$$P_X = MC_X - \frac{\Delta Q_Y}{\Delta Q_X}(P_Y - MC_Y) - \frac{1}{2}\left[\frac{\Delta Q_X \Delta P_X + \Delta Q_Y \Delta P_Y}{\Delta Q_X} \right] \tag{6.6}$$

Because as $\Delta P_X \to 0$ so $\Delta P_Y \to 0$, the last term in the equation will also tend towards zero and can, therefore, be ignored. The importance of

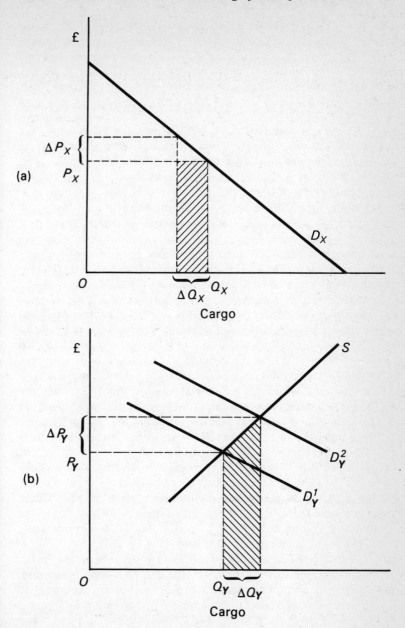

Figure 6.4   The problems of second best pricing

the remainder of the equation is that if the competing sector, Y, sets its prices equal to marginal cost (i.e. $P_Y = MC_Y$), then the pricing rule for shipping line X reduces to the standard marginal cost rule. If, however, shipping line Y charges rates above marginal cost (i.e. $P_Y \rangle MC_Y$), and on the assumption the lines are substitutes (i.e. $\frac{\Delta Q_Y}{\Delta Q_X} \langle 0\rangle$), then the UK line, X, should also charge above marginal cost. The reverse holds if $P_Y \langle MC_Y$. If, on the other hand, the services of the two shipping lines complement each other then the change in X's price will cause the demand for Y's services to shift inwards in Figure 6.4b. Under these circumstances it is easy to show that should Y have been pricing in excess of marginal cost then optimally X should price *below* its marginal cost.

In many cases a transport undertaking itself provides a number of different types of service (e.g. first and second-class rail services) and is also under a remit to make a prescribed level of profit. Given these conditions and assuming that the cross-elasticity of demand for the different services is negligible, Baumol and Bradford (1970) have demonstrated that the price of any services should be set equal to its short-run marginal cost plus a mark-up inversely proportionate to the service's price elasticity of demand. Hence, where the demand for a service is highly inelastic a substantial addition should be added to marginal cost. Where the demand is perfectly elastic, short-run marginal cost pricing is applied. In this way revenue above *SRMC* can be obtained to meet the financial target without distorting the allocation of traffic between services. (As we see in Chapter 9 the use of this type of approach has been prescribed in the UK for deciding between priorities in road and rail investments.) If cross-elasticities are not zero, then the simple rule must be modified to ensure that the relative quantities of goods sold correspond to the proportions which would occur if marginal cost pricing were applicable. The rule, for example, for substitutes is that optimal prices should be derived so that 'all output be reduced by the same proportion from the quantities which be demanded at prices equal to the corresponding marginal costs' (Baumol and Bradford, 1970, p.267).

The existence of monopoly and other distorting influences in the economy has been shown to necessitate some variations to marginal cost pricing in certain transport sectors. The key to the degree to which prices should deviate from marginal cost is clearly the sign and magnitude of the cross-elasticities of demand between transport and other goods and services in the economy. The practical difficulty in many cases is not the derivation of the appropriate theoretical model but rather our inadequate knowledge of the size of the cross-elasticities. The evidence that is coming forward tends to be piecemeal.

Additionally, most of the evidence is only related to intra-transport cross-elasticities with extremely few estimates of transport/other goods cross-elasticities.

6.4 Price discrimination

The adoption of marginal cost pricing can, in certain circumstances, result in an undertaking making a financial loss. The classic example of this is the decreasing cost industry where, because of high initial capital costs, the setting of charges equal to short-run marginal cost will result in a financial deficit. The railways are often cited as an example of an industry where marginal cost pricing may ensure optimal utilisation but leave the undertaking with a financial deficit. This is seen in Figure 6.5a where, for simplicity, the revenue and cost curves are depicted as linear. The railways are assumed to be a monopoly supplier and, indeed, if monopoly profit maximising prices (i.e. P_1) were adopted could return a super-normal profit (*wxyz*). The adoption of marginal cost pricing with the downward sloping *AC* and *MC* curves, however, result in a loss of *abcd*. A breakeven situation could be attained by average cost pricing (i.e. charging P_3) but this would mean $Q_2 - Q_3$ potential rail travellers, willing to pay the additional costs they impose, are priced off the service.

In these circumstances the adoption of marginal cost pricing is essentially a welfare decision and it is clear that if the undertaking does make a financial loss this is attributable to the pricing policy pursued rather than the incapacity of the service to be financially viable. The fixed costs of the service may be met in these cases by subsidy or by operating a 'club' system with potential users paying a fixed sum for the right to travel by rail and mileage rate (or some other 'cost'-related variable fee) to reflect use. It could be argued that the fixed rates of road vehicle taxation combined with fuel duties reflect a type of club arrangement but, if so, the system is extremely imperfect (Labour Party Study Group on Transport Policy, 1975).

Figure 6.5b illustrates a somewhat different situation, but one which is thought to be increasingly common in certain forms of transport. Here at *no level of output* does average revenue exceed average cost. It is impossible in this type of situation for costs to be recovered by charging a *single price* to all users even if monopoly pricing policies are adopted. In this case even a club arrangement is incapable of preventing the service from being unprofitable. An option here, and one which can also be employed in Figure 6.5a is to charge different customers different rates. Essentially, price dis-

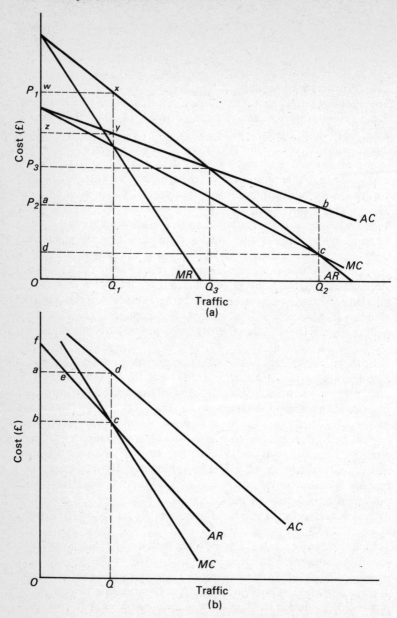

Figure 6.5   Price discrimination in transport

crimination involves charging 'what-the-user-will-bear'; in other words attempting to define the maximum amount each customer or, more realistically, each identifiable group of customers, is willing to pay for the service. The demand curve reflects willingness of users to pay and a perfectly discriminating supplier will charge down this curve. In Figure 6.5b output would be fixed at the level comparable to simple marginal cost pricing (i.e. Q) but each user would pay a different price dependent upon demand. This would yield a total value of $OfcQ$ which may be compared with the total cost of providing the service, namely $OadQ$. Quite simply if $afe \rangle cde$ when pursuing such a pricing policy, the service becomes financially viable.

It is not always possible for practical reasons to discriminate perfectly: the administrative costs of operating the system may be too high or exact knowledge of the demand curve unavailable. These, for example, are the reasons cited in the 1960s by British Rail for their reluctance to adopt more sophisticated costing and pricing policies – the diversity of services provided made it impracticable (Foster, 1975). In other cases it may be felt socially undesirable to charge 'what-the-user-will-bear' because of distributional consequences. Passengers with a low elasticity of demand may be from the poorer sections of the community and unable to transfer to alternative modes of transport. It may still be justified, even in these circumstances, to provide services even if not all costs are recovered by the operator providing that the *potential* revenue if discrimination were adopted exceeds the costs of the service. If this is the case, a subsidy is required to bring actual revenue up to potential revenue and, to some extent, the British government accepted this in the 1968 Transport Act when it introduced specific social subsidies to maintain a number of railway services.

While price discrimination is uncommon outside of the transport sector it is a familiar feature of pricing policy within it. A well documented example of price discrimination in practice is provided by shipping conferences. These act as monopoly suppliers of regular liner services between major ports. The possibility of airline competition tends to increase the elasticity of demand for their services to carry high price–low volume goods while tramp shipping becomes competitive for low price–bulk cargoes. Consequently, one can hypothesise an inverted S-shaped demand curve for liner services over any route. Given the high capital costs associated with shipping, there is adequate evidence that, without price discrimination, most conference lines would become unprofitable (Board of Trade, 1970). A detailed look at the Australia–Europe Conference by Zerby and Conlon (1978) produced a breakdown of rates which clearly shows the high degree of price discrimination exercised by these maritime cartels. Figure 6.6 reproduces their average revenues for each type of cargo carried in 1973/4 and it is clear that traced out this corresponds closely to the type of demand curve hypothesised. The low value–bulk cargoes (i.e. ores and metals) are carried at (or sometimes below if ballast is required) the average incremental costs of loading and unloading. While the high value products are carried at considerably higher rates, the tapering off in rates caused by potential competition from air transport is seen to be effective at the top of the price range.

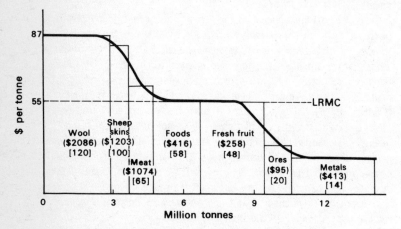

Notes: Average value per tonne in round brackets.
Storage factor in cubic feet per long ton shown in square brackets.

Figure 6.6   Average revenues from cargoes carried by the Australia/Europe conference 1973/4

Price discrimination does not only permit suppliers to recover their costs, it also helps travellers and consignors in that services can be retained even if, in some cases, it is necessary to differentiate the quality of service provided as well as the fare charged. International air travel offers some examples of this type of situation where differential prices are charged over a route according to the specifications of the types of service the travellers are willing to pay for. The gradual breakdown of the International Air Transport Association's (IATA) system of regulating air fares across the Atlantic in the 1970s was accompanied by the introduction of cut-price services such as 'Skytrain' (operated by Laker Airways). No-frill flights were introduced at low fares with seat allocation dependent upon the willingness of potential passengers to queue – tickets could not be purchased until six hours prior to take-off. A clear segmentation of the market had been recognised which permits services of the Skytrain type to operate alongside the rather more traditional scheduled services where prior booking, greater convenience and more comfort are offered (Abe, 1979). If, for example, there are three different groups of potential travellers with separate demand curves D_1, D_2 and D_3 as in Figure 6.7, then three separate fares should be charged (P_1, P_2, P_3) to maximise the consumers' surplus enjoyed. P_i is charged for the highest quality flight, equalling the marginal cost of service, with lower fares for poorer quality flights. On the surface it appears that ON_1 passengers will travel first

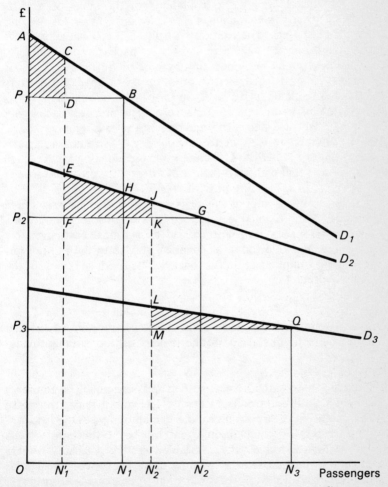

Figure 6.7   Price discrimination according to service quality

class reaping a consumer surplus of ABP_1 and N_1N_2 passengers will pay P_2 for the slightly lower quality of service and enjoy consumers' surplus of HIG. This ignores the possibility that first-class travellers may switch to the poorer quality but cheaper services (i.e. there may be some 'revenue dilution'). In fact, travellers $N_1'N_1$ could switch and increase their welfare. Similarly, $N_1'N_2$ passengers appear to be the probable number of customers for the poor quality 'Skytrain' service but again a further $N_2'N_2$ may be induced into joining them by the lower fare. Whether people actually do take advantage of the possibility of switching to cheaper but less convenient forms of service is uncertain, but the availability of the range of services means the total *potential* consumer surplus in Figure 6.7 is the sum of the shaded areas. The consumer surplus enjoyed will exceed that generated if only a single price and service package were available.

Price discrimination is not only by type of traffic or quality of service but may also be by length of journey. Friedman (1979) offers a classic example of such a policy in the context of long-haul/short-haul differentials on American railways. The practice of charging short-haul traffic a higher mileage rate on railways than long-haul, despite attempts to legislate to the contrary, was common in nineteenth century America. Friedman's justification for this practice demonstrates that without it there may arise quite serious distortions in transport infrastructure provision.

As an example, suppose there is a railway link between three towns, A, B and C where B is located between the other two towns. There is also river transport (priced at marginal cost) available between A and C offering an identical service to the railway but offering no communication for town B. The fixed, sunk cost of the rail link is such that

$$C_{AC} = C_{AB} + C_{BC}$$

i.e. the sunk cost of the line from A to C is the sum of the two component sub-links. Also, on the same basis, the variable cost is

$$V_{AC} = V_{AB} + V_{BC}$$

Figure 6.8 shows the respective demand schedules for transport between the different pairs of towns. The railways may maximise their profits by charging down the demand curves D_{AB} and D_{BC}, where there is no competition from river-borne transport, to the point where marginal (i.e. variable) cost is reached. Where competition does exist over the long route between A and C, the railways, to attract customers, will want to charge *at most* the rate offered by river transport (call this R_{AC}). The railways will, however,

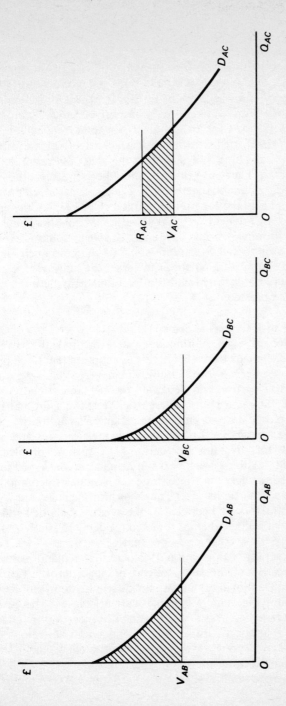

Figure 6.8   Railway revenues from discriminate pricing according to length of haul

accept traffic at rates below R_{AC} but above the variable cost. The shaded areas show the revenues enjoyed by the railways on different links. If R_{AC} is lower than either the highest position of D_{AB} or D_{BC}, then there exists long-haul/short-haul discrimination in addition to discrimination *within* each type of traffic. In other words, *identical* goods with *identical* demand for transport schedules would be charged more per mile for a short haul than for a long haul.

The sum of the shaded areas in the diagram offers a measure of the social value of building and operating the *ABC* railway line. The aggregate producer surplus generated should be set against the fixed costs of provision, which together with calculations for *AB* and *AC* separately, indicate the long-term desirability of keeping the entire line open or only segments of it. Without long-haul/short-haul discrimination the railway would have either to give up some of its long-haul business or to fail to capture some of the consumer surplus generated on short haul. Whatever the case, the railway's incentive to invest would be distorted and some economically desirable lines would not be operated.

6.5 Pricing with stochastic demand

Our discussion of price discrimination as a method of recovering costs has to date made the rather heroic assumption that the supplier of transport – be he ship-owner, railway manager, airline operator or whatever – has perfect knowledge of the demand situation confronting him. In practice this is unrealistic. Most transport managers have, from past data and employing 'managerial intuition' some notion of the average level of demand for their services and some idea of how this demand fluctuates. (The specific problem of systematic and regular *known* peaks in demand is considered in the following section; here we concentrate on irregular fluctuations in demand of a stochastic nature.) They may, for instance, know that fluctuations are about 20 per cent of the average daily demand but have no way of telling whether tomorrow's demand will be, say, 7 per cent above the average or 14 per cent below it.

The introduction of this notion of 'stochastic' demand requires a slight modification to the marginal cost pricing approach (Turvey, 1975). The conventional arguments for discriminate pricing revolve around the idea that simple marginal cost pricing will, because of declining average cost, result in the supplier incurring a financial loss. Turvey's position is that the problem should be expressed in terms of the difficulties associated with matching the services supplied (usually vehicle journeys) with those which are demanded (usually passenger journeys) when a fixed timetable is operative.

Approached from this way, the problem is seen as one of defining a price structure which will cover all relevant costs but which will, at the same time, ensure reasonable utilisation of the transport capacity available. Two broad approaches emerge. The first of these depends upon fairly reliable information about demand and its range of fluctuation while the second is reliant upon good information on all relevant costs. Here, we concentrate on the first approach and, in particular, the load factor for a service. If fares are fixed so high that the number of people wishing to use the service *never* exceeds the available capacity then, as a result of the fluctuating demand condition, there will frequently be substantial numbers of empty seats and resources are wasted. Alternatively, if the fares are set so low that capacity is fully utilised *all* of the time then many people, who often have spent time queuing for the service, will, again because of demand fluctuations, find themselves unable to obtain a seat. Clearly, common sense suggests a compromise between these extremes which will meet the requirements of both supplier and potential traveller. Turvey's pragmatic solution is that operators should structure their fares so that on *average* a certain percentage of seats will remain empty.

To some extent this is the situation which developed with the introduction of 'Skytrain' – as discussed in the previous section – where passengers have even greater flexibility by being able, via the premium charged on normal scheduled services, to ensure themselves a seat if they wish or, at a lower fare, to risk disappointment. The situation is also evident on the streets of central London where parking meter fees are fixed so that *on average* 15 per cent of spaces are vacant although, of course, from experience we know that at times it is impossible to find a vacant parking space while at others they are in abundance. One might also point to the 'stand-by capacity' kept by British Rail until the 1968 Transport Act which, it was claimed, acted to cope with long-term fluctuations in demand for railway services. The official Ministry view ran counter to this particular argument (Ministry of Transport, 1967).

To cover costs in this type of situation without recourse to either direct or cross-subsidisation it is likely that price discrimination is necessary. Any of four standard types of discrimination (i.e. by (i) type of passenger, (ii) degree of comfort, (iii) regularity of use and/or (iv) seat availability) could be used for this purpose.

Where knowledge of demand fluctuations is less precise, then Turvey's (1975) second and rather more pragmatic approach may be applicable. Here fares can be determined by simply dividing available costs of the service by the passengers carried and the service only runs if such fares *broadly* correspond to those on the remainder of the transport system. Additional revenue may then be gained on an *ad hoc* basis by raising fares for those groups where willingness-to-pay exceeds the cost-based fare. The actual avoidable costs can be estimated, where there is uncertainty about initial traffic levels, using the following formula which for simplicity is couched in terms of a railway service:

$$\left[\left\{\begin{matrix}\text{Probability that marginal passenger}\\\text{will necessitate an extra carriage}\end{matrix}\right\} \times (\text{Cost of extra carriage})\right]$$

$$+\left[\left\{\begin{matrix}\text{Probability that marginal passenger}\\\text{will necessitate an extra train}\end{matrix}\right\} \times (\text{Cost of extra train})\right]$$

Because this probability long-run marginal cost curve represents costs as an increasing function of the number of passengers and also since this is itself a decreasing function of the fare charged, there is likely to be a fare structure where such marginal costs are recovered.

Whether the fare is optimal, however, depends upon time-table flexibility; so far we have implicitly assumed a *given* time-table. The overall fare is set at the level of the marginal *social* cost of an extra passenger – in other words equal to the frustration and inconvenience he causes to other potential but disappointed travellers by occupying a scarce seat. The combination of time-table and fare that equates the marginal cost, so defined, with the marginal financial cost is thus an overall optimum. In practice, of course, imperfect knowledge of demand situations, plus the need to make time-tabling and pricing decisions simultaneously, makes it unlikely that such an overall optimum will be attained except by chance.

6.6 The problem of the peak

Most forms of transport, both freight and passenger, experience regular peaks in demand for their services. Urban public transport (upon which our attention is focused later) experiences peaks in demand during 'rush hours' each weekday morning and evening. Table 6.1, for instance, tabulates daily demand for bus services on three routes in Southampton. Urban freight transport also has peaks in demand to match the needs and operating practices of customers. In London, for example, the majority of deliveries are made between 11.00 a.m. and noon while clear peaks are revealed for Newbury and Camberley in Table 6.2. Over a year, air, bus and rail services meet peaks in demand from holiday traffic during the summer months and over public holidays, while within a week there are marked differences between weekend and weekday demand levels. Over an even longer period shipping is subjected to cyclical movements in demand as the world economy moves between booms and slumps.

Table 6.1   Buses required from Portswood, Shirley and Woolston Depots in Southampton, 1967

Time	A	B	C	Time	A	B	C
6.00– 6.30	63	76	—	13.30–14.00	103	103	83
6.30– 7.00	139	169	136	14.00–14.30	103	103	83
7.00– 7.30	132	139	112	14.30–15.00	105	105	85
7.30– 8.00	147	154	124	15.00–15.30	110	112	90
8.00– 8.30	159	165	133	15.30–16.00	147	160	129
8.30– 9.00	146	152	123	16.00–16.30	143	146	118
9.00– 9.30	121	139	112	16.30–17.00	140	142	115
9.30–10.00	98	102	82	17.00–17.30	137	137	111
10.00–10.30	93	93	75	17.30–18.00	128	136	110
10.30–11.00	92	92	74	18.00–18.30	105	120	—
11.00–11.30	92	92	74	18.30–19.00	84	89	—
11.30–12.00	98	100	81	19.00–19.30	72	79	—
12.00–12.30	98	98	79	19.30–20.00	60	65	—
12.30–13.00	103	105	85	20.00–20.30	55	55	—
13.00–13.30	104	105	85	20.30–21.00	54	54	—

Notes: A – Bus half hours performed
B – Sum of buses on road and entering or leaving termini
C – Index of B with 6.30 to 18.00 needs = 100

Source: Walshe, 1970

Table 6.2   Urban freight deliveries in Newbury and Camberley

Time of arrival	Newbury %	Camberley %
07.30–07.59	3.1	0.8
08.00–08.59	12.3	8.5
09.00–09.59	12.7	11.2
10.00–10.59	12.1	15.3
11.00–11.59	15.5	16.4
12.00–12.59	12.3	9.4
13.00–13.59	11.9	11.2
14.00–14.59	8.4	11.7
15.00–15.59	7.1	7.6
16.00–16.59	4.2	4.3
17.00–17.30	0.4	1.7
Unknown		1.9

Source: Christie *et al.*, 1973

The difficulty in all these situations is to determine a pattern of prices which (i) ensures that transport infrastructure is used optimally, (ii) provides a guide to future investment policy, and (iii) ensures that all relevant costs are recovered. Unlike the previous section, we are concerned here with problems arising from *systematic* variations in demand, frequently over a relatively short time period during which adjustments cannot be made in capital equipment to ensure that price is always equated with long-run marginal cost. (The problem is essentially one of indivisibility in the time dimension of supply relative to demand and is, therefore, a particular form of the joint production problem.) Problems of this kind do occur in other sectors of the economy but transport (like electricity and some other forms of energy) cannot be stored to reconcile systematic changes in demand with smooth, even production. Reconciliation can only be through price.

Before proceeding to look at the peak-load pricing problem it is worth noting that there exists a parallel spatial/directional problem of joint costs in transport which can be treated in an identical way to that of the peak. This involves the question of deriving appropriate rates for front-hauls and back-hauls – a situation often found in the provision of unscheduled road haulage, or freight and shipping services. Basically there is a high demand for a service in one direction (the front haul) but a lower one for a return service (the back haul); i.e. demand is uni-directional in nature whereas supply consists of round-trip journeys. This situation is directly analogous to the peak-load situation, with the front-haul being the spatial/directional equivalent of the peak, and simple substitution of words yields the appropriate analysis (see also Waters, 1980).

Perhaps the most widely discussed peaking problem involves urban public transport and particularly bus services. The size of most urban bus fleets is determined by the demand for public transport services during the morning and evening commuter rush hours. Typically over half the passengers carried during a day travel during the main peak periods. In Manchester, for example, 1090 buses were required to meet rush-hour demands in 1966 while only 400 were used during the midday period. Comparable figures for Birmingham Corporation Transport Department in 1969 were 1500 and 327 vehicles respectively. Bus road crews may also be considered as a joint cost since numbers are determined by peak demand. It is seldom possible to cover both daily peaks with one shift, hence either two shifts are required, or else split-shifts must be introduced usually involving inconvenience payments (often equal to the standard wage) being paid for time between peaks. The total wage bill for road staff, which amounts to about 50 per cent of total cost of most British bus operators, is, therefore, almost invariate with demand and may be treated as a joint cost of providing peak and non-peak services.

To determine optimal prices let us assume that during a twelve-hour period a bus operator is confronted by two different demand situations, each of six hours' duration. In Figure 6.9 D_1 is the low, off-peak demand situation and D_2 the peak level demand curve. The short-run marginal costs of operation (fuel and mileage dependent depreciation) are assumed constant at level Oa until the capacity of the bus fleet, which initially is assumed as fixed, is filled whereupon they become infinite. Expansions of capacity do not influence *SRMC* except to the extent that the capacity constraint is pushed further to the right. Long-run capacity costs (*LRMC*) are treated as constant at a level A. In the short term, with fleet size and, *ipso facto*, fixed costs given, the optimal prices to charge are P_1 and P_2 to non-peak and peak users respectively. Following these marginal cost principles means that while the entire vehicle fleet is fully used during peaks, (i.e. OQ_P) there is under-utilisation during the non-peak periods (i.e. OQ_N). The social surplus generated, given that all short-run costs must be recovered (i.e. $abc + adef$), is, however, maximised. The higher peak fare is charged to ration the scarce seats

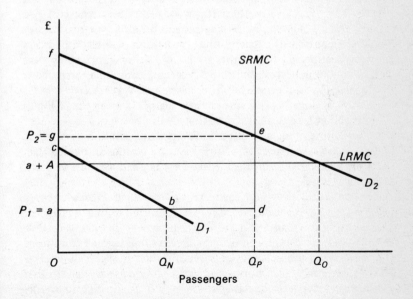

Figure 6.9 Peak load pricing – the standard case

available – if a price lower than P_2 is levied, then the demand for seats would exceed those available and a 'dead-weight' welfare loss would result. The fact that different fares are charged at peak and non-peak times should not be seen as a form of price discrimination of the type discussed in previous sections – discrimination involves varying price according to elasticity of demand but elasticities do not enter into fare determination here.

In practice, the situation is often somewhat more complicated than that depicted, because passengers are not rigidly confined to either period but may switch trips between them if differential fares are levied. Thus our implicit assumption that D_1 and D_2 are independent is often unrealistic and allowance needs to be made both for their own and also cross-elasticities. Also, of course, it may be necessary to take cognizance of interdependencies between the demand for urban bus travel as a whole and the possibilities of switching with private transport (Glaister, 1974).

In Figure 6.9 the fare structure generates a producer surplus of *adeg* for the operator which may go towards the cost of fixed elements which are joint to both peak and off-peak services. With long-run costs of the type illustrated the bus operator earns enough to cover all fixed costs plus make a super-normal profit above *LRMC*. In other words the sum of the prices levied exceeds the sum of the variable costs for the two periods plus the fixed cost (i.e. $(P_1 + P_2) \rangle (2a + A)$). As we saw in section 6.2 this type of situation justifies expansion of capacity until, at the new, adjusted marginal cost prices, super-normal profits are no longer being earned. In other words, assuming perfect divisibility, capacity should be expanded so that peak capacity becomes Q_o (i.e. at the point where $D_2 = LRMC$) and where no super-normal profits are earned. If we compare Figure 6.9 with Figure 6.3 it is clear that, with the types of demand functions illustrated, one can always generate additional consumer benefit by using capacity at off-peak or idle periods (provided fixed costs are recovered from peak travellers) at fares that are equal to immediate running costs.

Complications, however, can arise if the relative differences in peak and non-peak demand are less pronounced than in Figure 6.9. These conditions can result in 'shifting peaks'. In Figure 6.10 we have much less pronounced differences between demand conditions. Our previous arguments suggest fares of P_1 and P_2 should be charged at off-peak and peak times and further, since $(P_1 + P_2) \langle (2a + A)$, there is a case for contracting the capacity of the bus fleet – the problem is deciding upon the degree of contraction. The previous argument suggested that optimally the peak fare should be equated with *LRMC* and the off-peak fare with *SRMC*. However, if this is adopted the optimal off-peak capacity appears as OQ_{no} which is greater than the optimal peak capacity OQ_{po}, i.e. the peak has shifted. Hirschleifer (1958), however, produced the optimal pricing policy for this situation. Since the capacity is joint to both sub-periods, changes in capacity should be determined by the *combined* demand of peak and off-peak periods, i.e. the full cycle of activities. Consequently, it is D_{cycle} which is the relevant demand curve in Figure 6.10 (because this represents the vertical summation of D_1 and D_2 and $LRMC_{cycle}$ the relevant long-term cost curve (because this represents the combination of the short-run costs in the two periods plus fixed costs; i.e. $2a+A$). In essence the situation is analogous to that of a collective good. The optimum long-run capacity is OQ_o with non-peak travellers paying $\bar{P}_1$ and peak travellers, $\bar{P}_2$, which will

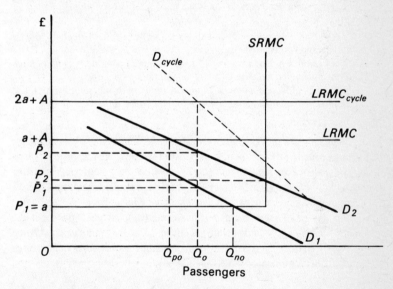

Figure 6.10 Public transport pricing with shifting peaks

together yield total revenue of $2a+A$. It is noticeable that the differential between the peak and off-peak fares is much smaller than in the firm peak case. Also $\bar{P}_1$ now exceeds *SRMC* and capacity is fully utilised around the clock, the pricing differences reflecting differing strengths of demand. Changes in capacity, because it is joint to both periods, now depend upon the sum of the differences between price and the capacity's operating costs per period relative to the cost of providing new capacity (A) for the entire cycle (i.e. investment is justified if $[(\bar{P}_1 - a) + (\bar{P}_2 - a) \rangle B)$. It is relatively simple to extend the analysis to any number of sub-periods, which may be of unequal duration, by weighting the different periods according to their fractional importance in the entire cycle.

While there is a firm economic basis for peak-load pricing, its implementation has been piecemeal to date. (An example was the pricing policy pursued in the Manchester–Salford area between the summers of 1970 and 1975 – see Tyson (1975) for details.) One reason may be the lack of a real understanding of the basic problem and the actual function served by price. A survey of 250 British economists, government officials and public opinion makers conducted by Brittan (1973) included the following question,

> In order to make the most efficient use of a city's resources, how should subway and bus fares vary during the day?
> (b) They should be relatively low during the rush hour to transport as many people as possible at that time.
> (a) They should be relatively low during rush hour to reduce costs for the maximum number of people.
> (d) They should be the same at all times to avoid making travellers alter their schedules because of price differences.
> (c) They should be relatively high during rush hour to minimise the amount of equipment needed to transport the daily travellers.

The 'correct' economic answer, (c), was given by 91 per cent of academic economists while the remainder declined to answer, usually on the grounds of insufficient information. Government and business economists answered (c) 84 and 90 per cent of the time respectively. In contrast 17 per cent of Labour Members of Parliament and 35 per cent of Conservative Members answered (c) – in fact 60 per cent of the latter answered (d). Only 25 per cent of journalists and TV commentators gave (c) as the answer. Quite clearly the prospect of marginal cost pricing for peak services being adopted on a large scale is a long way off.

6.7 Transport subsidies, operational objectives and pricing

Many sectors of transport enjoy quite substantial levels of government subsidy (some tentative indication of the total aid given in Great Britain is seen in Table 6.3 while Ruppenthal (1974) offers some USA statistics) which can complicate the pricing problem. To some extent the type of problem created depends upon the form of subsidy given. If the subsidy is for a specific service, then it may be seen as representing government demand for the particular service and treated alongside the demand of other customers – the social service subsidies given by the government to British Rail under the

1968 Transport Act may be categorised in this way. From a pricing – operational point of view such subsidies are relatively easily assimilated into standard economic models. When lump sum subsidies are given to transport undertakings for general revenue purposes, problems arise in deciding upon the best methods of using the subsidy and the appropriate charge to levy on customers. In particular, it is difficult to devise pricing and operational objectives which ensure that the management uses the fixed subsidies efficiently to attain the welfare objectives for which they are intended.

Table 6.3 Transport subsidies in Great Britain

	£ million out-turn prices	
	1971/2	*1976/7*
Local bus and underground transport		
Revenue subsidies	3	176
Fuel tax rebate	21	45
Excise duties	30	45
New bus grants	11	42
Investment grants	35	140
Concessionary fares	5	82
School travel	12	30
British Rail		
Revenue subsidies	74	366
Fuel tax	40	50
Investment grants	1	57
Capital write-offs	120	120
Pension payments	—	88
Concessionary fares	—	n.a.
School travel	1	3
Total	353	1244

Source: British Road Federation, 1978

It has been argued that commercial criteria (with profit-maximising pricing) in this situation would lead to monopoly exploitation and be counter-productive in terms of the social objectives justifying the subsidy, while a Paretian criterion (with marginal cost pricing) would break the link between costs, prices and output and lead to probable X-inefficiency (Nash, 1978). To circumvent these problems, and to provide clear pragmatic guidelines for lower level management, London Transport has attempted to maximise passenger mileage subject to a budget constraint (i.e. that costs are recovered after the fixed sum subsidy has been taken into account). Operationally, when the criterion is applied at the margin, this means:

> Reduce price as long as the increase in passenger mileage resulting exceeds the loss of revenue multiplied by the shadow price of public funds. Increase bus mileage as long as the increase in passenger mileage resulting is greater than the net addition to the financial loss multiplied by the shadow price of public funds. (Nash, 1978, p. 77).

The criterion, therefore, permits adjustments to the system operated so that costs are met (after allowing for the subsidy) and relatively junior management can assess the desirability of alternative courses of action. The criterion is, however, demonstrably inferior in theoretical terms to a pure marginal cost pricing strategy – price discrimination and cross-subsidisation may result which push fares on inelastic services above marginal operating costs so that revenue is available to finance services which exhibit a relatively high elasticity (and thus easily provide an increase in passenger miles). It is quite possible, therefore, for a service to be operated for which the level of demand is *never* high enough to permit price to cover marginal costs (Glaister and Collings, 1978). It is possible, at the expense of complicating the criterion, to devise weighting schemes which can be attached to passenger miles on various routes to reflect their importance to the decision-maker and schemes do exist which yield the same results as marginal cost pricing. Whether it is justified to adopt such weights must be an empirical question, depending on the loss of welfare which may accompany the simple unweighted passenger miles maximisation approach relative to the administrative costs of implementation. Bos (1978) also points to the distributional implications of the criterion and suggests that positive distributional effects may justify a certain level of welfare loss although, again, the exact distributional effect cannot be determined by *a priori* argument. (Empirical evidence in London suggests, however, that the London Transport scheme does have desirable distributional implications.)

6.8   Further reading and references
A comprehensive, but rather difficult, account of the principles of marginal cost pricing is presented in Millward (1971, Chapters 7 and 8). This reference looks in more detail at both the long and short-run pricing decision and also at specific difficulties associated, for example, with peaked demand. Attempts to devise operational pricing rules for urban transport are reviewed both cogently and in depth by Nash (1978). This reference usefully contrasts the

theoretically ideal with a set of second-best but pragmatic approaches to public transport pricing. Subsidies in transport are often alluded to in the literature but, despite their quantitative importance in the real world, are seldom rigorously assessed. Ruppenthal (1974) offers data on subsidies but the parent volume in which it is published also contains several analytical papers which look at subsidies and their associated problems in much more detail.

References

Abe, M.A. (1979), 'Skytrain: competitive pricing, quality of service and the deregulation of the airline industry', *International Journal of Transport Economics*, Vol. 6, pp. 41–47.

Baumol, W.J. (1962), 'On the theory of the expansion of the firm', *American Economic Review*, Vol. 52, pp. 1078–87

Baumol, W.J. and Bradford, D.F. (1970), 'Optimal departures from marginal cost pricing', *American Economic Review*, Vol. 60, pp. 265–83.

Beesley, M.E. (1973), 'Regulation of taxis', *Economic Journal*, Vol. 83, pp. 150–72.

Bennathan, E. and Walters, A. (1979), *Port Pricing and Investment Policy for Developing Countries*, Oxford, Oxford University Press.

Board of Trade (1970), *Report of the Committee of Enquiry into Shipping*, Cmnd 4337, London, HMSO.

Bos, D. (1978), 'Distribution effects of maximisation of passenger rules', *Journal of Transport Economics and Policy*, Vol. 12, pp. 322–9.

British Road Federation (1978), *Who Pays the Fares? – The Transport Subsidy Labyrinth*, London, BRF.

Brittan, S. (1973), *Is There an Economic Concensus*? London, Macmillan.

Christie, A.W., Bartlett, R.S., Cundhill, M.A. and Prudhoe, J. (1973), 'Urban freight distribution: studies of operations in shopping streets at Newbury and Camberley', *Transport and Road Research Laboratory Report*, LR.603.

Davis, O.A. and Whinston, A.B. (1967), 'Piecemeal policy in the theory of second-best', *Review of Economic Studies*, Vol. 34, pp. 323–31.

Foster, C.D. (1975), *The Transport Problem*, London, Croom Helm.

Friedman, D.D. (1979), 'In defence of the long-haul/short-haul discrimination', *Bell Journal of Economics*, Vol. 10, pp. 706–8.

Glaister, S. (1974), 'Generalised consumer surplus and public transport pricing', *Economic Journal*, Vol. 84, pp. 849–67.

Glaister, S. and Collings, J.J. (1978), 'Maximisation of passenger miles in theory and practice', *Journal of Transport Economics and Policy*, Vol. 12, pp. 304–21.

Hirschleifer, J. (1958), 'Peak loads and efficient pricing – comment', *Quarterly Journal of Economics*, Vol. 72, pp. 451–462.

Labour Party Study Group on Transport Policy (1975), *Report* Socialist Commentary, London.

Lipsey, R.G. (1979), *An Introduction to Positive Economics*, London, Weidenfeld and Nicolson.

Millward, R. (1971), *Public Expenditure Economics*, Maidenhead, McGraw-Hill.

Ministry of Transport (1967), *Railway Policy*, Cmnd 3439, London, HMSO.

Mishan, E.J. (1962), 'Second-thoughts on second best', *Oxford Economic Papers*, Vol. 14, pp. 205–17.

Nash, C.A. (1978), 'Management objectives, fares and service levels in bus transport', *Journal of Transport Economics and Policy*, Vol. 12, pp. 70–85.

Ruppenthal, K.M. (1974), 'Transport subsidies in the United States – some statistics', in K.M. Ruppenthal (ed.), *Transportation Subsidies – Nature and Extent*, Vancouver Centre for Transportation Studies, University of British Columbia.

Shreiber, C. (1975), 'The economic reasons for price and entry regulation of taxicabs', *Journal of Transport Economics and Policy*, Vol. 9, pp. 268–79.

Shreiber, C. (1977), 'The economic reasons for price and entry regulation of taxicabs', *Journal of Transport Economics and Policy*, Vol. 9, pp. 11, pp. 298–304.

Simon, H.A. (1959), 'Theories of decision-making in economics and behavioural science', *American Economic Review*, Vol. 49, pp. 253–83.

Sturmey, S.G. (1975), *Shipping Economics*, London, Macmillan.

Turvey, R. (1971), *Economic Analysis and Public Enterprises*, London, Allen & Unwin.

Turvey, R. (1975), 'A simple analysis of optimal fares on scheduled transport sources', *Economic Journal*, Vol. 85, pp. 1–9.

Tyson, W.J. (1975), 'A study of the effect of different bus fares in Greater Manchester', *Chartered Institute of Transport Journal*, Vol. 37, pp. 334–8.

Walshe, G. (1970), 'A stagger enquiry', *Journal of Transport Economics and Policy*, Vol. 4, pp. 284–308.

Waters, W.G. (1980), 'Output dimensions and joint costs', *International Journal of Transport Economics*, Vol. 7, pp. 17–35.

Wiseman, J. (1957), 'The theory of public utility price – an empty box', *Oxford Economic Papers* (New Series), Vol. 9, pp. 56–74.

Zerby, J.A. and Conlon, R.M. (1978), 'An analysis of capacity utilisation in liner shipping', *Journal of Transport Economics and Policy*, Vol. 12, pp. 27–46.

7 The Containment of the External Effects of Transport

7.1 Introduction

Chapter 5 offered evidence of the magnitude and diversity of the external costs associated with transport. In this chapter we are concerned with methods of containing the externality problem and, if possible, optimising the environmental and congestion costs of transport. It should be emphasised at the outset that the focus on the external costs of transport, while glaring in the developed world, is much less intense in less wealthy countries. The affluence of the western world has transferred part of the desire from improving material living standards to that of improving (or retaining) environmental quality. The marginal utility of additional financial income, it is often argued, is, for the majority of people in the West, possibly of less value than a cleaner, quieter and safer environment in which to live. This is a comparatively recent phenomenon and books on transport economics written in the pre-war period gave scant attention to externalities. Third world countries still retain this comparative indifference to environmental factors – their generally poor living standards and inadequate transport systems necessitate that effort be directed almost exclusively at improving material output.

We have seen in Figure 5.1 that ideally, externalities should be contained to the point where the costs of further reductions exceed the marginal social benefits ('pollution should be reduced to the point where the costs of doing so are covered by the benefits from the reduction in pollution', Royal Commission on Environmental Pollution, 1972, para. 20). It should be re-emphasised that this is unlikely to mean zero pollution or zero congestion but rather optimal levels of external cost. To achieve this optimum a number of possibilities recommend themselves and the objective of this chapter is to evaluate the effectiveness of each. While it is useful at times, both for illustration and to retain the link between theory and policy, to refer to actual measures employed by transport authorities the emphasis is on the direct economic implications of the alternative approaches rather than their political or social virtues. We begin by looking at the traditional 'Pigouvian solution', namely internalising external costs by charging those who generate them.

7.2 The 'polluter pays' principle

Let us assume we are simply concerned with the problem of traffic noise – the general principles derived can equally well be applied to other forms of externality as we see in section 7.3. In Figure 7.1, *MPC* is the marginal private cost of transporting goods (in tons) by lorries in an area (i.e. the labour, fuel, maintenance costs, etc.), *MEC* is the marginal environmental cost, representing the money value of the marginal noise nuisance at each traffic level and *D* is the demand curve for road haulage services. *MSC* is the summation of the private and external costs. If road hauliers are unaware (or take no account) of the external cost of their carriage then Q_A goods will

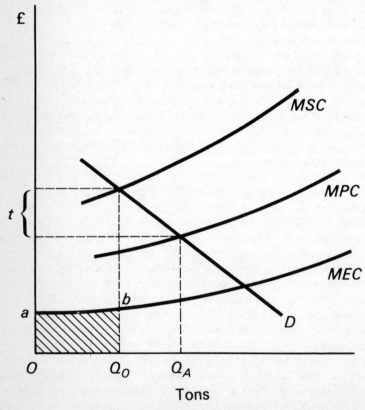

Figure 7.1   *The optimum pollution charge*

be transported which exceeds the socially optimal level of Q_O when *all* costs are taken into consideration. The 'polluter pays principle' suggests that the hauliers should be made aware of the external costs they generate by paying a charge equal to the MEC (i.e. t at the optimal level of output). This would reduce the amount carried to the socially optimal level. In practical terms this may mean some goods will be transferred to other modes or that longer-term relocations of industry will take place reducing the total transport input.

It may seem that application of pricing rules could never by implemented because of practical difficulties. Mills and White (1978), albeit in the specific context of atmospheric pollution associated with cars, concentrate on this practical aspect of the policy. They suggest that there should be no restriction on vehicle production but that each type of vehicle should be charged according to the *average* emissions associated with its use. Samples of each model, tested over some 50 000 miles, would provide the basis for estimating average carbon monoxide, hydrocarbon and nitrogen oxide emissions. The charge would be added to the *showroom* price of cars so that prospective purchasers would be fully cognizant of the costs of their driving with periodic checks made on vehicles to ensure that their performance has not deviated significantly from the average. Different charges may be applicable in different regions of a country. While such an approach does not offer an ideal 'polluter pays' scheme – in particular it does not relate to the actual use made of a car – it does offer a pragmatic device for pricing pollution externalities.

Two important general points regarding the pricing approach however need to be made immediately. Firstly, in order to calculate the optimal pollution charge or price it is necessary to have reliable information about the *MEC* curve. As we have seen in Chapter 5 knowledge in this area is scant and although the use of, for example, hedonic house price indices may shed some light on the monetary importance of noise nuisance they are far from perfect. Additionally, evaluation of the marginal environmental costs of many other forms of pollution is even more primitive should the principle be applied to externalities other than noise. We return to this problem below. Secondly, the revenue generated by the tax or price does not go directly to those affected by the noise nuisance that remains. (In terms of the criteria laid out later in Chapter 8, the policy does not result in a genuine Pareto improvement but rather a hypothetical one.) It is the government or local authority who enjoy a 'windfall' gain of t times O_o which *may* be used in compensation payments.

At a rather more theoretical level, it is possible to question whether the 'polluter pays principle' is being correctly applied in Figure 7.1 (Coase, 1960). We have implicitly assumed that the hauliers should buy the right to pollute the atmosphere with lorry noise, but this could be turned on its head, and the proposition presented that non-hauliers should buy the right to relative peace and quiet, i.e. the hauliers should be *paid* a subsidy of *t* in the diagram to curtail their activities. The question is essentially a moral-legal one involving property rights although where there are actual administrative costs of introducing either prices or subsidies these should also be considered.

As Baumol and Oates (1975) have stressed, one of the problems of charging polluters is that information about the *MEC* curve is imperfect and that, even if some initially arbitrary price is charged, there is no indication of whether this is too high or too low. The usual 'trial and error' method of pricing used in industry is, therefore, not appropriate. Since information about the *MEC* curve is necessary for virtually all optimal containment of noise, irrespective of the method used, Baumol and Oates argue in favour of pricing on the grounds that it will cause less distortions than other policies. Their arguments have recently found favour with the Organisation for Economic Co-operation and Development (1975), who argue, 'The costs of these measures (to ensure that the environment is in an acceptable state) should be reflected in the cost of goods and services which cause pollution in production and/or consumption.'

We extend our arguments to embrace two modes of transport, road haulage and railways and in Figure 7.2 relate the marginal net private benefits (*MNPB*) associated with using each mode to the noise nuisance emitted. (The *MNPB* is simply the difference between the marginal private benefit and the marginal private cost. With each level of transport there is a certain amount of noise emission and since increasing transport can be expected to generate successively lower incremental private benefit, the curve will be negatively sloped.) These curves are unknown to the Department of Transport but it may be decided that it would be beneficial to do something about pollution rather than leave it at a high level. In these circumstances one may wish to reduce noise emissions by say 15 per cent and to use polluter charges to achieve this. Baumol and Oates (1975) demonstrate that a uniform charge on both road and railway noise is the appropriate 'second best' policy to pursue. In Figure 7.2 we assume *OT* to be the optimal charge in this context (of course, the authorities may initially charge above or below this but since the objective is specified 'trial and error' modifications are possible until the 15 per cent reduction in noise is attained). This means a greater reduction in noise level from roads than the railways but since the *MNPB* from noise emissions is equal this is quite sensible. If road noise were reduced less and railway noise more the welfare loss to those near roads would exceed the benefit to those adjacent to railways. (See Alexandre *et al.*, 1980 for a more detailed discussion of this point.) We should perhaps note that the Baumol–Oates argument is something of a hybrid approach to pollution policy and only resolves the problem of the inappropriateness of the 'trial and error' method by adopting an arbitrary target for abatement. Consequently optimal pollution levels are unlikely finally to evolve.

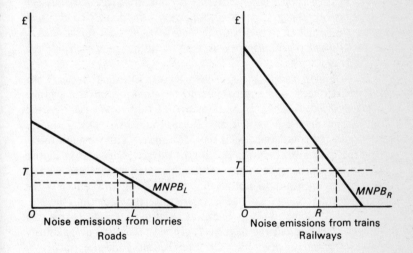

Figure 7.2   A common pollution price for roads and railways

While the 'polluter pays' principle tends to be favoured by many academics, it is not without its critics. Sharp (1979), for example, questions the distributional implications and argues that in some instances an environmental improvement may be obtained as efficiently by means of progressive taxation without the possible regressive effects of pollution charges. Essentially, the argument revolves around the fact that the benefits from any environmental improvement are closely related to income. A poor person would probably have a preference for no pollution charges (and *ipso facto* lower final money prices) than a wealthier person whose marginal utility of income is lower. Hence, from a distributional point of view, a subsidy of *Ot* in Figure 7.1 to hauliers to suppress vehicle noise, financed from a progressive taxation system, will have the same environmental effect but none of the regressive features of the pollution charge.

7.3   Congestion charges – theory and practice

It is not only in the context of pollution that externality pricing has been advocated. One idea for optimising the level of congestion is to use the price mechanism to make travellers more fully aware of the impedence they impose upon one another. This notion was first suggested in the context of urban road traffic over sixty years ago by Pigou (1920). The idea is that motorists should pay for the additional congestion they create when entering a congested road. Ideally, as with pollution charges, they should pay the actual road users affected but practically this is quite clearly impossible so the idea is that the relevant road authority or agency should be responsible for collecting the charges.

The optimal road price, as such a charge is called, reflects the difference between the marginal cost of trip-making and the average cost (as defined in Chapter 5). This means that in Figure 7.3a the optimal road price per vehicle is AB, i.e. the charge which equates the demand for road space with the MC curve. With demand intersecting the backward bending portion of the cost curve, as in Figure 7.3b, the same principles apply and the price that should be levied as $A'B'$. It is important to notice that the relevant MC curve is the upward sloping one (see Chapter 5) despite the fact that the AC curve is cut by demand on its backward sloping section. This is still valid even if D had cut the negatively sloped MC curve quite simply because one can always find an intersection with the positively inclined curve which offers a higher social benefit.

In the simple case (Figure 7.3a) road pricing generates a welfare gain of $(WxvB) - (uxy)$. This is because the traffic flow is reduced by $(Q_1 - Q_2)$ resulting in some motorists losing consumers' surplus of uxy but, at the same time, the road authority collects revenues of $BvuA$. This revenue is not all a social benefit; a part of it (equal to $AuxW$) represents a transfer of consumers' surplus enjoyed by road users to the providing agency in the form of additional revenue. Providing the relevant section of the demand curve has a degree of elasticity then $(WxvB) - (uxy)$ must be positive and road pricing increases social surplus. It is important to note that it is the *providing agency* which directly benefits from the scheme not road users. Of course, since it is either local or central government which collects the revenue, the monies raised *could* always be given back to motorists through some distributional mechanisms.

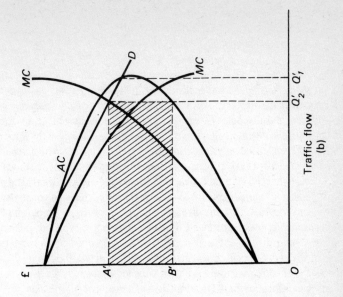

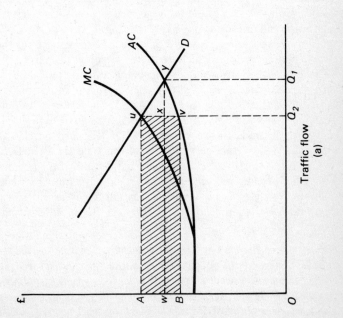

Figure 7.3   Optimal road pricing levels

While the basic theory of road pricing is comparatively straight-forward, its detailed implementation has been subject to debate. There are six main areas of controversy.

(1) *The difficulty of devising a practical method of collection.* Congestion varies across urban areas but it is quite clearly impossible to make a separate charge for each segment of the road network. Some general attempt at this may be practicable in the long run if vehicles are fitted with auto-matically activated meters, charging rates that vary with traffic conditions, but there then arises the problem that motorists are only retrospectively made aware of the congestion costs of their trips. Such systems are also likely to prove expensive to install and administrate. Crude area licensing is cheaper and, since permits must be purchased before entering specified urban zones, the full cost of a journey is made known to motorists before they enter congested streets – if they are still prepared to do so. The disadvantage of this simpler system is its insensi-tivity to changes in traffic conditions throughout the day.

(2) *The possibility of undesirable distribution repercussions.* With road pricing the use of roads depends upon the capabilities of potential users to pay the congestion charge. Whether this would result in undesirable regressive effects on social welfare is an empirical question. It is likely that public transport, which could move more freely, would provide a better service for the lower income groups which tend to patronise it. Also, the wealthy are likely to benefit from being able to 'buy' uncon-gested road space, a situation they value because of the importance they attach to time savings. In contrast, middle income groups could be forced to switch from private to public transport, a mode they consider inferior (Richardson, 1974). Inter-personal welfare comparisons of this type are difficult to make but it is possible, for example, that if some of the revenue from road pricing were directed towards further improvements in public transport (which may or may not mean heavily subsi-dised fares), then the adverse effects on the middle income group could be substantially reduced.

(3) *There are difficulties in disposing of the revenues raised.* Sharp (1966) pointed out that the revenues from road pricing need to be reallocated with a degree of circumspection. While it has been suggested above that some of the money could be used, on distributional grounds, to improve public

transport, strictly direct transfer payments to former road users are more efficient in achieving this objective. (Subsidies also pose problems for management in defining their operational objectives.) Direct transfers back to former motorists, however, pose the problem that they are likely to use at least part of the money to 'buy-back' road space. An alternative method of compensating motorists adversely affected may be to use the road pricing revenues to construct more roads. Indeed, revenues from different areas offer a useful *general* guide to road building priorities. Despite this, investment decisions should be based upon a much wider range of criteria than simply the revenues raised from road pricing (see Chapter 9). Possibly a less controversial approach would be to treat the revenues as a pure tax income and to use them as part of general public expenditure, in this way wider problems of efficiency and distribution may be tackled.

(4) *The impact on freight costs may prove inflationary if the road price is passed on to final consumers.* In fact, the inflationary impact is unlikely to be as great as some people suggest (Button, 1978). Urban transport costs only form a small part of final retail prices and, therefore, the imposition of road pricing is unlikely to have a significant effect on final prices. Additionally, since many of the costs of urban freight transport operations are time related, the reduced congestion which results from road pricing is likely to reduce substantially many costs of urban distribution and offset the financial cost of the road price. A desk study forming part of the Coventry Transportation Study confirms this, producing the predictions

Table 7.1   The impact of road pricing on transport costs in Coventry

Vehicle type	Charge in cost of a round trip in pence	Charge weight (pcu)
Private car	+ 16.0	1
Business car	− 124.0	1
Light commercial vehicle	− 46.0	1
Medium commercial vehicle (3.5–8.5 tons)	− 6.0	2
Heavy commercial vehicle (over 16 tons)	− 37.5	2

Source: Goode, 1975

of the impact of a cordon road pricing scheme shown in Table 7.1 – a charge of 35p per passenger car unit being the proposed toll.

(5) *The demand functions for road use are more complex than the simple analysis suggests.* The analysis above has assumed that the demand for road space may be represented by a continuous function but in practice there may be kinks or discontinuities. Sharp (1966) implies that there may be no optimal road price because the demand situation is such that pricing would result in either too much traffic or too little depending upon the levy charged. This is a theoretical possibility. After all the smooth curves used in basic analysis are only expositional aids, but, in fact, the actual form of the demand function is an empirical question which can only be resolved in the light of practical experience. There is, however, no *a priori* reason to suspect the demand for road space is *atypical* of demand curves in general.

(6) *Road pricing is a first-best solution in a second-best world.* Marginal cost pricing of road space is only strictly optimal if all other goods in the economy are also marginal cost priced. However, since the overall demand for urban transport tends to be independent of the demand for other commodities providing that urban public transport pursues marginal cost pricing policies, no serious distortions within the transport sector should arise (see also Chapter 6).

Despite the theoretical speculation about the economic pros and cons of road pricing, practical implementations have been limited. Desk-top studies of possible schemes have been conducted in a number of British cities (most notably, Bristol, Coventry and London) but political concern, combined with worries about distributional consequences, has discouraged implementation. One of the difficulties in the UK is the close economic interdependence of adjacent urban areas which makes the unilateral introduction of road pricing in one area extremely difficult. While there is only academic speculation about the probable effect of road pricing on British cities a limited number of road pricing experiments have been conducted elsewhere. Valletta (Malta), for instance, has for some time operated a simple scheme in which the annual licence is more expensive for vehicles used in the city. Since May 1975 Singapore has operated an area licensing system for rush hour traffic.

The Singapore scheme offers some practical evidence of the effects of congestion pricing (Watson and Holland, 1978). The initial policy of simply charging for vehicles entering the central zone (see Figure 7.4) between 7.30 a.m. and 9.30 a.m. was found to be inadequate as traffic spread to either side of the licensing period and in August 1979 the period of licensing was extended to between 7.30 a.m. and 10.15 a.m. The impact of the scheme was, nevertheless, impressive from its inception. There was an initial reduction of 24 700 cars travelling during the peak period, rising to a reduction of 30 800 after the licensing period was extended. Traffic speeds during the peak rose by about 22 per cent. While Table 7.2 indicates that there have been subsequent increases in traffic volume since 1975, these are considerably below the levels anticipated in the absence of road pricing. There was also some initial geographical spread of traffic to 'escape corridors' outside of the licensing area, but this was contained by adjusting traffic signals etc. on circumferential routes.

The Singapore scheme was initially a comprehensive package of measures embracing ring route designations and public transport, park-and-ride facilities. The latter proved singularly unsuccessful as commuters took to car pooling – since full cars were exempt from the licensing fee – rather than public transport. The rise in car pool trips is seen in Table 7.2. The eighty-nine mini buses forming the park and ride fleet were eventually diverted to other uses and the parking sites transformed into housing estates, tennis courts, etc.

It was anticipated that the reduced morning traffic flow would be mirrored in the evening but evening peak hour traffic flow only

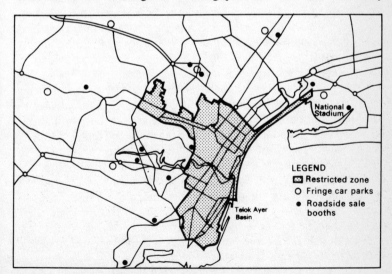

Figure 7.4   The licensing area in central Singapore

Table 7.2   The long-term effects of road pricing in Singapore

Time	Vehicle	May 1975	May 1976	May 1977	May 1978	May 1979
0700–0730	Cars	5384	5675 (+5.4)	6488 (+14.3)	6723 (+3.6)	5723 (−14.9)
	Car pools	617	509 (−17.5)	636 (+25.0)	606 (−4.7)	492 (−18.1)
	Total	9800	10332 (+5.4)	11489 (+11.2)	11692 (+1.8)	10596 (−11.9)
0730–1015	Cars	42790	10754 (−74.9)	10350 (−3.8)	11350 (+9.7)	13181 (+16.1)
	Car pools	2369	4641 (+95.9)	5337 (+15.0)	5684 (+15.0)	5756 (+1.3)
	Total	74014	37587 (−49.2)	44318 (+17.9)	47503 (+7.2)	49606 (+4.4)
1015–1045	Cars	n.a.	6459	6636 (+2.7)	6326 (−4.7)	5527 (−12.6)
	Car pools	n.a.	320	280 (−12.5)	281 (+3.2)	232 (−19.7)
	Total	n.a.	13441	13805 (+2.7)	14308 (−3.6)	15179 (+6.1)

Source: Seah, 1980

declined by 3–4 per cent. This is because commuters diverting to escape corridors or travelling earlier in the morning had no incentive to do so at night while others engaging in car pooling were collected in the evening by other members of the family who, by adjusting their own daily routine, acted as chauffeurs after making trips into the city for shopping, recreation or other purposes. Road pricing, it appears, needs to be applied *directly* at times congestion occurs.

The Singapore scheme does indicate that road pricing can reduce congestion successfully although the actual effect of any scheme seems rather more difficult to forecast than some advocates suggested. The actual details of this scheme are obviously tailored to the geography and political climate of Singapore and replication elsewhere may result in somewhat different effects. It is also questionable whether the actual prices charged are truly optimal or whether they are excessively high (Toh, 1977), acting as a method of revenue collection for the government as much as an instrument of microeconomic resource allocation. Quite clearly transport may be a legitimate field for pure indirect taxation but in assessing the effectiveness of a road pricing scheme it is important to isolate the price efficiency aspect from that of taxation *per se*.

Roads are not the only area where congestion pricing has been advocated. Walters (1976), for example, has argued that appropriate marginal cost pricing (including congestion charges) is 'no panacea for ailing or congested ports, but it does supply *a useful set of principles to deploy in the discussion of port pricing policy'* (emphasis added). The general principles are identical to road pricing (a rigorous framework has been provided by Vanags, 1977), but in some circumstances the nature of the shipping industry may result in complications. In the road context there is a monopoly supplier adopting social pricing policies coupled with competition for road space amongst many, unco-ordinated potential users. While the majority of ports conform to this type of market situation, in some instances the port authorities are confronted by a monopoly (or, more likely, a cartel of) shipping companies.

Figure 7.5 shows the demand curve for shipping (the demand for port services may be seen as proportional to this) in terms of total import and export traffic. The port is assumed to have constant marginal handling costs, *OH*, which are passed to the shipowners as port charges. The shipping companies, if competitive, would then charge these customers an additional amount, *RH*, to reflect their own average costs, to give a total shipping rate of *OR*. The *AC* of shipping will itself rise after a certain point as port congestion forces queuing to load and discharge. Since the *AC* curve does not reflect the true costs of increasing traffic the port authority should, on welfare economic grounds, levy a congestion charge of *AB*. Assuming there is no potential for modifying the types of ship in service or methods of cargo handling this will reduce the tonnage passing through the port from T_1 to the optimal level T_2. This is identical to the road pricing case.

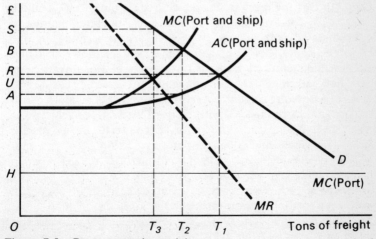

Figure 7.5　Port congestion pricing

Suppose that instead of a competitive shipping market, the port was used exclusively by a closed liner conference. There are now two important differences. Firstly, the conference, being the sole operator, will bear the costs of congestion itself – the congestion costs are internalised. Secondly, the conference is likely to act as a monopolist (although, as we have seen in the previous chapter countervailing powers act as a limited constraint in practice) and be more concerned with the marginal revenue curve than with demand. Thus the shipowner will charge customers a rate of *OS* for his services which comprise (i) port fees, *OH*; (ii) his own costs, including that of congestion, *HU*; and (iii) economic, monopoly, rent, *US*. The tonnage passing through the port is now sub-optimally small at OT_3.

Although one might argue that in this situation the optimal use of the port could, technically, in some situations, be achieved by *not* charging a congestion toll and by *reducing* port fees below *OH* (see Bennathan and Walters, 1979), this rather evades the real problem, namely the monopoly power of the shipping conference. Such a policy also places excessive power in the hands of the conference when negotiating with port authorities the fees (and, *ipso facto*, the subsidy) to be charged. The solution here is to tackle distortions at source, namely, in the shipping market, rather than maladjust port prices.

7.4   Emissions standards

Figure 7.1 indicates that external costs can be optimised by charging a pollution price of *t*. It is equally possible, however, that rather than operate the pricing mechanisms the desired output of OQ_O could be obtained by, for example, setting emissions standards limiting the noise generated by the lorries. In practice this has been the approach of the UK authorities with the establishment of 'noise abatement zones' and the controls embodied in a series of Road Traffic Acts which have, since 1973, laid down regulations regarding car silencers and exhausts. Noise standards were introduced at the manufacturing stage for new lorries in 1970 with limits of 91*dB(A)* for vehicles with engines over 200 hp and 89*dB(A)* for less powerful lorries while by March 1983 new vehicles coming into production must meet more stringent requirements of 88*dB(A)* and 86*dB(A)* respectively. The Heavy Commercial Vehicles (Controls and Regulations) Act 1973 requires local authorities to prepare comprehensive plans for dealing with heavy lorries 'so as to preserve the amenities of their areas'. The Civil Aviation Act 1971 lays down regulations about night movements over built-up areas and specifies over-fly patterns for aircraft. The speed limits operative on roads are primarily designed to reduce accident risk – with some supplementary effects on fuel economy. The compulsory wearing of seat-belts in many countries is also to reduce accident costs. Similarly, the periodic testing of vehicles and the licensing of lorries, aircraft, etc. are to ensure that minimum safety and environmental standards are achieved. In many overseas countries the regulations are more stringent (e.g. the removal of lead from petrol in the USA, and annual checks on pollution emissions from internal combustion engines in New Jersey and Oregon) or take different forms but their intended effect is the same, to reduce the marginal environmental cost of transport.

While all the above represent physical regulations to contain pollution they should strictly be divided between those controls that act directly to contain the externality (e.g. noise emission legislation) and those that control transport in such a way as to reduce the external costs (e.g. lorry routes and aircraft flight path regulations). The effects of these alternative broad sets of physical controls are not the same. Actual emission standards act directly to limit the external effects permitting other characteristics of operations to be adjusted freely. The operational regulations impose much more stringent controls, severely limiting the alternative courses of action open to the operator. With noise emissions standards for aircraft flying over an area, for instance, an airline can either conform and pay the costs of suppressing noise or avoid the area in question – with operational controls only the latter option is available. This point should be borne in mind during the more general discussion of physical controls which follows. We return to the question of operational restrictions and vehicle routing in a more general context in section 7.6.

While in the simple case illustrated in Figure 7.1 the effect of an optimal standard produces an identical level of road transport activity (and, *ipso facto*, environmental intrusion) to an optimal pollution charge, it can be argued that, with more realistic assumptions, the pricing approach offers a superior solution to the externality problem. Lowe and Lewis (1980) argue that even if full information permitted the alternative policies to be applied optimally, the standards/regulation approach can lead to excess capacity in the road haulage sector. The argument is that while any haulage undertaking would have to conform to the standard, the fact that there is no need actually to pay for the cost of remaining pollution (i.e. area OQ_Oba) may result in too many hauliers operating in the area. (Counter to this, if the argument is taken to its logical conclusion, is the fact that with a charging regime only a single uniform pollution charge is levied which could result in an overall capacity *below* the optimal level, i.e. $(t \times Q_O) \rangle (O Q_O ba)$. This type of problem is only likely to occur in sectors such as road haulage or inter-urban bus services which are highly competitive and fragmented, and where the size of the industry depends mainly upon new entrants or firms leaving, it is less relevant to monopoly or oligopolistic modes of transport where mobility into and out of the sector is less important.

When information about the exact shape of the *MEC* curve is poor, the use of standards is demonstrably less efficient than the Baumol–Oates charging approach seen in Figure 7.2. If, in order to achieve the 15 per cent reduction in transport noise used in our example both road and rail were compelled to cut their noise emissions by a quarter (i.e. to *OL* and *OR* respectively), then it is clear from the diagram that the marginal net private benefits generated by the two modes are no longer equal (at the new emission levels, $MNPB_R \langle MNPB_L$). Consequently, social welfare could be improved by lowering the standard for railways and increasing it for roads. Unfortunately in the real world lack of perfect knowledge of the *MNPB* curves means that the optimal differentiation of standards is likely to be impossible to define. Thus in this imperfect situation, the 'polluter pays principle' is almost certainly going to prove superior to the use of emission standards.

It is probable that pollution pricing will prove more flexible than standards. While transport infrastructure may impose external costs of visual intrusion it is normally the mobile unit which generates the greatest external costs. Given the differing income levels and pre-ference patterns in various parts of the country one could re-interpret the *MNPB* curves in Figure 7.2 in terms of the marginal net private benefit associated with a *single mode* but operating in *different parts of the country*. In this case the uniform emissions charge would be both theoretically superior and, in addition, reduce the costs to transport undertakings of reducing their noise emissions. The imposition of different standards for each area means that operators must either ensure that vehicles moving between areas conform to the most stringent standards or have specific, variously suppressed vehicles designed to conform with local regulations. Both options are likely to be wasteful. With a charging regime, the operator can select a vehicle mix that minimises his overall costs of operation – vehicles may be suppressed *or* pay the emissions price *or* they may be sub-jected to a combination of the two. This line of argument has been strongly presented by Peltzman and Tideman (1972) in the context of environmental optimisation in different sizes of urban area.

Moving to a more dynamic situation, where technology is

variable, Maler (1974) has suggested that pollution prices have important advantages over regulations for the encouragement of a rapid adoption of cleaner technologies. His argument rests upon the implicit assumption that transport suppliers, when confronted with either a pollution price or emissions standard, assume this price or standard to be fixed in the medium term irrespective of their individual action. Consequently they will always assess the benefits to themselves of adopting new operating methods or technologies against *existing* prices or standards. In Figure 7.6 we show the marginal private costs of reducing exhaust fumes for a road haulier confronted with the existing technology (MC_1) and with the new technology (MC_2). The MC_2 curve is inside MC_1 because it is cheaper to quieten vehicles with the new technology at *all* noise levels. On the assumption that the authorities have full information on *MEC* and can, therefore, define the optimal level of traffic noise we see that

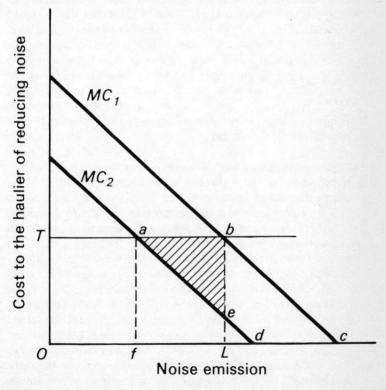

Figure 7.6 *Pollution charges, emission standards and technical change*

either a pollution charge of *OT* or a standard of *OL* will ideally be in force. If the pricing policy is pursued the haulier will find it financially worthwhile to quieten his vehicle by *Lc* (costing *Lbc*) and pay *OTbL* in charges. With a standard he pays no pollution charges but it costs him *Lbc* to conform to the noise regulation. However, if the new technology is available an individual haulier will perceive, *ceteris paribus*, the benefits of adopting it as *abcd* if there is a charging policy operative, i.e. he will reduce his emissions with the new technology to *Of* (costing *fad*) and pay charges of *OTaf*. The incentive to adopt the alternative technology with the emissions standard is only *debc*, i.e. the cost of conforming to the standard with the new technology rather than the old. Thus the pollution charging policy offers an incentive of the shaded area, *abe*, in excess of an emissions standard to move to the cleaner technology.

One possible option is a combined environmental tax/standards approach whereby all vehicles are obliged to meet a set standard and there is a scale of emissions-related 'fines' for vehicles which exceed this. If the standard were rigorous and well below the existing level of emissions (i.e. consistent with the optimal level of pollution with the cleaner technology in our example above), then this would be as effective as the pricing approach and at the same time offer a *firm* target for vehicle operators to aim at. Such a tax/standards approach may, however, be particularly appealing at the vehicle manufacturing stage where new technology can most easily be injected into the transport sector.

7.5   Transport subsidies and the environment
An alternative to operating directly upon the transport undertaking generating externalities (either pollution or congestion) is to offer a carrot for transport users to switch to more socially desirable modes. This line of reasoning has been widely used as a partial justification for the large subsidies given to support the railways and urban transport services (see Table 6.3). The Railways Act 1974, for example, permits government grants of up to 50 per cent of the costs to be paid to British Rail customers for the installation of rail sidings and provision of rolling stock on the basis of an assessment of the environmental harm of the lorry movements which would be avoided if the investment concerned went ahead. The 1968 Transport Act initiated a system of centrally and locally financed public transport operating and capital subsidies (the latter of which has subsequently been abandoned) with the objective of containing the growth in private motor traffic in the large urban areas. In a perfectly competitive world there would be no justification for this type of

policy but in a situation where marginal cost pricing is *not* universal and where political expedience leans against the introduction of measures such as road pricing, subsidies may offer a pragmatic second-best approach to the externality problem.

Where the cross-elasticity of demand between transport and other goods is negligible and the overall demand for transport is totally inelastic – a situation not unrealistic in the context of commuter travel in many large urban areas – the optimal subsidy to a zero externality generating transport mode will have the same effect on the use of an externality generating mode as pollution charges. In Figure 7.7, the total demand for transport is fixed at D_D. Mode X has associated with its use external costs to the difference between the MPC_X and the MSC_X. Mode Y has no such externalities associated with its use (i.e. $MSC_Y = MPC_Y$) and for simplicity we assume it is a constant cost form of transport. This situation may be thought to represent car travel (mode X) in a city, with extensive congestion and pollution aspects, competing with a fixed fare, pollution free, independently tracked public transport system (mode Y). The free

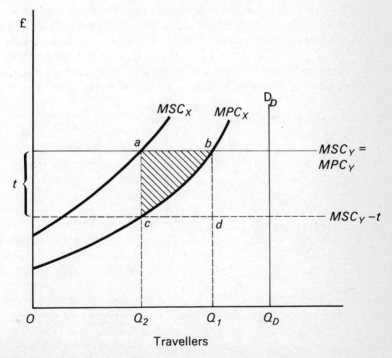

Figure 7.7 Optimal subsidy with fixed aggregate demand for travel

market outcome, where no cognizance is taken of externalities, will be OQ_I people using cars and Q_IQ_D people using public transport. The optimal solution is a split of $OQ_2:Q_2Q_D$ which may be brought about by charging a pollution price of t or alternatively subsidising the public transport mode by t. The modal split effects are the same.

While the subsidy and road pricing may have the same visible effects on traffic, the subsidy in this situation involves real financial costs. The Q_2Q_I travellers switching mode have effectively been 'bought' for a sum equal to *abcd* in the diagram. (The existing passengers are better off as a result of the reduced fare level, but this is just a transfer of welfare from the contributors to the subsidy – the taxpayers – to the public transport users.) The welfare benefit enjoyed by these Q_2Q_I travellers is reflected in the cost saving gained by switch from car to public transport (i.e. *cdb*) which is less than this bribe (by an amount *abc*). Thus the subsidy is clearly 'second-best' to road pricing in this case.

If aggregate demand is not perfectly inelastic then the optimal subsidy is more difficult to define although it may still offer a second-best solution to the externality problem. Figure 7.8a shows the cost conditions for the externality generating mode with a demand curve for its services of D_X. Figure 7.8b shows the cost and demand for the public transport mode. A subsidy for mode Y will cause D_X to shift to the left (say to D'_X), reducing the dead-weight welfare loss associated with the sub-optimally high level of car usage. (Unless, however, the demand for car use is pushed so far left that it

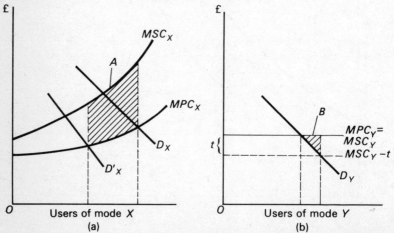

Figure 7.8 Optimal subsidy with elastic aggregate demand for travel

intersects the cost curves in some area where $MPC_X = MSC_X$, a dead-weight loss will remain.) As with Figure 7.7 the subsidy itself will also result in some loss of welfare. If we say the dead-weight loss saving associated with the reduced level of demand for mode X is equal to A (i.e. the area between MSC_X and MPC_X as D_X shifts to the left) and the welfare loss directly associated with the subsidy is B (A and B representing the two shaded areas in Figure 7.8), then the optimal subsidy, t, is defined as

$$\max \{A - B\}$$

The practical difficulty with this approach is that the optimal subsidy may be extremely large and theoretically, if the cross-elasticity of demand between modes is low, may even result in negative fares. The use of public transport subsidies in urban areas has been questioned for this very reason. Kemp (1973) found that in general the direct fare elasticity for urban public transport was low (-0.1 to -0.7) suggesting that substantial subsidies are necessary to attract passengers to public transport irrespective of whether they constitute new travellers or those diverted from private cars. Baum's (1973) work is even less optimistic yielding fare elasticities in the range from -0.1 to -0.4 for Britain, the US and West Germany. At the extreme, evidence from Chicago (Moses and Williamson, 1963) indicates that even free public transport would encourage only 13 per cent of motorists to switch mode. While these results give little support to fare subsidies in urban areas as a means of containing the external costs of private motoring (although the work of Sherman (1972) and Glaister and Lewis (1977) runs counter to this trend) they do not necessarily mean that fare subsidies cannot achieve other objectives nor that non-fare subsidies may not produce the desired transfers. Travellers often appear more sensitive to service quality and reliability than monetary cost; hence subsidies to provide good transport facilities at relatively high prices may be more successful at attracting people to public transport than cheap but poor quality services. It should also perhaps be remembered after reflecting on Chapter 4 that transferring people and goods to public transport may not be the panacea to the environment problem that some groups have claimed.

7.6 Protecting the sufferers
The strategies examined so far have relied upon either forcing the generator of externalities to change his production process or encouraging the adoption of a different method of operation. We have only touched upon the idea of insulating the public from en-

vironmental intrusion (i.e. in the context of aircraft landing path controls and lorry routes). Insulation in the short term may be achieved either by directing traffic away from sensitive areas or by physically protecting people and property (e.g. with double glazing for sound insulation) while in the longer term new investment permits a more efficient separation of transport from those sensitive to its wider impact (the main reason for the official rejection of the Roskill Commission's recommendations on the siting of a Third London Airport was that an inland site would be excessively damaging to the country's environment – see Chapter 8).

The Armitage Report (Department of Transport, 1980) goes as far as to recommend the establishment of 'Lorry Action Areas' to protect residents living in a limited number of areas but who suffer from the worst environmental effects of road freight transport. Specifically such areas would involve:

(1) the installation of double glazing in houses, which would reduce considerably the major problem of noise in homes;
(2) grants for repairs to houses physically damaged by lorries;
(3) maintaining road surfaces to high standards, which would reduce vibrations;
(4) minor road improvements to reduce accidents and to reduce noise, e.g. by the use of noise absorbing road surfaces;
(5) the building up of pavements or erection of bollards to reduce the problems of vehicles cutting corners and of damage to buildings through physical contact; and
(6) in the worst cases of intense local nuisance by a specific generator of lorry traffic, compensation for discontinuance action taken by a planning authority in respect of a site with planning permission or existing use rights.

The difficulty with protective options, both long and short-term, is that their effects are often much wider than simply protecting sensitive groups in the community and their overall cost may be considerable (as, for example, would be the 'Lorry Action Areas'). Limiting the flight paths of aircraft can both increase the risk of accident (by forcing the adoption of less safe climbing and turning patterns) and increase the cost of operations (especially energy costs). Similarly, lorry routing both necessitates higher infrastructure costs and often leads to longer trip distances. Table 7.3 looks at a selection of major long routing proposals and gives the range of effects experienced – it is clear that these are far from uniform and that in some cases perverse environmental results are found (i.e. more houses gain than lose). Insulation of housing is undertaken as part of the compensation for noise from new roads but if this extended to cover all dwellings experiencing noise from road traffic the cost, according to the Noise Advisory Council, would be £1.6 billion.

In the longer term it should, theoretically, be easier to design the spatial economy so that transport's effect on the environment is significantly lower. Many options are available (Foster and Mackie, 1970) including:

(1) sterilisation of land between nuisance and dwellings;
(2) use non-sensitive buildings (e.g. light industry) as barriers between nuisance and sensitive areas;
(3) design dwellings so that little used rooms confront the nuisance rather than living rooms or bedrooms;
(4) make use of self-protecting developments – for example patio style housing – to reduce intrusion.

Table 7.3 Range of effects of lorry operation restriction schemes

Item	Range
Road length protected	325 yards – 14 miles
Increase in trip length	0 – 10.5 miles
Increase in cost per trip	0 – £2
Total annual increase in costs	0 – £1 million
Reduction in lorries per day	50 – 1 700
Reduction as % of all lorries	33 – c.100%
Annual cost per house gaining	0 – £1 000
Ratio of houses gaining to houses losing	1:6 – 3.5:1
Violation rate	0 – 30%

Source: Department of Transport, 1980

Such designs obviously generate additional costs and only provide a partial solution to the environmental problem. Like most of the shorter-term protective measures they only ameliorate those aspects of environmental costs inflated while people are at home. Land-use planning may offer some limited protection at other times – especially in the reduction of accident risk – but it is unlikely to separate completely transport from the non-traveller.

7.7 Some conclusions
The optimisation of the external effects of transport is a complicated

matter. The previous sections have indicated the pros and cons of alternative courses of action, highlighting specifically the difficulties of putting theoretical solutions into practice. One of the biggest problems which has only been touched upon in passing is that many externalities are interrelated and cannot adequately be handled in a partial framework. Many of the relationships are joint and a reduction of vehicle noise, for example, is often accompanied by less air pollution but this is not always so. Larger lorries, for example, may involve greater individual intrusion but at the same time fewer lorries are required. Road pricing may act to optimise urban traffic congestion but in doing so diverts traffic through areas sensitive to noise and vibration; a faster traffic flow is also likely to result in fewer but more serious accidents.

To date policies have been piecemeal, usually focusing on modes of transport rather than directly on transport externalities and, generally, with the explicit objective of reducing the effect of different modes rather than optimising them. This suggests that the social objective of government policy has been one of satisficing rather than optimising although it has been argued that the actual effect of some regulations has been excessive. Schwing *et al.* (1980) have, for instance, suggested that the US Clean Air Act of 1970 imposed car exhaust emission levels which were far too stringent with a consequential welfare loss. Table 7.4 presents the results of their cost-benefit study. While the high benefit estimate suggests some welfare advantage from the Act, the underlying assumptions required to reach this conclusion are deemed very unrealistic. The optimal levels for the toxic exhaust emissions were estimated to be 0.73 per cent, 0.31 per cent and 0.82 per cent control for nitrogen oxides (NO), carbon monoxides (CO) and hydrocarbons (HC) respectively.

The acceptability of this piece of work would be questioned by environmentalists in terms of both the items included in the cost-

Table 7.4   The cost and benefit of the US Clean Air Act 1970

Benefit estimate	% Control level			Benefit	Cost	Net benefit
	HC	CO	NO	(10^9)	(10^9)	(10^9)
Low	0.98	0.97	0.94	9	65	− 56
Prime	0.98	0.97	0.94	34	65	− 31
High	0.98	0.97	0.94	102	65	37

Source: Schwing *et al.*, 1980

benefit calculations and the valuations placed upon them. The problem, common to most studies of environmental aspects of transport, is the inadequacy of knowledge both about the actual physical impact of the various external effects generated by transport and about the values society places upon them. Until some clear understanding of these matters is obtained it is difficult to see how the external effects of transport are likely to approach the optimal level.

7.8 Further reading and references

Road pricing is a well researched subject area but is still open to some controversy. A dated, but extremly well written and comprehensive review is contained in Beesley (1968) and this offers a useful extension of the material presented in the chapter. Singapore offers the only major application of road pricing and the reader is thoroughly recommended to read some of the references cited in the chapter, but should these be difficult to obtain, Holland and Watson (1978) offers a good survey of the work. The Armitage Report (Department of Transport, 1980) provides some useful comment on the relative merits of different policies towards the externalities associated with heavy lorries. The paper by Foster (1974) offers possibly the most thorough discussion of the different approaches to contain the specific externalities generated by urban traffic movement and extends the argument beyond the simple issue of economic efficiency.

References

Alexandre, A., Barde, J-Ph. and Pearce, D.W. (1980), 'The practical determinants of a charge for noise pollution', *Journal of Transport Economics and Policy*, Vol. 14, pp. 205–20.

Baum, H.J. (1973), 'Free public transport', *Journal of Transport Economics and Policy*, Vol. 7, pp. 3–19.

Baumol, W.J. and Oates, W.E. (1975), *The Theory of Environmental Policy: Externalities, Public Outlays and the Quality of Life*, New York, Prentice Hall.

Beesley, M.E. (1968), 'Technical possibilities of spatial taxation in relation to congestion caused by private cars', *European Conference of Ministers of Transport, 2nd International Symposium,* Paris, OECD.

Bennathan, E. and Walters, A.A. (1979), *Port Pricing and Investment Policy for Developing Countries*, Oxford, Oxford University Press.

Button, K.J. (1978), 'A note on the road pricing of commercial traffic' *Transportation Planning and Technology*, Vol. 4, pp. 175–8.

Coase, R.H. (1960), 'The problem of social cost', *Journal of Law and Economics*, Vol. 3, pp. 1–44.

Department of Transport (1980), *Report of the Inquiry into Lorries, People and the Environment* (Armitage Report), London, HMSO.

Foster, C.D. (1974), 'Transport and the urban environment', in J.R. Rothenberg and I.G. Heggie (eds.), *Transport and the Urban Environment*, London, Macmillan.

Foster, C.D. and Mackie, P.J. (1970), 'Noise: economic aspects of choice', *Urban Studies*, Vol. 7, pp. 123–35.

Glaister, S. and Lewis, D. (1977), 'An integral fares policy for transport in London', *Journal of Public Economics*, Vol. 9, pp. 341–55.

Goode, A.P. (1975), 'Restraining traffic – a study of some possible methods', in *Traffic and the Urban Environment*, London, Planning and Transport Research and Computation.

Holland, E.P. and Watson, P.L. (1978), 'Traffic restraint in Singapore', *Traffic Engineering and Control*, Vol. 19, pp. 14–22.

Kemp, M.A. (1973), 'Some evidence of transit demand elasticities', *Transportation*, Vol. 2. pp. 25–52.

Lowe, J. and Lewis, D. (1980), *The Economics of Environmental Management*, London, Philip Allan.

Maler, K.G. (1974), 'Environmental policies and the role of the economist in influencing public policy', in J.G. Rothenberg and I.G. Heggie (eds.), *Transport and the Urban Environment*, London, Macmillan.

Mills, E.S. and White, L.J. (1978), 'Government policies towards automotive emissions controls', in A.F. Friedlander (ed.), *Approaches to Controlling Air Pollution*, Cambridge, Mass., MIT Press.

Moses, L.N. and Williamson, A.F. (1963), 'Value of time, choice of mode and the subsidy issue in urban transportation', *Journal of Political Economy*, Vol. 57, pp. 211–21.

Organisation for Economic Cooperation and Development (1975), *The Polluter Pays Principle*, Paris, OECD.

Peltzman, S. and Tideman, T.N. (1972), 'Local versus national pollution control,' *American Economic Review*, Vol. 62, pp. 959–63.

Pigou, A. (1920), *The Economics of Welfare*, London, Macmillan.

Richardson, H.W. (1974), 'A note on the distributional effects of road pricing', *Journal of Transport Economics and Policy*, Vol. 8, pp. 82–5.

Royal Commission on Environmental Pollution (1972), *First Report*, London, HMSO.

Schwing, R.C., Southworth, B.W., von Buseck, C.R. and Jackson, C.J. (1980), 'Benefit-cost analysis of automotive emission reductions', *Journal of Environmental Economics and Management*, Vol. 7, pp. 44–64.

Seah, C.M. (1980), 'Mass mobility and accessibility: transport planning and traffic management in Singapore', *Transport Policy and Decision Making*, Vol. 1, pp. 55–71.

Sharp, C.H. (1966), 'Congestion and welfare: an examination of the case for a congestion tax', *Economic Journal*, Vol. 76, pp. 806–17.

Sharp, C. (1979), 'The environmental impact of transport and the public interest', *Journal of Transport Economics and Policy*, Vol. 13, pp. 88–101.

Sherman, R. (1972), 'Subsidies to relieve traffic congestion', *Journal of Transport Economics and Policy*, Vol. 6, pp. 22–31.

Toh, R. (1977), 'Road congestion pricing: the Singapore experience', *Malayan Economic Review*, Vol. 22, pp. 52–61.

Vanags, A.H. (1977), 'Maritime congestion: an economic analysis', in R.O. Goss (ed.), *Advances in Maritime Economics*, Cambridge, Cambridge University Press.

Walters, A.A. (1976b) 'Marginal cost pricing in ports', *Logistics and Transportation Review*, Vol. 12, pp. 99–105.

Watson, P.L. and Holland, E.P. (1978), 'Relieving traffic congestion: the Singapore Area Licensing Scheme', *World Bank Staff Working Paper* No. 281.

8. Investment Criteria – Private and Public Sector Analysis

8.1 Basic principles

The preceding chapters have been primarily concerned with making the best use of an existing transport network or fleet of vehicles. They have primarily focused on short-term problems involving the management, regulation and pricing of an established transport system. In particular, they were concerned with emphasising the central role of marginal cost pricing (including social costs) in encouraging the optimal utilisation of transport facilities. There is, however, a longer-term aspect to be considered, namely possible changes in the size or nature of the basic transport system by either investment or disinvestment. In the case of road haulage, airline and shipping operations, the commercial nature of decision-making bodies means that changes are normally analysed in terms of their financial repercussions. With road track, railways and port authorities, which in most countries are owned by public agencies, the provision of basic infrastructure is usually determined by looking at much wider considerations.

Simple economic theory provides straightforward guidelines for investment; essentially they involve pricing and output decisions where the constraints of a fixed production capacity (e.g. a given fleet or rail network) cease to be binding. In Figure 8.1, for example, we consider a profit-maximising airline with a fleet exhibiting short-run average and marginal cost characteristics of $SRAC_1$ and $SRMC_1$ respectively, and confronted by the demand curve D (with marginal revenue MR). Ideally, a price P_1 will be set and seat-kilometres Q_1 offered. The long-run marginal cost ($LRMC$) is, however, below MR at this output and, with this size of fleet, gives an inducement to expand output in the long term by acquiring more capacity. Higher seat availability will force price down but, and this is important in the example, it may also make it more economical to increase the aircraft fleet size. In the diagram, and assuming throughout that profit-maximising prices are charged, the fleet could be expanded to correspond to $SRAC_2$ and $SRMC_2$. Here the long-run optimum situation is achieved with marginal revenue equated to long-run and short-run costs and with profit maximisation resulting. If the firm were concerned with social rather than commercial, profit maximisation, criteria and adopted instead marginal cost pricing, then the $SRMC_3$ and $SRAC_3$ curves become relevant because with this objective function it is the setting of $D = LRMC = SRMC$ which is important. Greater capacity still is needed for this (hence the $SRMC_3$ and $SRAC_3$ curves) and optimal long-run output will be higher at Q_3 seat kilometres with fares lowered to P_3. At this price and output, social surplus is maximised although, since $P_3 \langle LRAC$, in the long run a financial loss will be made.

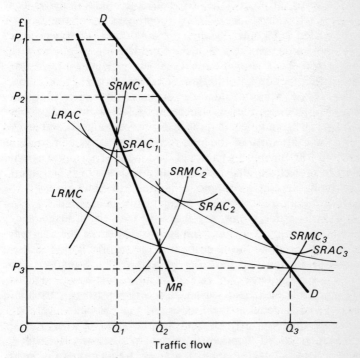

Figure 8.1   Optimal investment:- profit maximisation and social surplus maximisation

The basic principles are simple and come straight from the elementary literature (e.g. Webb, 1973); the difficulty comes in the transport context in putting them into practice. In many cases investments are not divisible and, hence, the $LRAC$ and $LRMC$ curves are not the smooth envelopes depicted in Figure 8.1 but rather a series of disjointed segments, or even points, which do not intersect with demand. This is an extremely common situation in transport and it does pose serious problems in many operational cases. It is not difficult, for example, to envisage routes where the available vehicles (be they planes, buses or whatever) are either too small or too large to be optimal and it is even more common in the case of infrastructure where, for instance, a two-lane motorway may be inadequate to cope with normal demand but a three-lane one is too capacious. Further, there is the problem of what exactly is meant by 'cost'. While we have treated the commercial and social criteria of profit maximisation and marginal cost pricing as amenable to presentation on one diagram, in practice most socially orientated undertakings look at a much wider range of costs (notably many of the externalities discussed in Chapter 5) when deciding upon investment than do those motivated by purely financial considerations. Coupled with this is the fact that the diagrammatic analysis assumes that, irrespective of the operational criteria, prices are optimal in the short term and thus can act as an aid and guideline to investment decision-making. Also, despite the sophistication of forecasting techniques (see Chapter 9) it is unlikely that the transport provider is completely aware of the exact form of the long-run demand curve confronting him. Indeed, the fluctuating nature of demand for transport (especially long-term cycles in demand associated with national and international economic conditions) mean that it is rather more of a stochastic concept than a deterministic phenomenon as depicted.

Given all these difficulties, together with the general inadequacy of information enjoyed by most transport suppliers of their current levels of cost, let alone future costs, it is not surprising that investment analysis in transport has received considerable attention. The high costs and long-term implications of infrastructure investments in road and rail track, and sea and airports has led to particular attention being directed at these areas. At the academic level they also pose particularly difficult questions because, in many cases, facilities are provided at prices unrelated to cost, or made freely available to users. Additionally, there are frequently widespread ramifications for transport users elsewhere or for the non-users living in surrounding areas.

8.2 The discounting formulae – the commercial and social approaches
The administrative structure of transport in many countries means that most types of infrastructure are supplied with the intention of maximising economic efficiency – i.e. they are appraised in terms of

their social value assuming they are optimally utilised at marginal cost prices. There are clearly exceptions to this, however, where profit maximisation is seen as the primary objective. The distinction between the two approaches may be seen by contrasting the discounting approach used by large profit-oriented firms (and public corporations instructed to operate commercially) with the discounting approach of undertakings concerned with economic efficiency. (The discounting process is a simple weighting of different items of cost and income according to the time period at which they occur – more distant items being given less emphasis in the calculations.) The commercial firm will, in the absence of a budget constraint, accept investments when the financial net present value is positive, i.e. where

$$NPV_f = \sum_{n=1}^{K} \left[\frac{P(R_n - P(F_n)}{(1+i)^n} \right] \tag{8.1}$$

where NPV_f is the financial net present value;

$P(R_n)$ is the probable revenue that would be earned from the investment in year n;

$P(F_n)$ is the probable financial cost of the investment in year n;

i is the rate of interest reflecting the cost of capital to the undertaking; and

K is the anticipated life of the investment.

A positive NPV_f, therefore, tells the businessman that it is worthwhile undertaking an initial investment – i.e. it tells him that a movement from zero output in Figure 8.1 to output Q_1 with the associated short-run costs of $SRAC_1$ and $SRMC_1$ is commercially desirable and that a profit above both long and short-run costs will be earned. A more normal case, where an expansion of operations is being considered involving some new capital outlay, requires the *additional* discounted profits from the investment to be compared with the *additional* discounted costs. If the resultant incremental NPV_f is positive then the investment is justified on profitability grounds. In terms of the diagram a movement down the *LRMC* curve to output level Q_2 with the short-run marginal costs of $SRMC_2$ would yield a positive *incremental NPV_f* but subsequent investment to take one down the *LRMC* curve to output Q_3 would not.

In contrast, economic efficiency is assessed using some form of cost-benefit analysis which, again in the absence of a budget constraint, suggests schemes with a positive social net present value should be undertaken where

$$NPV_s = \sum_{n=1}^{k} \sum_{m=1}^{j} \left[\frac{P(a_m B_{nm}) - P(b_m C_{nm})}{(1+r)^n} \right] \qquad (8.2)$$

where NPV_s is the social net present value;

$P(a_m B_{nm})$ is the probable social benefit to be enjoyed by individual m in year n as a result of the investment's completion. B_{nm} is given a weighting a_m to reflect society's welfare preference;

$P(b_m C_{nm})$ is the probable social cost to individual m in year n associated with the project. C_{nm} is given a weight b_m to reflect society's welfare preference;

$(1+r)^n$ is the relative social weight attached to a cost or benefit occurring in a given year;

K is the anticipated life of the investment;

j is the total number of individuals affected.

In terms of Figure 8.1, a positive NPV_s implies that the social surplus associated with an investment exceeds the discounted costs – i.e. the demand curve at the final output is equal to or above the *LRMC* curve. An additional investment will be economically justified as long as the discounted value of incremental social benefit exceeds incremental costs. Contrasting this with the commercial criteria, the NBV_f associated with moving down the *LRMC* curve from output Q_2 to Q_3 is negative but the incremental NPV_s would be calculated to be positive.

Not only is the cost-benefit type of analysis more comprehensive in terms of the items considered but it also redefines many of the items retained from commercial criteria. For example, the costs of imported raw materials used in a potential road construction project in a third world country would be valued at market prices if a commercial undertaking were responsible for road investment decisions. If a public body undertakes road investment using wider social criteria, then it would look beyond the immediate financial indicators and at the 'shadow' prices of imports so that the scarcity of foreign exchange and the limitations of adequate finance for imports is reflected in the decision-making. In some investments use is made of formerly unemployed factor services – e.g. unemployed labour – where the opportunity cost of employment in a transport scheme is really zero or the opportunity cost of the leisure they now forgo. A commercial concern would cost such inputs at the wages that have to be paid, but in a cost-benefit study they may not be considered a cost at all or, more probably, would be costed so that genuine resource costs are incorporated in the calculations.

A further very important distinction is that the social efficiency approach takes cognizance of the distributional effect of the investment (the a_m and b_m terms in equation 8.2). This is often difficult to do in reality although various schemes for weighting costs and benefits have been advanced by theoreticians (e.g. McGuire and Gain, 1969). In practice there is a tendency to employ rather crude methods, often, as in the case of the Planning Balance Sheet approach used in several urban infrastructure investment appraisals (Lichfield and Chapman, 1968), involving the simple setting out in tabular form of the impacts of a scheme on the different user and non-user groups affected or, as with inter-urban road appraisal in the UK (Department of Transport, 1978), carrying out a partial CBA with no allowance for distributional effects and subjecting the results of this to further debate at public inquiry.

8.3 The theory of cost-benefit analysis
While there are many complexities in undertaking commercial investment appraisal (e.g. allowing for risk of unexpected changes in demand, deciding upon appropriate methods of raising capital, etc.), it is public sector transport investment which has attracted the greatest attention. The wide-ranging and long-term effects of most major changes in transport infrastructure necessitate the employment of sophisticated methods of project appraisal and of comprehensive techniques for decision-making. The underlying notion of cost-benefit analysis, which forms the explicit (and, on occasions, implicit) foundation for much of this work has already been alluded to in previous sections. While the algebra set down there suggests a comparatively simple set of standard calculations, the theoretical model is itself based upon a set of much more complex assumptions which makes the application a far more tortuous exercise than it might at first appear. Indeed, there is evidence that the optimism once felt for CBA as the panacea for all transport investment appraisal problems has gradually evaporated and the confidence felt in the strength of CBA calculations no longer exists.

This and the following sections attempt, in broad terms, to explain the CBA methodology and to point to recent innovations in theory and practice. The subject matter of CBA has now become so vast that the treatment here must, by necessity, be rather limited. A comprehensive and rigorous assessment of CBA at the theoretical level is offered by Lesourne (1975) while Harrison (1974) provides a useful and thorough guide to its applications in transport.

The simple outline of CBA in the previous section emphasised the notion of selecting investments which maximise social surplus rather

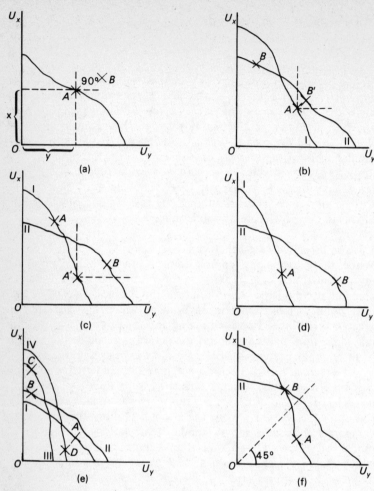

Figure 8.2   Compensation criteria

than just pecuniary returns. One of the major problems in this is that of interpersonal comparisons of welfare. Is it really possible to say social welfare has risen if one group becomes better off at the expense of another? This represents a common situation in transport where users tend to benefit at the expense of non-users. CBA attempts to circumvent this conceptual problem by making use of 'hypothetical compensation tests'. Strictly, since we only have a notion of the ordinal ranking of individuals' priorities, interpersonal welfare comparisons can only be made in very limited circumstances. The Pareto criterion, which underlies most modern welfare economics, states that an action can only definitely be said to be socially desirable if at least one agent benefits and *none* suffers diminution of welfare.

Diagramatically, in Figure 8.2(a) we have two individuals, x and y, who enjoy various levels of welfare recorded on the horizontal and vertical axis as U_x and U_y. If we have a finite collection of goods and services available (including transport services) together with a fixed level of costs, then the well-being of x and y will depend upon how these goods, services and costs are distributed between them. The utility possibility frontier I represents the maximum possible welfare they could enjoy given different distributions of the goods, services and costs. Initially, the goods etc. are distributed so that point A on the frontier is achieved (i.e. x enjoys a utility of O_x and y of O_y). The goods, services and costs could be redistributed so that any other point on I *could* be obtained but no point outside of it. Suppose now a transport investment results in the bundle of goods, services and costs changing and that position B beyond frontier I is reached. This would be deemed a Pareto improvement because *both* x and y are better off. Indeed, any *ex post* position within the 90° zone marked would be Pareto superior to A since, even on one of the limits, at least one person is better off while the other at worst retains his original utility level.

The strict Pareto criterion is of little use in practice – most transport schemes have either direct or indirect net adverse effects on some members of the community. The suggested method of allowing for this is to adopt a hypothetical Pareto criterion and decide whether after the investment it *would* be possible to redistribute the impacts in such a way that no one is worse off but there is still some residual gain to others. Whether such redistribution actually occurs is felt to be a normative issue and should be treated as within the domain of politics rather than economics. There are two broad approaches to the hypothetical compensation criteria. The first, initially advanced by Kaldor (1939), forms the basis for most CBA studies and suggests that a scheme is socially desirable if the beneficiaries could compensate the losers and still remain better off. In Figure 8.2(b), B is Kaldor-superior to A (although not strictly Pareto-superior) because B is on a new post-investment utility possibility frontier II which passes outside of A. Hence, the bundle of goods, services and costs which generate II *could* be redistributed from B to B' which is Pareto-superior to A. Whether the government instigates a tax/subsidy scheme to cause such a movement along II is considered a political issue; Kaldor (in a discussion of the repeal of the nineteenth century Corn Laws!) simply argues that it *could* be done. Hicks (1940) favours a similar approach but adopts *pre-invest-ment* weights for his criteria. Specifically he argues for a project's acceptance if those who lose as a result of its implementation cannot bribe the gainers not to do it without becoming worse off themselves. In Figure 8.2(c), *B* is Hicks-superior to *A* because, with the *pre-investment* package of goods, services and costs which permitted frontier I to be attained, it is impossible for *x* (the loser) to bribe *y* (the beneficiary) not to support the investment. *B* is always above I and hence will be Pareto-superior to any point, such as *A '* which can be achieved by redistributing the pre-investment package.

The problem with the Kaldor and Hicks approaches is that they may, in some circumstances, contradict one another. For example, in Figure 8.2(b) although *B* is Kaldor-superior to *A*, we can see that *A* is Hicks-superior to *B*. Further, even if one only used the Kaldor test and the investment was completed and position *B* attained, it then becomes possible to show that it is, again following the Kaldor criteria, socially beneficial to disinvest and return to *A*. (Similar types of problem exist in 8.2(c) with the Hicks test.) Samuelson (1961) argues that the problem will always exist as long as the pre and post-investment utility possibility frontiers cross and that compari-sons in such circumstances are invalid. This is an extremely restric-tive view. As long as the two actual positions being compared are on the same side of any intersection of the frontiers then the two criteria give consistent assessments and there are no problems of 'revers-ibility' (Skitovsky, 1941). Figure 8.2(d), for instance, shows a situ-ation where *B* meets both the Hicks and the Kaldor hypothetical compensation tests and may, therefore, be considered socially superior to *A*. There is also no question of advocating reversibility once the investment leading to *B* has been undertaken. Whether, in practice, transport analysts need to test for these problems is an empirical question which has, to date, been inadequately explored. At least one experienced economist in the CBA field suggests that the Skitovsky criteria may be violated on more occasions than is some-times supposed (Graaf, 1975).

A different problem may arise when appraising a series of piece-meal investments. It is possible because of the relative nature of con-sumer surplus – which underlies all these tests – for a series of small investments each to pass the Skitovsky test but for the eventual out-come to be socially inferior to the initial position (Gorman, 1955). In Figure 8.2(e), if we have an initial position of *A* on frontier I, then an investment which permits *B* to be reached satisfies the Skitovsky criterion (and, indeed, Samuelson's); further, a move from *B* to *C*, following additional investment, may be approved and, likewise, a subsequent move from *C* to *D*, which again meets the Skitovsky test. However, despite the fact we have seen that *A* ⟨ *B* ⟨ *C* ⟨ *D* in terms of hypothetical compensation tests, it is clearly evident in Figure 8.2(e) that *A* is preferable, on Skitovsky grounds, to *D*. Each of the series of small changes appear desirable but the final, overall outcome leaves society worse-off than before.

If this problem was only a theoretical curio there would be no need for concern, unfortunately this does not seem to be the case. Numerous examples of piecemeal decision-making leading to a subsequent diminution of social welfare can be cited in urban planning, but in the context of transport perhaps the most worrying problem concerns the growth in car use since the Second World War at the expense of urban public transport (Mishan, 1967). For simplicity, we take a concentric shaped city with employment concentrated in the centre. The core is surrounded by a ring of residential estates. The analysis is short-term and assumes that this land-use pattern is fixed. It is now possible to define three phases:

Phase I   All commuters have only one mode of transport available and travel to work by public transport – taking 10 minutes – is the norm.

Phase II   One commuter (*X*) buys a car and drives to work taking 5 minutes, leaving the other travellers unaffected by his action and still taking 10 minutes to reach work by public transport.

Phase III   Many commuters, observing the advantage enjoyed by *X*, begin to buy and use cars which, with the resultant congestion generated, increase driving time to work to 15 minutes and, due to the impedence caused by the cars, slows public transport so that commuters using this mode now suffer a 25-minute journey. In the longer term, because of the technologically unprogressive nature of public transport, the service may be withdrawn (following the syndrome of few passengers – higher fares and poorer service – even fewer passengers etc., etc.) leaving a choice of car purchase or walk trips to work. The result is a 'prisoner's dilemma' type of situation where individually each commuter would prefer the original situation, rather than the new undesirable equilibrium, but cannot attain it by unilateral action.

The example illustrates the difficulties which may arise as the result of decisions based upon relative welfare measures: each commuter thought that he would benefit by investing in a car because he did not take cognizance of the whole set of decisions being made. Ideally, a CBA study should appraise *all* the systems or sequences of potential investments other than assess individual components of a programme of events. The urban planning process, discussed in Chapter 9, is an area where this is particularly relevant.

While most CBA studies of transport projects have concentrated on efficiency considerations, relying upon the hypothetical compensation criteria, it has been suggested by Little (1950) that some allowance for distributional impact should be incorporated. Specifically, it is argued that a project should only be accepted using the hypothetical type of criteria if the final outcome improves the income distribution. For example, in Figure 8.2(f), we assume that an improved income distribution means greater equality of welfare and thus corresponds to a movement closer to the 45° line depicted. Thus, *B*, on the post-investment policy frontier, is both Skitovsky-superior to *A* and also Little-superior because it is closer to the 45°, equal utility, line. It is important to note that it is the *actual* outcome which is being considered and not potential, redistributed packages of the post-investment collection of goods, services and costs. As we see in section 8.5 there are several ways in which this distributional element may be incorporated within CBA studies.

8.4 CBA and network effects

One of the particular difficulties of applying CBA to transport investment decisions is to incorporate adequately the wide-ranging effects a change in one part of the transport system has on the rest of the network. Most transport infrastructure forms a link in a much larger, interacting network and, consequently, changes in any one link tend to affect demand on competitive and complementary links. Although this sort of complexity exists for virtually all forms of transport, the problem of assessing the overall effect on road transport of improving a single link has, because of the dominance of this form of transport in modern society, attracted the majority of attention.

If there are two roads, one from X to Y and the other X to Z, then an improvement in route XY will affect three groups. We will assume for simplicity that all demand curves are linear and that the pre-investment traffic flows on XY and XZ are T_{XY} and $(T_{XZ} + R)$ respectively. The three groups of users to consider are then:

(1) Existing users who remain on their original routes (i.e. T_{XY} and T_{XZ}). These will enjoy a gain in consumers' surplus because

those on route XY will now be using a higher quality facility while those on XZ will benefit from reductions in demand for this route as some former users switch to the improved XY. If this latter traffic which has diverted from XZ to XY is denoted as R, then the total benefit to those remaining loyal to their initial routes may be represented as:

$$T_{XY}(C_1 - C_2) + T_{XZ}(D_1 - D_2)$$

where C_1, C_2, D_1, D_2 are the pre and post-investment costs by roads XY and XZ respectively.

(2) Generated traffic consisting of people who did not previously travel (i.e. G_{XY} and G_{XZ}). On average (given the linear demand curves) each of these groups of new road users will benefit by half as much as existing, non-switching traffic. (Some will obviously be marginal trip-makers and only just gain by making a trip while others are intra-marginal and enjoy nearly as much additional consumer surplus as the non-switchers.) The total benefit of the investment to this group will thus be

$$\tfrac{1}{2} G_{XY}(C_1 - C_2) + \tfrac{1}{2} G_{XZ}(D_1 - D_2)$$

(3) Diverted traffic which switches from route XZ to route XY as a consequence of the investment (i.e. R). Obviously the switch, given the free choice situation open to travellers, must leave this group better off – they would not have switched otherwise – and the additional welfare they enjoy can be seen to equal half of the difference in benefit between the cost reductions on the two routes, i.e.

$$R\left[(D_1 - D_2) + \tfrac{1}{2}\{(C_1 - C_2) - (D_1 - D_2)\}\right]$$

which may be reduced to:

$$\tfrac{1}{2} R\{(C_1 - C_2) + (D_1 - D_2)\}$$

The total benefit (TB) of the investment is the summation of these three elements namely:

$$
\begin{aligned}
TB = T_{XY}(C_1 - C_2) + T_{XZ}(D_1 - D_2) + \tfrac{1}{2} G_{XY}(C_1 - C_2) \\
+ \tfrac{1}{2} G_{XZ}(D_1 - D_2) + \tfrac{1}{2} R\{(C_1 - C_2) + (D_1 - D_2)\}
\end{aligned}
\tag{8.3}
$$

Figure 8.3 shows this diagramatically, Figure 8.3(a) representing the supply and demand situations on route XY and Figure 8.3(b) those on route XZ. On route XY we see that demand has increased the supply of road space but demand has declined because the relative

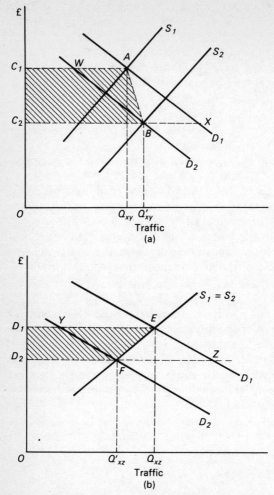

Figure 8.3   Social benefits over a transport network

generalised cost of using XZ changes as traffic diverts from it to the improved facility. Using the notation in the diagram, we know that $Q_{XY} = T_{XY}$ and that $Q'_{XY} = (T_{XY} + G_{XY} + R)$, therefore:

$$\tfrac{1}{2}(Q_{XY} + Q'_{XY}) = (T_{XY} + \tfrac{1}{2}G_{XY} + \tfrac{1}{2}R).$$

Similarly, since $Q_{XZ} = (T_{XZ} + R)$ and $Q'_{XY} = (T_{XZ} + G_{XZ})$, we know that

$$\tfrac{1}{2}(Q_{XZ} + Q'_{XZ}) = (T_{XZ} + \tfrac{1}{2}G_{XZ} + \tfrac{1}{2}R).$$

Substituting this into equation 8.3 we discover:

$$TB = \tfrac{1}{2}\,(Q_{XZ} + Q'_{X:}) \, (C_1 - C_2) + \tfrac{1}{2}(Q_{XZ} + Q'_{XZ}) \, (D_1 - D_2)$$

or more generally, this can be seen as the 'rule of half',

$$TB = \tfrac{1}{2}\Sigma_n \;\; (Q_n + Q'_n)(C_n - C'_n) \, \} \qquad (8.4)$$

This is equivalent to the shaded areas in Figure 8.3. The rule of half can be applied to all transport schemes that interact with other components of the transport system where demand curves are linear. (It must, however, be used with a degree of circumspection when routes are complementary, where demand for the non-improved links may shift to the right, but the broad principle applies.)

The method of handling interdependencies outlined above was initially developed as part of the London Transportation Study (LTS) in the late 1960s, but it does rely upon a rather strong implicit assumption that the income elasticities of demand for routes XY and XZ are equal (Foster and Neuburger, 1974). The problem is that there are many possible sequences in which the price changes on routes XY and XZ could follow; each would yield a different level of aggregate social welfare. For instance, if the chain of price changes is $(C_1, D_1) \to (C_2, D_1) \to (C_2, D_2)$ then the consumer surplus gain in the diagram would be $\{(C_1 A X C_2) + (D_1 \, YF D_2)\}$. But if the sequence is $(C_1, D_1) \to (C_1, D_2) \to (C_2, D_2)$ then the aggregate benefit would be $\{(C_1 WB C_2) + (D_1 EX D_2)\}$. The general measure set out in equation 8.3 and used in the LTS assumes that the demand fluctuations are linear in their own prices and with respect to cross-price effects – if this is so then the measure would give identical results to both the sequences outlined above (which would themselves yield identical benefit estimates). Whether such assumptions are valid is debatable but Foster and Neuburger argue that any deviation is unlikely to be of any practical significance in actual evaluation exercises. Certainly, given the other major difficulties of evaluation and measurement, the 'rule of half' provides a robust and useful guide to the user benefits of transport schemes.

8.5 CBA in practice and variations on the theme

Our attention, to date, has focused on the theoretical ideas underlying CBA, we now turn to look at its actual application in transport fields. The equation set out above (equation 8.2) gives a formal mathematical definition of CBA, while Prest and Turvey (1965) give the verbal counterpart:

CBA is a practical way of assessing the desirability of projects, where it is important to take a long view (in the sense of looking at repercussions in the further as well as the nearer future) and a wide view (in the sense of allowing for side effects of many kinds on many persons, industries, regions, etc.) – i.e. it implies the enumeration and evaluation of all the relevant costs and benefits.

CBA has formed the basis of investment appraisal of many major transport schemes in the UK (e.g. the M1 motorway, the Victoria Line underground railway, the Channel Tunnel, London's system of ringway urban motorways and the siting of a Third London Airport) and has also become a tool in more routine decision-making (e.g. to assess railway social service subsidies in the late 1960s and as a component of inter-urban road investment appraisal).

The Third London Airport Study (Commission on the Third London Airport, 1971) characterises the traditional CBA approach although here, since it was assumed that a new facility was necessary anyway, the benefits were deemed virtually equal for all possible sites, i.e. the question posed involved considering where and when an airport should be built – *not* whether. This meant that in some ways it became a social cost effectiveness study – finding the site with the lowest social costs attached to it. The present values of the various cost and benefit items for each alternative discounted from 2006 to 1975 are given in Table 8.1. While the study team favoured Cublington as marginally superior to the other sites, subsequent Parliamentary debate overruled this in favour of Foulness (i.e. Maplin). Although even this revised proposal was later abandoned, the study proved useful in showing up some of the practical difficulties in conducting a CBA study of a scheme which has extremely wide-ranging and diverse impacts – many of them posing serious problems of evaluation. (For more details of this study see Flowerdew, 1972.)

Despite the widespread adoption of CBA by the transport sector, there has been a gradual disillusionment with the all-embracing, stereotype appraisal implied by Prest and Turvey. This has manifested itself most strongly since the rejection of the Roskill Committee's recommendation regarding the siting of a Third London Airport and became particularly noticeable at public inquiries into new road proposals in the late 1970s. While the criticisms of CBA as a method of socially evaluating transport investments have been extensive, they are perhaps most adequately summed up by Wildavsky (1966, p.297), 'Although cost–benefit analysis presumably results in efficiency by adding the most to national income, it is shot through with political and social value choices and surrounded by uncertainties and difficulties of computation.' The Chairman of British Rail summarised the attitude evolving in the UK when he argued that

Table 8.1   *Social costs and benefits (£m) associated with alternative sites for a Third London Airport*[a]

	Cublington	Foulness	Nuthampstead	Thurleigh
Capital costs				
Construction of airport	184.0	179.0	178.0	166.0
Airport services	14.3	9.8	14.5	11.6
Extension/closure of Luton Airport	– 1.3	10.0	– 1.3	– 1.3
Road and rail development	11.8	23.4	15.5	6.5
Relocation of defence and public scientific establishments	67.4	21.0	57.9	84.2
Loss of agricultural land	3.1	4.2	7.2	4.6
Impact on residential conditions	3.5	4.0	2.1	1.6
Impact on schools, hospitals, etc.	2.5	0.8	4.1	4.9
Other	3.5	0.5	6.7	10.2
Total	288.8	252.7	284.7	288.3
Current costs				
Aircraft movement costs	960.0	973.0	987.0	972.0
Passenger user costs	931.0	1041.0	895.0	931.0
Freight user costs	13.4	23.1	17.0	13.9
Airport services, operating costs	60.3	53.1	56.2	55.6
Travel costs to/from airport	26.2	26.5	24.4	25.4
Other	12.4	7.5	8.5	7.2
Total	2003.3	2124.2	1988.1	2005.1
Benefits (relative to Foulness)				
To common/diverted traffic (net of costs)	—	—	—	—
To generated traffic	44.0	—	27.0	42.0
Total (costs less differential benefits)	2248.1	2376.9	2245.8	2251.4

[a]The table is only a partial reflection of the results obtained and does not, for example, reflect the sensitivity analysis conducted.

Source: Commission on the Third London Airport, 1971

there is a need for an approach that 'can be understood by ordinary intelligent people . . . incorporates the methods of analysis developed by welfare economists over the last decade or so . . . gets away from the naive position adopted by the early cost–benefit men which seemed to imply that every consideration could be perfectly weighted and that, therefore, there was a single best solution' (Parker, 1978).

The response of analysts to these dissatisfactions with mechanical CBA procedures have taken two broad lines. The first is an attempt to modify the original CBA framework (as exemplified by equation 8.2) so that some allowances are made for the major criticisms. In particular, greater effort has been put into evaluating the externality items included in a CBA account (see Chapter 5) and to placing more reliable values on time-saving attributes of schemes (see Chapter 3). Additionally, techniques have been evolved that introduce allowances for the distributional effects of schemes – an area neglected in earlier work which concentrated on overall impact – and for the risk and uncertainty that the predicted cost and benefit streams will diverge from that forecast.

Distributional effects can be allowed for, as we saw in section 8.2, by weighting the costs and benefits according to the different groups affected. Unfortunately, it has been demonstrated at the theoretical level (Mishan, 1974) that in many investment situations the applications of such weights (which may, in particular, be based upon measures reflecting income tax liability) to cost and benefit items can still lead to the acceptance of projects which benefit the rich to the detriment of the poor. Consequently, there is a case for treating distributional considerations independently of efficiency.

Risk and uncertainty about probable outcomes pose even more difficult problems. With risks there is some knowledge about the likelihood of errors in forecasts and this can be incorporated in the analysis by indicating the range of probable long-term effects of investment, together with an indication of the probabilities of different levels of costs and benefits occurring. Unfortunately, there is no such knowledge of possible error with uncertainty and consequently adjustments tend to be made according to intuition or 'skilled judgement'. With many transport projects, the costs of under-engineering are likely to be higher than those of comparable over-engineering (the 'premature' physical disintegration of the UK motorway system being a good example) and thus there is a tendency to over-react to the possibility of uncertain outcomes.

While these advances in traditional CBA techniques go some way towards meeting criticism of early studies in the field they tend to complicate the estimation and decision-making frameworks and, hence, to move even further from the openness sought by Peter Parker and also the Leitch Committee on trunk road investment appraisal (Department of Transport, 1978). One offshoot of CBA which retains the notion of social welfare maximisation but also makes the CBA account accessible to the proverbial 'educated layman' is the Planning Balance Sheet (Lichfield and Chapman, 1968) which was initially devised and developed over a series of case studies to help urban planners. We discuss the PBS in more detail below.

The second response to the critics is to move entirely away from the notion of a social welfare maximisation CBA approach and to adopt a lower level, but possibly more operational and manageable, approach to investment appraisal. Broadly, it is argued that, like most large private companies, public transport undertakings have insufficient information about the stream of costs and benefits (including social items) associated with the different policy options open to them and should, therefore, attempt to meet broad minimum levels of achievement rather than to maximise net benefits. This notion of 'satisficing' fits in with the attitude of most mature industrial concerns towards managerial decision-making (Simon, 1959). Although this second type of response to the critics of CBA is, to date, still comparatively under-researched in the transport field, a number of multi-criteria investment appraisal techniques have been developed, often only at an abstract level, in related areas of study such as regional and national resource planning (Button, 1979).

The Planning Balance Sheet approach mentioned above, although firmly founded in the CBA tradition, offers a methodology which is sufficiently flexible to adaption for both maximising and satisficing frameworks. It has two main merits; firstly it shifts the emphasis of analysis away from the total measure of net benefit to the distribution of the costs and benefits among affected groups and secondly, it circumvents many of the problems associated with expressing all costs and benefits in money terms.

The technique involves setting down, in tabular form, all of the pros and cons associated with alternative investment options. These socio-economic accounts are expressed in monetary values wherever possible but should this prove impracticable then physical values are used and, if quantification is not possible, ordinal indices or scales. The accounts are subdivided to show the effect of different schemes on the groups affected and this offers guidance to distributional implications. The accounts are compared with pre-determined planning goals (and these instrumental objectives may imply either maximisation or satisficing objectives) which are selected as reflective of community preferences. Alternative investment plans are ranked under each objective heading using ordinal ranking procedures and the ranks are then added together to produce a ranking of the investments with respect to the objectives taken as a whole.

A technique of this general kind has met with approval from the Leitch Committee as a tool in inter-urban road investment appraisal. The Committee felt 'the right approach is through a comprehensive framework which embraces all the factors and groups of people involved in scheme assessment' (Department of Transport, 1978,

Table 8.2   The project impact matrix suggested by the Leitch Committee

Incidence group	Nature of effect	Number of measures	
		Financial	*Other*
Road users directly affected	Accident savings	1	3
	Comfort and convenience		1
	Time savings	6	
	Vehicle operating cost saving	5	
	Amenity		2
Non-road users directly affected	Demolition or disamenity to owners of residential commercial and industrial properties		22
	Demolition or disamenity to users of schools, churches, public open space		15
	Land-take, severance and disamenity to farmers		7
Those concerned with the intrinsic value of the area	Landscape, scientific and historical value	3 (plus verbal description)	
Those indirectly affected	Sterilisation of natural resources, land-use planning effects, effects on other transport operators	6 (plus verbal description)	
Financial authority	Cost and financial benefits	7	
Total		19	59

Source: Adapted from Department of Transport, 1978

p. 133). The project impact matrix, as the Leitch Committee called their variation, sets out a 'general framework' of about eighty relevant measures of the effects of transport schemes. As with most PBS studies the final account produced was extensive but Table 8.2 provides a summary. The intention is to use such an account to make pairwise comparisons between the magnitude of the effects associated with different investment alternatives or, where the problem is deciding upon a specific project in isolation, to compare them with some instrumental objectives.

The PBS type approach has, despite its attractions, some inherent limitations. In particular it depends upon crude ranking criteria and scaling methods. The selection of instrumental objectives is itself highly subjective and, although it does force the decision-taker to make his underlying value judgements explicit, it can result in some conflict between interested parties. There is also the danger that the subjectivity of these objectives and trade-offs is forgotten in the mass of data incorporated in the accounts. The PBS has the advantage over some of the more mechanical CBA approaches where numbers are simply fed into some computer programme (such as COBA which was developed in the UK for trunk road investment appraisal) that the construction of the initial socio-economic account can often, in itself, be educational and shed considerable light on salient questions the decision-taker should be asking.

While PBS has been seen as an extension of CBA, it may also be viewed as a primitive form of a 'multi-criteria decision-making technique'. Multi-criteria decision making techniques fall into the second category of advances outlined above in that they are concerned more with the meeting of certain low level aims than maximising social welfare. They involve weighting the different effects of an investment to reflect social priorities but the weights reflect the success at attaining certain objectives rather than maximising an output. A number of multi-criteria approaches have been devised, each attempting to achieve a multi-dimensional compromise between the wide diversity of goals and objectives which are embodied in any form of public choice (Nijkamp and van Delft, 1977). Approaches differ in their methods of presentation, the level of mathematical sophistication involved and the amount of data input required. Several of the techniques rely upon geometrical representation to produce multi-dimensional scalings while others involve a considerable degree of intuition. Of greatest practical value in transport are some of the weighting techniques of which there are numerous variations. Hill's (1968) goals achievement matrix, for example, offers an explicit treatment of various goals and applies a set of predetermined weights to them so that each option can be assessed in terms of goals achieved. To facilitate this, the goals are related to *physical measures* (e.g. minimum traffic speeds, acceptable accident rates, reduced levels of specified toxic exhaust emissions, etc.) to reflect the extent to which they have been achieved. The final goals achievement account employs the weighted index of goal achievement to determine the preferred course of action.

The problem with all useful multi-criteria procedures is the derivation of weighting schemes which reflect the relative importance of physical 'goals' or 'objective instruments' – seldom will a public sector transport scheme do all which is hoped for. The traditional CBA approach, albeit in a maximising context, avoids this problem by using monetary values as weights. While there is evidence that those actually responsible for decision-making in the publicly controlled sectors of transport favour movement towards multi-criteria appraisal techniques, the practical problems are unlikely to permit the widespread use of such approaches – beyond the project impact matrix type of analysis – in the near future.

8.6 Comparability ratios

If scarce investment funds are to be allocated to best effect within the overall transport sector and between it and the rest of the economy, it is clearly important that in some way comparisons are made between the potential effect of using funds in projects evaluated on commercial criteria and using them where social evaluation techniques such as CBA are employed.

Accepting that for institutional or administrative reasons there is no hope of a common method of assessment being employed in practice, then one possible method of comparing projects between sectors is to develop comparability criteria that reduce social and financial costs and benefits to a common denominator. Essentially a mathematical relationship between net social and net financial returns must be found. In certain, highly restrictive, situations this may prove to be feasible (Peaker, 1974). It is theoretically possible, under simplistic assumptions, to reduce everything to either a common financial or common social basis; we will assume, however, that we are assessing a potential investment aimed at improving an inter-city rail service (where profit maximising levies are charged) and wish to convert the net reserves obtained into social welfare terms. Social welfare is assumed here to refer to social surplus (i.e. combined consumer and producer surpluses) as is standard practice in welfare economics.

Figure 8.4 shows the demand curve for the existing rail service to

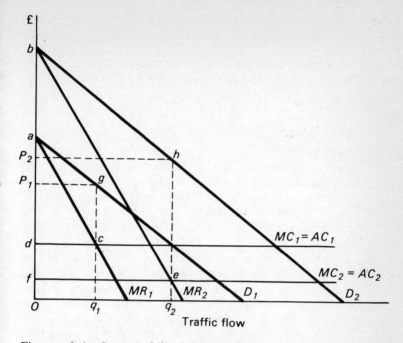

Figure 8.4 Comparability between commercial and social investment criteria

be linear (D_1 with marginal revenue curve MR_1) and that the improvement will result in a parallel shift of this curve to D_2. The average and marginal costs of using the service are assumed constant irrespective of custom with MC_1 ($=AC_1$) being the relevant curve prior to improvement and MC_2 ($=AC_2$) being operative afterwards. With these assumptions the demand curves are easily represented:

D_1 is $p = a - kq$
D_2 is $p = b - kq$

where p is price, q is the level of traffic flow and k is the slope of the parallel demand curves. With profit maximisation (i.e. $MC=MR$) it is seen from Figure 8.4 that $q_1 = \dfrac{a-d}{2k}$ and $q_2 = \dfrac{b-f}{2k}$. Integrating under the relevant marginal revenue curves shows that the improved rail service would increase profits by {Area (*bef*) – Area (*acd*)}. This equals

$$\tfrac{1}{2}[b-f]q_2 - \tfrac{1}{2}[a-d]\,q_1 = \frac{1}{4k}[(b-f)^2 - (a-d)^2]. \qquad (8.5)$$

The increase in consumers' surplus associated with the improved rail service is obtained from integrating under the relevant demand curves but above price. In this case the integration yields Area (bhp_2) – Area (agp_1) which equals

$$\tfrac{1}{2}[b-p_2]q_2-\tfrac{1}{2}[a-p_1]q_1=\frac{1}{8k}[(b-f)^2-(a-d)^2]. \tag{8.6}$$

Since total social surplus is composed of producers' surplus (i.e. profit) plus consumers' surplus it is apparent from adding equation 8.5 to equation 8.6 (and then comparing back to equation 8.5) that the gain in social welfare as a result of the rail investment in this profit-maximising situation is 1.5 times the profit which would be earned. It seems possible, therefore, in the circumstances to be able to convert profits earned into a comparable social surplus by multiplying by 1.5.

How useful is this conversion factor likely to be in practice? It is clear that it only applies to user costs and does not permit the inclusion of external factors, either in terms of pollution or congestion, which limits its usefulness in urban transport appraisal or for certain types of infrastructure, such as airports, which are particularly environmentally intrusive. Further, even within the strict confines of user benefit analysis the conversion factor crucially depends upon a series of limiting assumptions. The factors which have been found to influence the ratio include (Harrison and Mackie, 1973):

(1)   The shape of the MC curve before and after the investment;
(2)   The shapes of the demand curves before and after the investment;
(3)   The extent of price discrimination;
(4)   The pricing policy actually pursued and the nature (if any) of its deviation from profit maximisation;
(5)   The consistency of the pricing policy employed as investment alters the cost and demand conditions;
(6)   The incidence of externalities including network effects; and
(7)   The extent to which revenue and benefit streams differ in their availability for reinvestment.

Given the sensitivity of the '1.5 rule' to these various factors, it can hardly be seen as a practicable method of introducing comparability into transport investment decision-making.

8.7 The adjustment to price approach
The comparability ratio approach assumes an investment is under-

taken and then prices set to achieve some economic objective, usually profit maximisation. Financial returns are then compared to social returns. Starkie (1979) argues that a more practicable approach is to determine a common basis for pricing first and then adjust capacity accordingly. The basic idea stems from work on the railways by Joy (1964) which looked exclusively at freight investment, but Starkie generalises the approach to all forms of transport investment. It is assumed that the correct economic price for each mode is determined along the second-best pricing lines formalised by Baumol and Bradford (1970) and that investment (or disinvestment) should be adjusted until long-run marginal costs are equated with the revenues obtained. This means that prices are set to cover short-run marginal cost with a mark-up in proportion to the inverse of the price elasticity of demand for each mode. The mark-up then reflects 'what-the-user-will-bear' towards the cost of capacity provision (i.e. consumer surplus above *SRMC*). If this mark-up, combined with the revenue covering *SRMC*, does not meet the full *LRMC* then capacity should be reduced until an equality is established. If such a pricing regime produces a surplus in excess of *LRMC* then, *ceteris paribus*, there is a case for expanding capacity.

The fundamental idea is that if sufficient price discrimination is applied then *all* potential consumers' surplus is transferred to the supplier and, *ipso facto*, net revenue can be equated with social surplus. Its main advance is the importance which it places on pricing and the recognition that in the long run it is possible to fine-tune investment at the margin. Such an approach obviously removes the need to conduct comparability studies but it has its limitations. The main difficulty is that while it may be possible in some areas to apply the discriminate pricing Starkie advocates – mainly those undertakings directly controlled by government – in other cases private provision of transport facilities makes it rather difficult to ensure that the Baumol-Bradford rules are being applied. Consequently, it is difficult to see how it could be decided what is the correct level of overall investment in the publicly owned sector of transport *vis-à-vis* the aggregate for the private sector. Because much public investment is assessed on social criteria and virtually all private sector investment on commercial criteria, many of the problems of comparability remain. (This problem is avoided in Starkie's empirical work which focuses on road track and railway investment.) Further, the approach once again emphasises user benefits but does not allow for external factors, especially the environmental effects of transport on non-users (Button, 1980).

8.8 Assessing the effect on national income

It has been suggested that rather than expand financial surplus by a comparability ratio, or force some form of common pricing on all sectors of transport, an entirely different measure of the net value of investment, applicable to all forms of transport project irrespective of ownership, may be preferable. The effect of transport on national income, for example, could be used as a substitute for the combined consumers' and producers' surplus generated (e.g. see work by Bos and Koyck (1961) and Friedlaender (1965) on trunk road appraisal). However, besides the practical difficulties involved in estimating the change in national income associated with alternative transort investments, the measure throws up an additional problem that involves the more fundamental question of whether the national income approach really does offer a reasonable and acceptable guide to the relative desirability of alternative investments. (We should perhaps note at this stage that national income, in this context, refers to the accountancy concept used in macroeconomics rather than the wider

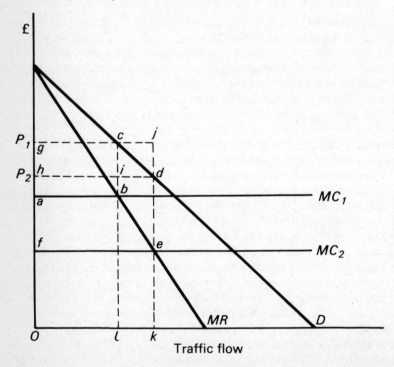

Figure 8.5   The national income change approach to transport investment appraisal

notion of national income referred to by Wildavsky earlier in the chapter.)

We can consider Figure 8.5 and assume D represents the demand (with MR the associated marginal revenue) for the transport service under consideration and that this will not shift following a change in capacity. Further, if we assume the transport undertaking acts as a monoplist in its pricing policy, then we can see that an investment that reduces marginal costs from MC_1 to MC_2 will increase social surplus by *abcdef* in the diagram and profits by $(abidef) - (gcih)$. The reduction in costs will also produce a higher national income. If the Laspeyres index is used (i.e. the change in output valued at the *pre*-investment price), the rise will be measured as *lcjk*. If the Paasche approach is favoured (i.e. the change in output is valued at the *post*-investment price), however, the addition to national income is found to be only *lidk*. There is no reason for the social surplus measure to correspond to the national income measure (or for different estimates of the latter to correspond) except in rather unrealistic circumstances. Nor indeed need it correspond to the profit generated. Of more practical importance, there is no reason why alternative investment possibilities will be ranked consistently by the different methods.

The reason that social surplus and national income measures (and, indeed, financial measures) need not correspond, nor rank consistently, stems from the fact that they measure entirely different things. Social surplus both includes leisure benefits emanating from a project and explicitly incorporates allowances for the diminishing marginal utility associated with the increased consumption of travel. The national income measure does neither: it concentrates exclusively on goods and services traded in conventional markets and assumes either a fixed pre or post-investment price level. Mohring (1976) has demonstrated that the only time the two types of measure yield identical numerical results is '*If* a change takes place which increases the output obtained from a given set of primary resources, and *if* the primary resources allocated to market activities do not themselves change, and *if* the same pricing rules are used in consumers' surplus as in national income change benefit calculations' (emphasis original). Clearly, this means that the national income measure is likely to differ in practice from either the financial or social surplus measure of benefit and, hence, is simply an alternative method of ranking and appraisal, different but not necessarily superior. Given the practical difficulties of estimation in most advanced economies its usefulness seems limited. In less developed countries, though, it may be seen as a more viable appraisal technique if distributional and welfare considerations are felt to be of secondary importance to boosting the national product (see Chapter 10). Transport projects that help stimulate national income growth in these circumstances may be given priority over others (Brown and Harrel, 1965).

8.9 Comparability in practice – UK inter-urban transport

The practical problems of incomparability between investment in different transport sectors has not gone unnoticed by UK transport authorities. The problem is particularly acute in publicly owned inland inter-urban transport where government policy since 1968 has clearly distinguished among different types of service, some of which must show a financial return and others a social return. The broad division is shown in Table 8.3.

Table 8.3   Division of investment by assessment technique

Financial appraisal	*Cost-benefit appraisal*
British Railways Board	British Railways Board
Inter-city services	Urban commuter services
Freight services	Closures
Ancillaries	Roads
National Bus Company	
Nation Freight Corporation	
British Waterways Board	

Source: Department of the Environment, 1976

Certain measures have been introduced that attempt to standardise some elements of appraisal procedures across the two groups. Since the late 1960s, for example, discounting techniques have been employed in all sectors (Treasury, 1967) using a nationally stipulated rate of discount. Some minor changes in the basis of calculation have taken place subsequently (e.g. Treasury, 1978) but such techniques remain the main tool of appraisal. The differences among sectors are really just the actual items discounted; in one case it is simply the fare revenues while in the other it is user benefits (usually calculated in terms of the financial value of the money, accident rate and travel time changes associated with the investment).

The official position, until recently, was that, although there may be a need to take distributional or environmental factors into account when doing *either* type of calculation, the pricing policies pursued mean that revenue may be equated with social surplus in the financially based calculation. Comparability then becomes unnecessary. The rationale behind this view was summarised by the Department of the Environment in evidence to a House of Commons Select Committee (1974), the argument being that although 'the mechanics of assessment differ . . . in ordinary circumstances British Railways pursue a policy of market pricing which ensures that *most benefits to users are fully reflected in the revenue collected*' (emphasis added). The Select Committee was not convinced, however, that inconsistencies do not remain and advocated the establishment of an Inter-Urban Directorate to tackle the problem.

Recently the Leitch Committee, looking specifically at trunk road investment (Department of Transport, 1978) has examined comparability in more detail and recommended that consistency could only be achieved if those undertakings employing financial techniques extended their analysis to embrace the wider social surplus based procedures of appraisal. As we have seen the type of CBA envisaged, however, is somewhat more comprehensive and transparent than that currently used for road investment appraisal in the UK which concentrates solely on user benefits. Further, to gain an even greater degree of consistency, there is a need to bring port and airport investment into the general CBA framework and widen the scope of appraisal away from the purely financial aspects which tend currently (with some significant exceptions) to dominate decision-making in these spheres.

While the notion of common CBA techniques being applied throughout the publicly controlled inter-urban transport system may have certain apparent advantages – indeed in the Federal Republic of Germany it is used for all inter-urban road, rail and waterway analysis – Leitch recognises the private ownership of coastal shipping and pipeline limits the degree of comparability. Essentially, the widespread use of CBA within the publicly owned sector (which, in fact, goes beyond the road/rail situation considered by Leitch) may produce consistent investment decisions within this sector but does not determine the optimal size of public *vis-à-vis* private sector investment. It seems unlikely, given the diversity of investment appraisal techniques employed in the private sector (small firms tending to use simple pay-back or average return calculations – Walton, 1978), that consistency between public and private sectors will occur in the foreseeable future.

8.10 Further reading and references
The available literature on investment appraisal is immense. Mishan (1971) is a classic volume on cost-benefit analysis and is almost encyclopaedic in its coverage – it is hard-going! An up-to-date and very clear discussion of investment appraisal is to be found in Pearce

and Nash (1981) and this provides possibly the most suitable follow-up reading to this chapter. It also contains useful case-study material. Specific consideration of investment in transport infrastructure is to be found in Harrison (1974), but this tends to be rather dated and lacks conciseness. Button (1979) provides a brief resumé of alternatives to the conventional CBA approach and has an extensive set of references. The Leitch Committee Report (Department of Transport, 1978) offers possibly the most readable and interesting discussion of transport investment appraisal in practice. It also offers stimulating ideas of the way that appraisal techniques may (should?) develop in the future.

References

Baumol, W.J. and Bradford, D.F. (1970), 'Optimal departures from marginal cost pricing', *American Economic Review*, Vol. 60, pp. 215–83.

Bos, H.C. and Koyck, L.M. (1961), 'The appraisal of road construction projects; a practical example', *Review of Economics and Statistics*, Vol. 43, pp. 13–20.

Brown, R.T. and Harrel, C.C. (1965), 'Estimating highway benefits in underdeveloped countries', *Highway Research Record* no. 115, pp. 29–43.

Button, K.J. (1979), 'Models for decision-making in the public sector', *OMEGA*, Vol. 7, pp. 399–409.

Button, K.J. (1980), 'Some comments on Starkie's method of allocating interurban road and rail investment', *Regional Studies*, Vol. 14, pp. 333–5.

Commission on the Third London Airport (1971), *Report*, London, HMSO.

Department of the Environment (1976), *Transport Policy: A Consultation Document*, London, HMSO.

Department of Transport (1978), *Report of the Advisory Committee on Trunk Road Assessment* (Leitch Committee), London, HMSO.

Flowerdew, A.D.J. (1972), 'Choosing a site for the Third London Airport: the Roskill Commission's approach', in R. Layard (ed.), *Cost Benefit Analysis*, Harmondsworth, Penguin.

Foster, C.D. and Neuberger, H.L.I. (1974), 'The ambiguity of the consumer's surplus measure of welfare change', *Oxford Economic Papers*, Vol. 26, pp. 66–77.

Friedlaender, A.F. (1965), *The Interstate Highway System: A Study in Public Investment*, Amsterdam, North-Holland.

Gorman, W.M. (1955), 'The intransitivity of certain "criteria" used in welfare economics', *Oxford Economic Papers* (new series), Vol. 7, pp. 25–35.

de V. Graaf, J. (1975), 'Cost-benefit analysis: a critical view', *South African Journal of Economics*, Vol. 44, pp. 233–44.

Harrison, A.J. (1974), *The Economics of Transport Appraisal*, London, Croom Helm.

Harrison, A.J. and Mackie, P.J. (1973), *The Comparability of Cost Benefit and Financial Rates of Return*, Government Economic Service Occasional Paper 5, London, HMSO.

Hicks, J.R. (1940), 'The valuation of social income', *Economica*, Vol. 7, pp. 105–24.

Hill, M. (1968), 'A goal achievement matrix for evaluating alternative plans', *Journal of the American Institute of Planners,* Vol. 34, pp. 19–29.

House of Commons Select Committee (1974), *First Report from the Expenditure Committee Session 1974, Public Expenditure on Transport*, HC 269, London, HMSO.

Joy, S. (1964), 'British Railways' track costs', *Journal of Industrial Economics,* Vol. 13, pp, 74–89.

Kaldor, N. (1939), 'Welfare proposition and interpersonal comparisons of utility', *Economic Journal*, Vol. 49, pp. 549–52.

Lesourne, J. (1975), *Cost-Benefit Analysis and Economic Theory*, Amsterdam, North-Holland.

Lichfield, N. and Chapman, W. (1968), 'Cost-benefit analysis and road proposals for a shopping centre – a case study: Edgware', *Journal of Transport Economics and Policy*, Vol. 2, pp. 280–320.

Little, I.M.D. (1950), *A Critique of Welfare Economics*, Oxford, Oxford University Press.

McGuire, M. and Gain, H. (1969), 'The integration of equity and efficiency criteria in public project selection', *Economic Journal,* Vol. 79, pp. 882–93.

Mishan, E.J. (1967), 'Interpretation of the benefits of private transport', *Journal of Transport Economics and Policy*, Vol. 1, pp. 184–9.

Mishan, E.J. (1971), *Cost-Benefit Analysis*, London, Allen & Unwin.

Mishan, E.J. (1974), 'Flexibility and consistency in cost-benefit analysis', *Economica*, Vol. 41, pp. 81–96.

Mohring, H. (1976), *Transportation Economics*, Cambridge, Mass., Ballinger.

Nijkamp, P. and van Delft, A. (1977), *Multi-Criteria Analysis and Regional Decision-Making*, London, Martinus Nijhoff.

Parker, P. (1978), *A Way to Run a Railway*, Haldane Memorial Lecture.

Peaker, A. (1974), 'The allocation of investment funds between road and rail: a conversion factor linking financial and surplus rates of return', *Public Finance*, Vol. 75, pp. 683–735.

Pearce, D.W. and Nash, C.A. (1981), *The Social Appraisal of Projects – A Text in Cost-Benefit Analysis*, London, Macmillan.

Prest, A.R. and Turvey, R. (1965), 'Cost-benefit analysis – a survey', *Economic Journal*, Vol. 75, pp. 683–735.

Samuelson, P.A. (1961), 'Evaluation of social income, capital formation and wealth', in F.A. Lutz and D.C. Hague (eds.), *The Theory of Capital*, London, St. Martins.

Simon, H.A. (1959), 'Theories of decision-making in economics and behavioural science', *American Economic Review*, Vol. 49, pp. 253–83.

Skitovsky, T. (1941), 'A note on welfare propositions in economics', *Review of Economic Studies*, Vol. 9, pp. 77–88.

Starkie, D.N.M. (1979), 'Allocation of investment to inter-urban road and rail', *Regional Studies*, Vol. 13, pp. 323–36.

Treasury (1967), *Nationalised Industries: A Review of Economic and Financial Objectives*, Cmnd 3437, London, HMSO.

Treasury (1978), *The Nationalised Industries*, Cmnd 7131, London, HMSO.

Walton, M. (1978), 'The investment decision: theory and practice', *Economics,* Vol. 16, pp. 71–3.

Webb, M.G. (1973), *The Economics of Nationalised Industries*, London, Nelson.

Wildavsky, A. (1966), 'The political economy of efficiency: cost-benefit analysis, systems analysis and program budgeting', *Public Administration*, Vol. 26, pp. 292–310.

9 Transport Planning and Forecasting

9.1 The development of transport planning

The preceding chapters have concentrated primarily upon pricing and investment decisions for individual modes of transport in isolation – the pricing of public transport, urban car-users, etc. Little has been said about the co-ordination of pricing and investment decisions across whole sectors of transport. Co-ordination, as Adam Smith pointed out, will come about automatically in a perfectly competitive market framework where marginal cost pricing principles are universally applied. Indeed, there is considerable emphasis on co-ordination through the market in the development of inter-urban transport in Britain. Concern over safety is the main interest of the authorities and, within a quality licensing framework, competition both within and among modes is encouraged. There is, however, some attempt to plan infrastructure provision although the idea of a strategic motorway network in the early 1970s has given way to rather more piecemeal planning of trunk roads. The main objective here is the avoidance of duplication, especially in relation to major development projects with a long period of gestation.

In other areas of transport activity, and particularly in the urban context, it has been felt necessary to introduce a high degree of planning and central/local government intervention to improve the overall efficiency of local transport provision. The role that transport may play in other spheres of economic activity is one reason for this (improved transport, for example, may form part of a social welfare policy and is currently seen as central to the revitalisation of local economies in depressed inner city areas), but a more general explanation may be found in the magnitude of the imperfections of the urban transport markets. The justification for urban transport planning is summarised in a white paper on *Transport Policy* (Department of Transport, 1977):

> The many activities concentrated in urban areas must be accessible to people and the economic and social life of cities depends on enormously

diverse and complex patterns of travel and destination. Yet there is not enough road space in large towns and cities for people to travel as much as they like and how and when they like. This in itself can be one source of grievance. Another is that intrusion of dense traffic brings objectionable and sometimes intolerable noise, fumes and vibration.

We have already seen the extent of the external effects of transport and considered ways in which they may be tackled individually. A comprehensive marginal pollution pricing regime combined with comparable social investment criteria would ensure optimality. Political resistance to such an approach combined with disquiet over the possible distributional repercussions and the practical problems of implementation have tended to rule out the full-scale use of market mechanisms to regulate the urban transport sector. This does not mean that the pricing mechanism is not used but rather that it forms part of a much larger package of policy instruments which are combined with the intention of improving the overall efficiency of urban transport in meeting the objectives of society.

The history of urban transport planning in the UK is comparatively short, originating in the recognition that urban life-styles and cities themselves would change once ownership of private cars became widespread. The physical planners of the immediate pre and post-Second World War periods were concerned with redesigning cities and transport infrastructure to meet the requirements of a motor-car age. Abercrombie, in the County of London Plan of 1943, for example, typified much of the philosophy of the period in his proposals for the university quarter of Bloomsbury and the area around Westminster where he advocated the application of the pre-cinctual principle. Traffic was to be diverted around these areas on good quality, arterial roads, with the precincts served by a limited number of local, access routes. While this idea, which was American in origin, was never applied to the two sites studied by Abercrombie, the broad principle was employed in the post-war reconstruction of Coventry.

The central theme of the physical planning approach to the urban transport problem was that traffic congestion could be alleviated by improving the local transport network. While the initial approach was a narrow one, two important developments occurred in the 1950s and 1960s which strengthened the concept. Firstly, although some planners, such as Abercrombie, took a broad geographical view of urban problems the focus of most early planners tended to be local, seeking piecemeal solutions to specific traffic problems. In the 1950s there was a widening out. Local highway authorities were encouraged by central government to produce joint plans for local road networks and the joint plans produced by the authorities in the Manchester area (the SELNEC Highway Plan of 1962) and by the Merseyside area authorities (in 1965) bear witness to the success of this policy.

Secondly, and not entirely independent of co-ordinated highway planning, came the recognition of the strong links between land-use and transport planning. The *Buchanan Report* (Ministry of Transport, 1963) provided firm evidence of the need to co-ordinate the two areas of planning. Buchanan was particularly concerned about the environmental cost of traffic, and argued that urban road networks should not be expanded to the extent needed to reduce congestion to some predefined levels, as was then the accepted practice, but rather changes in transport and urban land use systems should be assessed in terms of the costs of reducing congestion *while maintaining some predefined environmental standard.* If the costs of expanding the transport network without violating the environmental standard prove excessive to the community then traffic must be restrained until the environmental limit is attained.

Once it became recognised that not only was there a need to consider objectives other than simply congestion in transport planning, especially since transport is an integral part of a much wider urban economic system, it became apparent that physical planning needed to be replaced by a more comprehensive planning framework. The co-ordinated approach which resulted embodied 'structure planning' which sets out policies for the development of land, transport and the local environment. The Town and Country Planning Act of 1968 embodied the idea of structure planning while the creation of the Department of the Environment in 1970 integrated overall responsibility for urban and transport planning in one organisation. The 1968 Transport Act created a number of Passenger Transport Authorities in major conurbations which was given responsibility for public transport operations within their areas. The PTAs were themselves committed to drawing up policies (within a year) and plans (within two years) to provide 'a properly integrated and efficient system of public transport to meet the needs of [the] area'. While the commitment to draw up structure plans necessitated liaison and co-ordination between local planning and highway departments and the PTAs, in practice land-use, road building and public transport responsibilities remained separate – indeed in some cases the agencies had different boundaries. The Local Government Act, 1972 integrated the existing PTAs, plus three newly created ones, into a reformed local government structure. The Act placed further emphasis on the need for co-ordinated transport planning in urban areas and each urban authority was compelled to produce a Transport Policy and Programme (TPP) setting down the strategy and objectives which were being followed. The TPPs have been used since 1975 as a means of assessing the level of central government financial aid to local urban transport undertakings (via the Transport Supplementary Grant) and emphasis has been placed on integrating transport planning with the wider issues of land-use planning and social policy in the area.

The move to structure planning has resulted in two major changes in the types of approach adopted by local transport agencies. Firstly, there has been a trend towards more structured and phased planning; the Tyneside Study of 1968, for instance, produced an immediate action programme, a transportation plan for a fifteen-year horizon and a general urban strategy plan to the end of the century. The TPP framework encourages a continual monitoring and up-dating of plans within a rolling framework. Secondly, planning is no longer viewed simply in terms of investment but now embraces the short-term management of existing resources. In part this may be a reflection of the changing objectives of urban transport planning but it is also the consequence of a greater economic awareness in planning that there is an opportunity cost associated with all actions involving the employment of scarce resources.

9.2 The theory of transport planning

The movement away from physical transport planning to structure planning in the 1960s increased the economic input into the transport planning process, although the development of modern planning methods must be attributed mainly to civil engineers, statisticians and mathematicians rather than economists. One of the main problems of urban land-use/transport planning is the enormous range of possible options available, although this is much less of a difficulty in a country such as Britain, where urban land-use patterns are established and not susceptible to rapid change – in such cases one is seeking the optimal transport system for the existing urban structure. A sequential approach to urban transport planning may, therefore, be appropriate (House of Commons Expenditure Committee, 1972) with four different levels of planning taking place, namely,

(1) Design of broad land use plan;
(2) Design of strategic transport plan;
(3) Design of detailed land use plan; and
(4) Design of detailed transport plan.

(There may be some feedback between (3) and (4) in the sequence.)

The transport planning process itself can be broken down into a number of stages, each involving a certain amount of economic input to it. There is no firm or accepted best-practice method of drawing up a transport plan, different agencies favour different detailed approaches. Broadly, however, the process may be typified by the various stages set out in Figure 9.1 but this must be seen very much as a stylisation, intended rather more to show where economics can contribute to the transport planning process, than as a representation of any actual planning procedure. A few comments are justified on each of the stages.

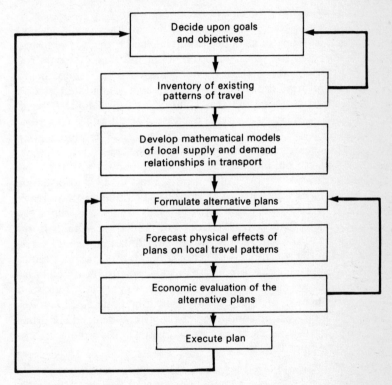

Figure 9.1   The urban transport planning process

Goals and objectives

As we have seen above the objectives of urban transport planning have changed over recent years, a greater emphasis being placed upon social and environmental considerations and somewhat less on improving the efficiency of the system. The general objectives of policy need to be made more specific to permit trade-offs among alternative goals at a later stage of the planning process. The economist's contribution at this stage is that of a balancing agent, often counteracting engineering pressures for the emphasis of the plan to be on improving traffic flow. He may also act as a sieve, pointing out the incompatibility or contrary nature of certain goals. Since goals and objectives are often formulated at the beginning of the planning exercise before full information on existing transport problems have been obtained, they may be redefined after later stages in the sequence.

Inventory of existing transport system
Information is gathered about the nature of the local transport system and travel patterns both by sampling and counting people actually in the act of transport and by obtaining information from firms and households about their travel behaviour and requirements. Additional information is often extracted from official sources such as the Census, the National Travel Survey and the Family Expenditure Survey. The types of surveys conducted and the questions asked have changed over the years as a result of important developments in transport forecasting. As we see in later sections much more emphasis is now placed on understanding why people travel rather than on modelling flows of traffic. Consequently, more detailed information of household characteristics are now sought although the greater efficiency of modern measuring techniques means that the actual sample size has tended to fall (from over 10000 households in the large studies of the late 1960s – the last substantial household survey in the UK, that of the West Yorkshire Transportation Studies, sampled 12 322 addresses – to less than 1000 today). The broad brush approach has given way to seeking greater insights into representative travel behaviour. Quite clearly, since the basic aim is to seek information on existing conditions of supply and demand for urban transport services, economists can contribute to formulating the types of questions to ask.

Mathematical simulations of the local transport market
The following sections look at modelling and forecasting techniques, and in particular their economic underpinnings, but it is important to emphasise at this stage the basic requirements of the simulation models. Transport markets are complex and to produce models which replicate all their details is both difficult and, more importantly, likely to be too cumbersome for later forecasting work. Heggie (1978) suggests that the pre-requisites of a good model are (i) that it assists in understanding and explaining behaviour; (ii) that it

aids policy formulation; and (iii) that it provides robust predictions. The models of travel and transport demand are used for forecasting; therefore it is important that the explanatory factors can themselves be predicted with some degree of certainty. The models are also used to assess the effects of different planning options; thus it is important that they are simple to use and permit the effect of several alternative strategies to be explored. One of the major limitations of early models was that they were cumbersome to manipulate, limiting the possible policy options which could be assessed.

Formulating alternative plans
The complex and wide-ranging effects of any change in an urban transport system makes it very difficult in practice for more than a limited number of detailed plans to be fully formulated. A comprehensive plan consists of a package of projects and schemes, and for a large city the possible combinations forming such a package is immense. In some cases (e.g. the Greater London Development Plan of the late 1960s and early 1970s) only one planning alternative is drawn up in detail after a preliminary sifting of other possibilities at an earlier stage in the planning process (again, the London Transportation Study had initially looked at more than twenty designs of motorway network). Usually the planning alternatives considered are a little more numerous and besides the 'do-nothing' situation, which may act as a bench-mark, generally involve at least one public transport orientated package, one private transport-based proposal and probably one rather more central alternative, offering a mix of private and public transport (witness, for example, the Merseyside Area Land-Use Transportation Study of 1969). Since the plans themselves are later evaluated, this approach should not be as restrictive as it appears. Following the forecasting and/or the evaluation stage new light may be shed on the detailed effect of alternative plans and new compromise packages of projects emerge. Without feedback of this kind it would be quite possible, given the vast range of alternative plans which are feasible for most large cities, to miss the potentially most beneficial alternative.

Forecasting the physical effects of alternative plans
Transport forecasting is looked at in detail in sections 9.3–9.6, the modelling and/forecasting stages being both central to the planning process and having a very substantial economics component. The key aspect of forecasting is that it provides the planner/decision-maker with useful information about the *long-term* implications of plans, emphasising in particular, those areas where there are signifi-

cant *differences* in the consequences of the alternative plans. Given the fact that transport is going to exist in the urban setting, irrespective of the plan adopted, and providing a 'do-nothing' option is assessed, then it is the *relative* performance of plans which is important. Additionally, it is important that the final decision-makers are aware of the underlying assumptions of the forecasts so that they can assess the reliability and strengths of the traffic forecasts.

Economic evaluation

The economic evaluation of plans normally involves employing some variant of the cost-benefit analysis approach outlined in Chapter 8. The comprehensive nature and emphasis on distributional effects which characterises the Planning Balance Sheet makes it a particularly attractive technique in the urban planning context. It is also sufficiently 'open' to permit the various consequences of plans to be related directly to the objectives of the planners. With traditional cost-benefit analysis, not only are there problems of placing monetary values on many items but also the final output of a single net present value of benefits is often viewed with suspicion by members of the urban community. General practice involves the inclusion of public participation at the evaluation stage, often in the form of public inquiries. In some cases – such as the Layfield Inquiry into the Greater London Development Plan (Department of the Environment, 1973) – such inquiries can result in quite substantial revisions of the plan to be adopted. Evaluation of something as complex as a transport plan is, by necessity, a political process but economists can assist the decision-maker by ruling out plans which are *clearly* inferior to others while at the same time giving a systematic presentation of the pros and cons of the final short list of alternatives. The inherent value judgements built into all forms of CBA make it a powerful aid in evaluation, but it is unlikely ever to provide an automatic, purely technical decision-making calculus, indeed it is debatable whether such a mechanical approach is to be desired.

Implementation

While it is often possible to implement some parts – usually traffic management components – of a transport plan almost immediately upon acceptance, other components – usually those involving infrastructure changes – are much longer-term in nature. It is important, therefore, that actions are phased so that costs are kept at a minimum. Additionally, over time objectives change and 'errors' in forecasts become apparent and this may necessitate revisions of the plan. Consequently, there are feedbacks from the implementation stage back to the early stages of the planning process; in other words modern planning is seen as an on-going, rolling process of adaptation and change. It is often important, in this context, to ensure the maximum flexibility in the implementation programme.

The preceding paragraphs have painted a thumb-nail picture of the transport planning process, highlighting the role economics can play. It is thin on detail and hides many of the subtleties of the planning exercise: readers interested in this specific aspect of transport economics are strongly advised to refer to one of the excellent texts now available on the subject. The following sections consider the economic problems of transport modelling and forecasting. These areas, together with plan evaluation, have become increasingly the preserve of economists and involve the application of modern microeconomic theory.

9.3 Modelling and forecasting travel demand

To conduct successful planning exercises it is essential to have reliable forecasts of the probable effect of different policy options. General qualitative assessments can often provide useful insights into the effects of different policies but good planning decisions require that we have more exact information of the detailed quantified relationship between travel and transport and the factors that influence them. Engineers, for example, need projections of future traffic flows when designing roads and other infrastructure. Recent years have witnessed a substantial growth in work attempting to specify and calibrate econometric travel demand models, a trend strongly encouraged by the introduction of structure planning in British urban areas in the late 1960s and the need for major transport planning agencies to produce statements of 'Transport Policies and Programmes'. Some general comments on the application of econometric analysis to transport forecasting highlight the difficulties that have been encountered in constructing travel demand models.

Traditional economic analysis specifies a demand relationship relating quantity demand to price and assume that this relationship only changes (i.e. shifts) when factors other than price vary. In transport demand analysis it is fairly easy to incorporate the 'shift' variables into a modelling framework because their values are essentially determined outside the transport system (e.g. income changes or changes in taste). The control 'price' variable is much more difficult. As we have seen, price is a broad concept in transport, embracing time, comfort and other factors, in addition to simply the monetary cost of a trip. While generalised cost offers one method of reflecting the multi-dimensional nature of the price variable there is a tendency in forecasting work to employ changes in the ease of access as a proxy for price. Accessibility is nothing more complicated than an index that reflects the ease with which people can achieve the various activities they wish.

Transport systems are extremely complicated, comprising many modes of travel, varieties of routes and combinations of different potential travel patterns. The sheer number of links and possibilities in any transport network has resulted in simplifications being adopted by forecasters to permit calculations to be reduced to manageable proportions. Further, the 'product' being offered by the transport system is also unique in that a passenger kilometre at a particular point on the network at a specific time may be performing a completely different function to another passenger kilometre.

Because of these problems, three broad types of forecasting framework have emerged (sequential, disaggregate and interactive), each with its own characteristics and each with its particular advantages and defects. These are looked at in turn. While the discussion is couched primarily in terms of forecasting the demand for person movements, much of the traffic carried by the transport system is freight. The demand to move commodities differs quite substantially from person movements in the sense that is, normally, unidirectional while person trips are usually circular (i.e. from home to work to home). The types of forecasting frameworks used to look at goods traffic are, however, essentially the same as for person movements, modified usually only in terms of the actual variables used (for a survey of work in the field of urban goods traffic demand forecasting see Button and Pearman, 1981). The three main approaches are now reviewed in turn.

9.4 Sequential travel demand forecasting

Sequential models attempt to reduce the complexity of travel demand forecasting by breaking the complicated patterns of demand for travel into, usually, four sub-models. Firstly, the trip generation/attraction model (the trip-end model) is used to forecast the number of trips originating and ending within predefined geographical zones of the study area (these might be countries in international travel studies or smaller areas within a city in urban land-use studies). The total zonal trips are then 'distributed' between origin–destination pairs of zones. Thirdly, for each flow between different zones, a modal choice model is calculated to explain the split of traffic between the alternative forms of transport available. Finally, the traffic flows between each pair of zones and by each mode of transport are assigned to specific routes on the transport network. In the context of freight modelling the parallel sub-models represent transactions, flows, means change and network assignment, with an industrial location model added to make the links between industrial activities and freight vehicle movements explicit. A vehicle loading sub-model is also sometimes added to shift the emphasis from the vehicle to the consignment.

Figure 9.2 provides an example of the sequential approach as developed by the Regional Highway Traffic Model team to assist specifically in national road planning. Mode choice sub-models are excluded because of the dominant position filled by motor-car traffic. The approach set out is particularly useful in distinguishing between the data analysis, computer simulation and calibration aspects of the overall modelling and forecasting process.

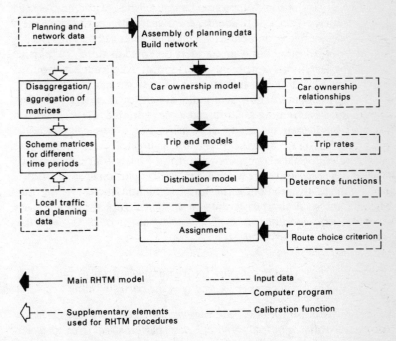

Figure 9.2   The regional highway traffic model

The sequential framework may, therefore, be seen as moving from aggregate to disaggregate forecasting with each successive sub-model in the sequence acting as a check on the one following. In econometric terms the sequence is recursive. Attempts have been made (e.g. in work forming part of the appraisal of the Greater London Development Plan) to introduce feedbacks from later to earlier sub-models in the sequence on the grounds that one cannot really fore-cast, say, mode choice without knowing probable levels of con-gestion on each route and this latter knowledge only becomes avail-able after the assignment stage. The transport model sequence is usually preceded by a land-use forecasting model which attempts to describe the effect of changing land-use patterns on transport. Ideally, because land-use is itself partly affected by transport con-ditions, there should also be feedbacks from the assignment sub-model to land-use patterns but to date this has proved to be practic-ably impossible.

Trip-end sub-models are now usually estimated on a household basis using either multivariate regression techniques or category analysis. The former statistically relates the number of trips made by households to the socio-economic characteristics of the households (e.g. income, number of residents, car ownership, social status, etc.) and the type of environment in which they are located. The concen-tration on the household is now widely accepted as standard practice to reduce statistical problems that appear when data is grouped excessively (e.g. by geographical zone). Category analysis is simpler, involving the construction of a multi-dimensional matrix with each dimension representing a socio-economic variable stratified into a number of discrete classes or categories. For example, households may be divided into four incomes classes, three car ownership classes and two locational classes, giving in total twenty-four categories of household, each with its own average trip-generation level. Forecasts are obtained by predicting the number of households falling into each category at the target date, and multiplying by the relevant average trip generation rate. The total zonal trips in the example above would be predicted as

$$T = \sum_{k=1}^{24} n_k r_k$$ where n_k is the future number of households in category k and r_k is the corresponding trip-rate.

Trip distribution models are of two broad types. Growth factor models involve extrapolating existing patterns of trips between alternative origins and destinations with projected trip-end estimates acting as constraints on the total number of trips leaving or entering any individual zone. They are little more than mechanical procedures based upon past behaviour patterns and suffer, in particular, from inabilities to allow for new zones being created. They have also gone out of favour because they require a substantial amount of data input.

The second group, simulation models, are more overtly economic in their nature. The gravity model is the most commonly used member of this group and has the attraction of having a precise economic interpretation (Cochrane, 1975). Gravity models differ in form but all exhibit terms reflecting the relative attractiveness of different destinations and terms that measure the effect of impedence caused by the nature of the transport system. In early work, attractions were specified simply in terms of population size but in more recent studies a multiplicity of factors have been included, frequently varying with the journey purpose under consideration. Similarly, the crude notion that distance is a full reflection of impedence has given way to the incorporation of various forms of generalised cost measures.

The interactive version of the gravity model takes the form:

$$T_{ij} = T_i\,T_j\,A_i\,A_j\,B_j\,\mathrm{f}\,(C_{ij}) \tag{9.1}$$

subject to $A_i = \left\{ \sum_j T_j\,B_j\,\mathrm{f}(C_{ij}) \right\}^{-1}$ and $B_j = \left\{ \sum_i T_i\,A_i\,\mathrm{f}(C_{ij}) \right\}^{-1}$

where T_{ij} is trips between zones i and j;

 T_i is the total number of trips originating in zone i;

 T_j is the total number of trips destined for zone j;

 C_{ij} is the generalised cost of travel between zones i and j;

 A_i and B_j are 'fuzz factors' – sometimes justified as indices of inverse accessibility – to ensure that total trips distributed across the whole study area originating from i do not exceed T_i and those destined for j do not exceed T_j.

This doubly constrained model assumes that trip-makers are competing for a limited number of opportunities in any specific zone and has clear applications to modelling the demand for work or school trips where job and educational opportunities can be assumed independent of the transport system. In many cases only one constraint (either T_i or T_j) is imposed; for example, with inter-urban freight demand one is often only interested either in the way movements fan out from a city or depot or in the way they converge on it. Urban non-work demand models are also often based upon origin constrained models with less concern about destinations. On other occasions it may prove necessary to relax the constraints to facilitate easier fitting of the models – constrained versions of the gravity model usually requiring specific computer software for calibration.

An alternative simulation model considers the opportunities available in different zones to meet the needs of travellers. The intervening opportunities model assumes that people try to keep their trips as short as possible and only lengthen them if nearer destinations do not prove acceptable to their needs. Individual residents in a given zone are assumed to consider opportunities for the location of their conduct of specific activities (residence, work, shopping, etc.) at various places, starting from the base zone and fanning out to other zones in increasing order of difficulty in reaching them. Each time an opportunity is considered, there is a given, constant chance that it will be selected. The model takes the general form:

$$T_{ij} = T_i \{\exp(-LV_j) - \exp(-LV_{j+1})\} \qquad (9.2)$$

where V is the possible destination just considered;
L is a constant representing the probability of possible destination being accepted (if considered).

While this type of approach has an intuitive appeal, it does suffer from the problem that, empirically, L seems to vary with V rather than remaining constant. Adjustment techniques to correct for the 'wandering' of L values are available but their use seems to violate the notion of constancy. Empirical studies indicate that the results obtained using the intervening opportunities model are no better than those from gravity models. Attempts to develop the opportunities framework by considering competing rather than intervening opportunities (by basing the underlying probability function on the ratio between the trip opportunities in a zone and its competing opportunities) offer no improvements in a forecasting context but complicate the estimation process considerably.

Modal split models allocate traffic flows to particular types of vehicles. In some cases, for example, with urban freight transport or long distance international passenger transport, one mode so dominates a particular sphere of transport activity that no mode choice sub-model is required although this is exceptional. The traditional method of splitting origin–destination traffic flows by mode involve the use of diversion curves. These show the proportion of traffic likely to favour a particular mode given its relative cost (or other) advantage over alternative modes. If we are concerned with two forms of transport, a and b, then a typical model might be

$$\frac{T_{ij}^a}{T_{ij}^a + T_{ij}^b} = \frac{1}{1 + e^{-\lambda\,(C_{ij}^b - C_{ij}^a)}} \qquad (9.3)$$

which yields a diversion curve of the form seen in Figure 9.3. Normally a series of curves are estimated by sub-dividing the travelling population (e.g. by income) and modes (e.g. by service ratios).

In some studies mode choice is modelled prior to distribution using trip-end or interchange models. The former are often used

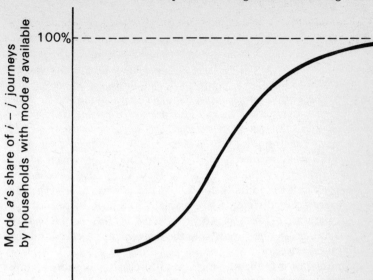

Figure 9.3   *Diversion curve of traffic between modes 'a' and 'b'*

in highway-orientated origin and destination studies where the emphasis is on car travel with public transport being treated as little more than a residual to be subtracted from the trip-end predictions prior to assignments being made. The emphasis on variables such as car ownership and income, and the general neglect of public transport characteristics, limits the usefulness of this approach in urban transport planning. Interchange models are more commonly used in public transport feasibility studies and, consequently, concentrate on comparative time, cost and service differentials between competing modes. Models of this type take the form:

$$T_{ijM} = a_0 X_{ij}^{a_1} (F_{ij}^M)^{a_2} (F_{ij}^b)^{a_3} (H_{ij}^M)^{a_4} (H_{ij}^b)^{a_5} \qquad (9.4)$$

where X_{ij} is a matrix of exogenous economic and social variables;
       F_{ij}^M is the financial cost by mode M;
       H_{ij}^M is the time cost by mode M; and
       the superscript b indicates the money/time cost by the best mode.

Models of this type have a foundation in economic theory (Quandt, 1970) but estimation of parameters $a_0 - a_5$ poses serious statistical problems.

The final sub-model, route assignment, compares the travellers' preferences for routes with the characteristics of the routes available. Early approaches relied upon diversion curves similar to those used in modal choice work but the development of minimum path algorithms combined with improved computing facilities has permitted the introduction of more sophisticated techniques. A major problem in assignment is the possible need to constrain traffic flows on each link in the transport network to the capacity of the link. If the capacity constraint is omitted then an 'all-or-nothing' assignment results and no allowance is made for the congestion which accompanies high traffic volumes (see Chapter 5). In reality, travellers use all routes, both the initially cheap and the not so cheap, especially when overall cost differentials are small. The introduction of capacity constraints permits this to be reflected in the model by adjusting link speeds (and hence costs) as the assignment proceeds and congestion levels rise.

In summary the sequential method of forecasting broadly involves developing a series of mathematical models taking the general form:

$$T_i = f(X_i) \; ; \; T_j = f(X_j) \tag{9.5a}$$

$$T_{ij} = f(T_i, T_j, C_{ij}) \tag{9.5b}$$

$$T_{ijM} = f(T_{ij}, C_{ijM}, C_{ijM}') \tag{9.5c}$$

$$T_{ijMP} = f(T_{ijMP}, C_{ijMP}, C_{ijMP}') \tag{9.5d}$$

where the prime notation refers to alternative modes (M') or routes (P'). Clearly, the series of calculations required to calibrate this set of equations places tremendous strains on the data base available and, in most studies, large and expensive surveys are needed to gather the necessary information. Also, as pointed out above, it is difficult to incorporate the desirable feedback from assignment to trip generation so that quality of service variables are adequately and consistently reflected in each sub-model of the sequence. Statistically, while it is possible to test the significance of the individual models in the sequence it is not possible to undertake statistical tests of the overall recursive system. Disaggregate models have been developed to avoid some of these problems and to approach more closely to the basic decision-making unit, the household.

9.5 Disaggregate modelling
The substantial data input required to calibrate satisfactorily the sub-models and the difficulty of transferring models once estimated from one data area to another, combined with dissatisfaction with the basically mechanistic and physical nature of the sequential

approach, has resulted in an alternative mathematical approach being developed (see Quandt, 1976). This *disaggregate* method of travel demand forecasting emphasises the economic – psychological influences on travel behaviour at the individual household level. The idea is that households are utility-maximizers who, mainly for mathematical convenience, are considered to make travel decisions in isolation from other activities. The emphasis is on short-run decisions rather than long-run mobility decisions. Small stratified samples of households (about 700 or so) provide the data input into the models which tend to be probabilistic, rather than deterministic, in nature (i.e. they forecast the probability of particular household travel patterns rather than the average number and type of trips to be undertaken). A personal disaggregate model of trip-making would be of the general form:

$$P(f,d,h,m,r) = P(f)P(d/f)P(h/f,d)\, P(m/f,d,h)\, P(r/f,d,h,m) \quad (9.6)$$

where $P(f,d,h,m,r)$ is the probability that an individual will undertake a trip with frequency (f) to destination (d) during time of day (h) using mode (m) and via route (r) out of a choice set comprising all possible combinations of frequencies, destination, time of day, modes and routes available to the individual (see Hensher, 1977). For actual planning or assessment, the forecasts produced from such models must be aggregated up to the level of the geographical zone – it is the inter-zonal level, for example, which determines the level of public transport. While there are claims that the approach can be used in comprehensive transport planning its main role to date has been in policy assessment (e.g. looking at car pooling proposals, pollution controls, public transport subsidies, etc. – see Ben-Akiva, 1977).

Broadly, disaggregate models are characterised by two main features. First, they explicitly recognise that travel decisions emerge out of individuals' optimising behaviour and, if it is pointed out that the final goods consumed as a result of travel are normal, then at a very minimum the demand for travel ought to be related positively to disposable incomes and negatively to the prices of transport services. Second, most have their origins in the 'attributal theory of demand' associated with Lancaster (1966). This approach to human behaviour assumes that people desire to maximise a utility function which has, as its arguments, *commodity attributes* rather than the quantities of the actual goods consumed. In other words, if we represent the amounts of attributes by the vector z, the amounts of commodities (in this case travel alternatives) by the vector x, posit a utility function, U(z), and a production of attribute function, G(x), which reflects the attributes of different travel alternatives, and assume that potential travellers are constrained by income, y, and the price of travel, p, then we can reduce the problem to solving:

$$\text{max} \qquad U(z) \qquad\qquad\qquad\qquad (9.7)$$
$$\text{subject to} \quad z = G(x),$$
$$x \geqslant 0,$$
$$p \cdot x \leqslant y.$$

As an example, if one is considering air transport between the UK and the USA, then the alternative commodities would be the different fare-packages offered by the airlines, and the attributes of each would be characteristics such as money costs, speed, period of advance booking, timing, type of aircraft, on-plane service (food, drink, films, etc.), stop-over regulations, required length of stay at destination, etc.

Direct attempts have been made to apply Lancaster's theory at the aggregate level by Quandt (1970) and associates in the context of abstract mode modelling. At the inter-urban level Quandt and Baumol (1966) attempted to construct an abstract mode model for air, bus and car journeys between sixteen city pairs in California using cost and time (both absolute and relative) as the determining attributes, but the results were inferior to those obtained from more conventional trip-distribution models. Howrey's (1969) study of air travel out of Cleveland produced an abstract mode model with correct signs, significant coefficients and a good overall fit to survey data. However, while its explanatory power proved statistically superior to a conventional gravity model it turned out to be inferior in terms of *ex post* forecasting quality. Talvitie (1973) concentrated on developing the framework to handle intra-urban travel while Baumol and Vinod (1970), by combining the attributed theory of demand with an inventory theory of goods handling, have adapted the approach to deal with urban freight transport demand.

While some of the calibration problems which were associated with the early aggregate abstract mode models have been resolved (see Quandt, 1970), it has been the introduction of disaggregate approaches which have marked the greatest advances. The major advance in this context was the realisation that each individual has a different utility function, partly because of quantifiable differences in their personal characteristics but also partly because of random factors. While the heterogeneous nature of the population poses serious problems, the work of Domenich and McFadden (1976) in modelling the random factors, and especially their theoretical work on justifying the use of 'multi-normal logit models', forms the basis of much modern disaggregate analysis. The forms of disaggregate model that have been developed along these lines, and the range of applications to which they have been applied, are many.

Most of the recent work on disaggregate modelling has centred on mathematical and calibration issues and there is no intention of taking discussion of such matters any further in this book. The mathematical complexity stems from the fact that one is looking at discrete choices – i.e. whether a person makes a trip or not – and this involves complications not normally encountered when considering continuous functions. A good indication of the current direction of work is to be found in the collection of papers contained in Hensher and Stopher (1979) although the reader should be warned that many of the contributions have a substantial mathematical content.

9.6 Interactive modelling

While the sequential and disaggregate approaches to transport demand analysis concentrate on developing sophisticated mathematical simulations, recently there has been a growth of interest in 'behavioural realism', and an emphasis on 'understanding the phenomenon' (Dix, 1977). The aim of this approach is to develop models that get closer to the essential decision process underlying travel behaviour. Rather than simply incorporate variables such as household status in mathematical models because the statistical 'explanation' of the model appears to be improved, interactive modelling seeks to explain *why* status affects travel behaviour. Theoretically, travel is seen as one of a whole range of complementary and competitive activities operating in a sequence of events in time and space. It is seen to represent the method by which people trade time to move location in order to enjoy successive activities. Generally, time and space constraints are thought to limit the choices of activities open to individuals. The technique is, however, still far from fully developed and has only been applied in a limited number of small-scale studies (e.g. by Jones (1978) in the UK to school bus operations and by Phifer *et al.* (1980) in the USA to energy constraints).

The emphasis of interactive models is upon the household (or individual) as the decision-making unit. Ideally, an interactive model should exhibit six main properties (Heggie, 1978):

(1) It should involve the entire household and allow for interaction between its members.

(2) It should make existing constraints on household behaviour quite explicit.

(3) It should start from the household's existing pattern of behaviour.

(4) It should work by confronting the household with realistic changes in its travel environment and allowing it to respond realistically.

(5) It should allow for the influence of long-term adaptation.

(6) It should be able to tell the investigator something fundamental that he did not know before.

In general, the approach is typified by a fairly small sample and careful survey techniques, often involving 'board games' (such as the 'household activities travel simulator' (HATS) developed by the Oxford University Transport Studies Unit) or other visual aids, to permit households to appreciate the full implications of changes in transport policy for their own behaviour. The HATS approach, for example, is to confront a household with a map of the local area together with a twenty-four hour 'strip representation of coloured pieces' showing how current activities of the household are spread over space and throughout the day. Changes to the transport system are then postulated (e.g. reduced parking availability in the local urban centre) and the effects on the household's activities throughout the day are simulated by adjustments to the strip representation. In this way changes in the transport system may be seen to influence the entire twenty-four hour life pattern of the household, and apparently unsuspected changes in 'remote' trip-making behaviour can be traced back to the primary change. It makes clear the constraints and linkages that may affect activity and transport choices. The emphasis is on the micro-unit and the hope is to develop fairly simple models which permit much clearer insights into the overall effects of transport policy. By asking respondents to trace the effect of changes in transport provision on the entire set of activities undertaken during a day (or week), information on important travel intentions can be seen and the relationships between travel and non-travel activities become explicit.

In contrast to the mathematical schools, advocates of this approach point to both the specific recognition that travel is a derived demand and the fact that transport policies have qualitative, as well as quantitative, effects on people's lives. In the longer term, when operational models are more fully developed, the framework may offer the much sought-after basis for integrating land-use and transport planning assessment. In the short term the approach has offered useful insights and verbal backing for more conventional statistical analysis.

9.7 Further reading and references

Heggie (1972) offers a useful extension to this chapter by setting out in more detail the methodology of transport planning and by outlining some of the basic techniques. Jones (1977) provides a terse but very useful guide to the contribution that economics may make to the transport planning process and also sketches out in more detail than has been possible above the various methods of transport demand forecasting. A useful extension of this is possibly Button and Pearman (1981, Chapter 4) which examines in some details the specific problems of forecasting the demand for urban freight transport and presents copious examples of actual demand models. The set of papers edited by Hensher and Stopher (1979) referred to in the text is perhaps the best indication of the present state of transport modelling and forecasting – the mathematics is formidable but a careful and selective 'picking' through the papers should prove invaluable to a reader specifically interested in this branch of transport economics.

References

Baumol, W.J. and Vinod, H.D. (1970), 'An inventory theoretical model of freight transport demand', *Management Science*, Vol. 16, pp. 413–21.

Ben-Akiva, M. (1977), 'Passenger travel demand forecasting: applications of disaggregate models and directions for research', in E.J. Visser (ed.), *Transport Decisions in an Age of Uncertainty*, The Hague, Martinus Nijhoff.

Button, K.J. and Pearman, A.D. (1981), *The Economics of Urban Freight Transport*, London, Macmillan.

Cochrane, R.A. (1975), 'A possible economic basis for the gravity model', *Journal of Transport Economics and Policy*, Vol. 9, pp. 34–49.

Department of the Environment (1973), *Report of the Panel of Inquiry into the Greater London Development Plan*, London, HMSO.

Department of Transport (1977), *Transport Policy*, Cmnd 6836, London, HMSO.

Dix, M.C. (1977), 'Report on investigations of household travel decision making behaviour', in E.J. Visser (ed.), *Transport Decisions in an Age of Uncertainty*, The Hague, Martinus Nijhoff.

Domenich, T. and McFadden, D. (1976), *Urban Travel Demand: A Behavioural Analysis*, Amsterdam, North-Holland.

Heggie, I.G. (1972), *Transport Engineering Economics*, Maidenhead, McGraw-Hill.

Heggie, I.G. (1978), 'Putting behaviour into behavioural models of travel choice', *Journal of the Operational Research Society*, Vol. 29, pp. 541–50.

Hensher, D.A. (1977), 'Demand for urban passenger transport', in D.A. Hensher (ed.), *Urban Transport Economics*, Cambridge, Cambridge University Press.

Hensher, D.A. and Stopher, P.R. (eds.) (1979), *Behavioural Travel Modelling*, London, Croom Helm.

House of Commons Expenditure Committee (1972), *Second Report: Urban Transport Planning*, House of Commons Paper HC.57 (I–III), London, HMSO.

Howrey, E.P. (1969), 'On the choice of forecasting models for air travel', *Journal of Regional Science*, Vol. 9, pp. 215–24.

Jones, I.S. (1977), *Urban Transport Appraisal*, London, Macmillan.

Jones, P.M. (1978) 'School hour revisions in West Oxfordshire: an exploratory study using HATS', *Technical Report*, Oxford, Oxford University Transport Studies Unit.

Lancaster, K.J. (1966), 'A new approach to consumer theory', *Journal of Political Economy*, Vol. 74, pp. 132–57.

Ministry of Transport (1963), *Traffic in Towns*, London, HMSO.

Phifer, S.P., Neven, A.J. and Hartgen, D.T. (1980), 'Family reactions to energy constraints', *Transportation Research Board Conference Paper*, Washington.

Quandt, R.E. (ed.) (1970), *The Demand for Travel: Theory and Measurement*, Lexington, Heath-Lexington.

Quandt, R.E. (1976), 'The theory of travel demand', *Transportation Research*, Vol. 10, pp. 411–13.

Quandt, R.E. and Baumol, W.J. (1966), 'The demand for abstract transport modes: theory and measurement', *Journal of Regional Science*, Vol. 6, pp. 13–26.

Talvitie, A.P. (1973), 'A direct demand model for downtown work trips', *Transportation*, Vol. 2, pp. 121–52.

10. Transport and Economic Development

10.1 Transport and economic development

Economists have long been concerned with assessing the links between changes in the transport sector and the evolving pattern of economic development within the area served. While the importance of transport in economic growth and development has never seriously been questioned, its exact role and influence have been subjected to periodic reappraisals (see, for example, Gauthier, 1970). Traditionally, it was argued that transport exerted a strong positive influence on economic development and that increased production could be directly related to improved transport. In the UK context, for example, over a century ago, Baxter (1866) argued that 'Railways have been a most powerful agent in the progress of commerce, in improving the conditions of the working classes, and in developing the agricultural and mineral resources of the country.' Over fifty years later we still find Lord Lugard (1922) writing, 'the material development of Africa may be summed up in the one word – transport'. Perhaps the strongest advocate of the positive role of transport, however, is Rostow (1960) who in accounting for economic growth maintains that 'The introduction of railroads has historically been the most powerful single indicator to take-offs. It was decisive in the United States, France, Germany, Canada and Russia.'

The linkage between transport provision and economic developments, according to this approach, can be divided between the direct transport input and indirect, multiplier effects. Good transport offers low shipping costs which have permitted wider markets to be served and the exploitation of large-scale production in an extensive range of activities. Hunter (1965), for example, postulates a causal linkage between low-cost transport and economic growth – the Industrial Revolution was successful because of a prior revolution in transport technology. Similarly, Owen (1964) argues that a widening of domestic markets through improved transport services is a necessary prerequisite for national economic development. Further, most undeveloped countries are, for a variety of geographical, economic and historic reasons dependent upon international trade and an expansion of this trade is an essential prerequisite for growth. In these circumstances the provision of efficient port facilities will, according to this school of thought, positively assist development.

The indirect, multiplier effects stem from the substantial inputs of iron, timber, coal, etc. required to construct a modern transport system and which, at least in the context of development in the nineteenth century, were supplied by indigenous heavy industries. Transport also often provided some initial experience of business, for many industrialists of the period. The potential multiplier effects for third world countries today are likely to be substantially less given the growth (itself a function of improved transport) of international trade and tied development aid. Additionally, the technical expertise required to engineer and plan modern transport systems is often unavailable in less developed countries and must be bought from more advanced nations.

This causal view of transport and economic development has become less credible in recent years. The econometric work of Fogel (1964) in the United States, for example, offers evidence that American growth in the nineteenth century would have been quite possible without the advent of the railways – waterways supplying a comprehensive transport system at comparable costs. The view that the railways were the motive force behind American economic development has given way to a weaker position, namely that good transport *permits* economic expansion. Economic development is, thus, seen as a complex process with transport *permitting* the exploitation of the natural resources and talents of a country; it is, therefore, necessary but not sufficient for development. Transport can release working capital from one area which can be used more productively as forced capital elsewhere, although a necessary prior condition is the existence of suitable productive opportunities in potential markets. The basic view of this school of thought is summarised by Ahmed *et al.* (1976):

> In many developing countries the inadequacy of transport facilities is *one* of the major bottlenecks to socio-economic development and a national integration. Often the lack of transport makes it difficult to introduce other social infrastructure such as education and medical services. The dissemination of the modern techniques and inputs of agricultural production and the linking of agriculture to other sectors of the economy through the market is hampered by the absence or inadequacy of transport facilities. As a result of these and other factors, the productivity of agriculture – the dominant sector in developing economies – is deplorably low. (emphasis original).

While the two approaches sketched out above ascribe a positive role to transport in economic development, albeit in different ways, there is a feeling among some economists that an excessive amount of scarce resources sometimes tend to be devoted to transport improvements. As with any scarce input it is possible to define an optimal provision of transport to facilitate development so that resources are not wasted by being drawn from other activities where they may be more productive. At a given point in economic development, a country requires a certain level of transport provision so that its growth potential is maximised – hence there is an optimum transport capacity for any development level. It has been argued, however, that there are economic forces that tend to lead to an excess of transport provision (especially high cost infrastructure) at the expense of more efficient and productive projects. More specifically, Wilson (1966) has pointed to the lumpiness of transport capital which together with its longevity and associated externalities make it particularly difficult to estimate future costs and benefits. Consequently, decisions to devote resources to transport are not easily reversible or readily corrected. The political acceptability of transport is highlighted by Hirschman (1958) who feels that the sector attracts resources quite simply because it is difficult for mistakes (of an economic nature) to be proved even after major projects have been completed. Also development planners tend to be mainly concerned with allocating public investment funds and it is, therefore, natural that they should claim transport, communications, energy, drainage, etc. as being of overriding and fundamental importance. Further, given the industrial composition of wealthier developed countries with an established heavy industrial base, tied aid for transport schemes has a firm attraction. Those adopting this rather sceptical approach to the role of transport, therefore, accept that an adequate basic transport system is an obvious *sine qua non* for modern economic development but question whether the opportunity costs involved in further improving transport are necessarily justified.

The following sections look at the role transport can play in economic development at successively different levels of aggregation. We look first of all at the general problem of stimulating economic growth in the third world before proceeding to consider the problems of formulating a common transport policy to foster the economic growth ambitions of the member states of the European Economic Community. At a more micro level there are also questions concerning the ways in which transport provision can stimulate economic growth *within* certain parts of a country or for a given urban area.

While the discussion of transport and economic development has been sectionalised for expositional convenience it is important to emphasise that in practice considerable trade-offs may be necessary between, say, devising a transport policy to stimulate national growth and one designed to assist the development of specified backward regions. The poorest countries especially often feel they must attempt to increase their national income. Indeed, if one were to accept the 'growth pole' approach to economic development, then national growth is attempted by concentrating effort in several strong regional centres. Hence, interregional inequality of growth is an inevitable concomitant and condition of growth itself. Consequently, although it may be possible to design a national transport strategy or investment programme that assists in the maximisation of national economic growth, it may need modifying to ensure that an acceptable degree of equity is retained among the different regions of the country. (An example of just such a situation at the international level arose in the European Coal and Steel Community – see section 10.3 – where agreements were reached to improve efficiency by the removal of transport subsidies from intra-community coal and steel trade *but* exceptions were made, notably to ease the regional burden on parts of Germany.)

10.2 Transport economics in less developed countries
Transport investment forms a major component of the capital formation of less developed countries, and expenditure on transport is usually the largest single item in the national budget. Up to 40 per cent of public expenditure is devoted to transport infrastructure investment with substantial supplements coming from outside international agencies such as the World Bank or in direct assistance from individual countries. At one level it is important to know whether this is, in aggregate terms, the most practical and efficient method of assisting the poor countries of the world while at another level it is necessary to be able to assess the development impact of individual transport schemes.

Broadly, transport may be seen to have four functions in assisting economic development (Fromm, 1965). First, it is an obvious factor input into the production process permitting goods and people to be transferred between and within production and consumption centres. Because much of this movement is between rural and urban areas it permits the extension of the money economy into the agricultural sector. Second, transport improvements can shift production possibility functions by altering factor costs and, especially, it reduces the levels of inventory tied up in the production process.

Third, factor mobility is increased permitting factors of production, especially labour, to be transferred to places where they may be employed most productively. The fourth factor is that transport increases the welfare of individuals, by extending the range of social facilities to them, and also provides superior public goods such as greater social cohesion and increased national defence.

Transport economists have made significant contributions in assessing in detail the role that transport may play in assisting economic development in third world countries. At the microeconomic level they have developed techniques of project appraisal that permit a more scientific assessment of the costs and benefits of individual transport projects to be conducted. Many of the techniques of investment appraisal employed in the developed parts of the world (see Chapter 8) are applicable in third world conditions but local situations often require changes of emphasis. This is not surprising considering these techniques were devised to look at transport systems based almost entirely upon mechanical modes while head porterage and canoes still account for the greatest proportion of goods movement in many less developed countries. The basic data are also often not so readily available or reliable in the third world as in most developed countries thus limiting the precision of any analysis. Nevertheless, the development of investment appraisal techniques of the type set down by Little and Mirrlees (1974) permit consistent analysis across investment alternatives both within the transport sector and between the transport sector and other areas of economic activity. Such techniques emphasise the importance of estimating appropriate shadow prices for both inputs into transport and the benefits derived from it. In particular, the shortage of foreign exchange suffered by many less developed countries is highlighted while it is recognised that higher levels of under-employment and unemployment require adjustments to the wage costs of labour. (The shadow price of labour being estimated as any lost production by diverting it from elsewhere in the economy – which is usually negligible – plus an allowance for the disutility associated with the work in the transport sector.)

At the macroeconomic level economists have pointed to the general influence that appropriate transport planning can have in assisting overall economic development. While it may be argued that ideally one should expand transport provision to balance developments elsewhere in the economy, this is not always possible. The balanced growth approach maintains that if transport services are inadequate, then bottlenecks in the economy will curtail the growth process, but if the services are excessive this is both wasteful, in the sense that the idle resources could be earning a positive return else-where in the economy, and can become demoralising if the antici-pated demand for transport does not materialise relatively quickly (see Nath, 1962 for a general defence of the balanced growth model). Hirschman (1958) takes a somewhat different view, arguing that the relationship between economic development and the provision of social overhead capital, such as transport, is less flexible than members of the balanced growth school believe.

In Figure 10.1, the horizontal axis shows the provision and cost of social overhead capital (which is normally provided by the public sector and will embrace transport as a major component) while the vertical axis measures the total cost of direct productive activities (which are normally undertaken on purely commercial criteria). The balanced growth approach assumes that DPA output and SOC act-ivities should grow together (i.e. along the growth path represented

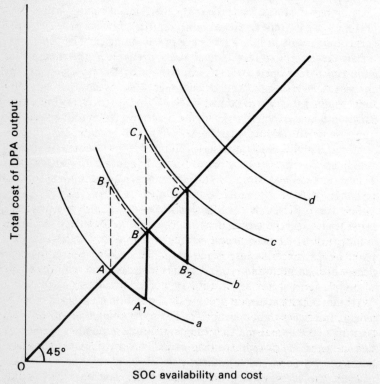

Figure 10.1   *Balanced and unbalanced growth of social overhead capital and direct productive activities*

by the ray from the origin), passing through the various curves from *a* to *d* representing successively higher amounts of DPA/SOC output. Hirschman, however, argues that less developed countries are in practice not in a position to follow such a path – partly because of the lack of necessary expertise to ensure the balance is maintained and partly because of inherent indivisibilities in the social overhead capital schemes available. Consequently, growth is inevitably unbalanced and may follow one of two possible courses; one based upon excess capacity of SOC (i.e. path $AA_1 BB_2 C$) the other upon a shortage of SOC (i.e. path $AB_1 BC_1 C$). If a strategy of excess SOC capacity is preferred it is hoped that this will permit DPA to become less expensive and encourage investment in that sector. Alternatively, with the second approach, DPA expansion occurs first and DPA costs will rise substantially. As a consequence considerable economies will be realised through the construction of more extensive SOC facilities. The actual effectiveness of the alternatives depends upon the strength of the profit motive in the DPA sector, and the responsiveness of the public authority in the SOC sector to public demand.

The actual type of transport provision most suited to developing economies is often of as much importance as the aggregate level of provision. Many developing countries tend to spend scarce development funds on prestige projects, especially international air transport, to demonstrate visually their capacity to emulate the performance of more developed nations; in other words X-efficiency is sacrificed for a modern, if superficial, image. More critical is the way in which funds are spent on internal transport provision and, in particular, whether there are advantages in concentrating limited capital resources in either the road or rail modes.

The appropriateness of different modes often depends upon the geographic–demographic nature of the country. Most less developed countries may be categorised as one of the following: (i) densely populated tropical lands; (ii) tropical land with low population density; (iii) mountainous, temperate lands with a low overall density of population but a concentration on a coastal plain or altiplane; or (iv) thinly populated desert areas with population concentrated along irrigated channels (Fromm, 1965). The appropriateness of different transport modes changes according to the type of country under consideration, thinly populated, tropic lands having different transport problems than areas of high density.

While the railways were important in the development of nineteenth century economies and characterised colonial development in many countries the emphasis in recent years has switched to the provision of adequate road infrastructure. This is particularly true in areas where a skeleton of roads already exists and resources can be devoted to improving and extending an established, if rudimentary, network. This approach may be especially fruitful if it links isolated agricultural communities both with each other and with the more advanced areas of the economy. Millard (1959) argues that unlike developed countries, in third world nations 'the benefits from road construction are almost entirely in the form of new development from traffic which the new road will generate'. The effect is not purely on immediate output but can stimulate a propensity for further development. Wilson *et al.* (1966) strongly supported road development in third world countries for this reason, arguing that 'Investment options might usefully be analysed in terms not only of their direct economic pay-off but also in terms of their influence on attitude' and that 'The educational and other spill-over effects of road transportation appear to be greater than those of other modes of transport. This is especially significant at low levels of development.' Having said this, however, there is a danger if integrated planning is not pursued that while improved road facilities may stimulate the agricultural economy, the new links between rural and industrial–urban areas could lead to increased polarisation in the spatial economy with an enhanced geographical, as well as sectional, dualism resulting.

Externally, improved port and shipping facilities permit less developed countries to export their products to wider markets, although, as we see below, there are some dangers here. Since the demand for shipping services is derived from that for the final product we can illustrate the benefits to LDCs from reducing maritime shipping costs by looking at the quantities of exports from a third world country and the imports into the market of a Western economy. Figure 10.2 shows a back-to-back diagram (after Shneerson, 1977) where S_i, D_i, are the supply and demand schedule for the commodity in the developed country and S_j, D_j, the supply and demand in the less developed nation. Demand for imports and supply of exports is obtained by subtracting horizontally the domestic supply from demand. The demand for imports (exports) at each price being the difference between quantity supplied and demanded assuming domestic and import commodities are perfect substitutes. D_e and S_e in Figure 10.2 are derived in this fashion – the vertical difference between these curves then represents the demand for shipping shown as D_s. (If shipping charges were zero, for example, then the free trade equilibrium would be F.) Suppose actual shipping rates were P^1, then at that rate the price of imports from country i confronting country j is

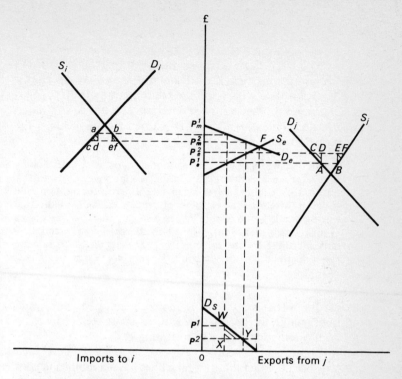

Figure 10.2   Welfare gains from improved shipping services

seen to be P_m^1 (the cif price) while the cost of exports to country j would be seen in country i to be P_e^1 (the fob price). Country i would then import an amount ab equal to country j's (our less developed country's) exports of AB.

There is now an improvement in shipping services, this may take the form of better port facilities or more efficient ships or it may be administrative (e.g. relaxation of high conference shipping rates). The effect is that shipping costs fall to P^2 resulting in exports from country j rising to CF to match the higher imports of cf into the developed country i. Trade has expanded for the less developed country. The benefit of this trade to the two countries is represented by the shaded areas in the figure. Area adc is the extra consumption enjoyed by the developed, importing country as a result of the fall in the cif price while bef is a positive production effect resulting from a contraction of country i's relatively high cost industry. The areas ADC and BEF are the symmetrical benefits to the less developed country. (Interestingly the sum of these benefits can be measured directly as the area *WXY* under the demand curve for shipping services.)

While it can be demonstrated that improved shipping facilities *can* aid development it should be noted that the analysis is crucially dependent upon the elasticities of demand for goods in developed and underdeveloped countries and the relative costs of supply. This often poses serious problems for less developed countries, as pointed out by UNCTAD (1969), with the LDCs often paying much of the costs of transport, i.e.

> For many of the world's agricultural products, on which developing countries rely for much of their export earnings, supply elasticities are low in the short run . . . Although overall demand elasticities for most of these commodities are also low, the elasticity of demand facing the individual supplier or the whole group of suppliers in a single country is likely to be relatively high, unless that country is the only source of supply, and there is no ready substitute for the commodity . . . *The supplier in these cases therefore normally bears the bulk of the transport costs.* (emphasis added).

In practice, the world is also a little more complicated, with trade involving not simply the production and transport sectors but also the system of international finance operating.

One of the practical problems experienced by many less developed countries has been the fact that shipping lines have combined in conferences to regulate prices and thus have often led to shipping costs – which are often borne by the less developed countries – being higher than in a free market situation. There are also arguments that the existence of non-pricing competition within conferences in itself produces a much higher quality of service (and *ipso facto* cost) than would prevail without collusion (Evans and Benham, 1975) and that this is again detrimental to third world countries. Empirical evidence produced by Devanney *et al.* (1975), looking at trade between the East Coast of the United States and Chile, Columbia, Ecuador and Peru, suggests that the conference system on these routes pushed up shipping rates by about $20 per ton in 1971, most of which would have been borne by the poorer countries.

It is not surprising that in these circumstances UNCTAD has negotiated a Code of Conduct for Liner Conferences (proposed in 1975) which allocates maritime traffic on 40:40:20 basis with 40 per cent of the trade allocated to the merchant marine of each of the trading nations and 20 per cent to cross traders (see Neff, 1980 for more detail). This is intended to give underdeveloped countries the chance to reap some of the financial rewards from shipping and also exert a more immediate influence on their own development. In 1978, for example, third world countries were in the disadvantaged position of only having 8.6 per cent of the world deadweight tonnage of shipping but generating over 30 per cent of the bulk cargoes and over 90 percent of the tanker cargoes. In the short term lack of capacity may prevent some nations from enacting the full implementation of the Code. Zerby (1979) has estimated, for instance, that of the twenty-six less developed countries he studied only nine had merchant fleets large enough to handle 40 per cent of their exports in 1975 and only fifteen had sufficient capacity to handle 40 per cent of imports (third world nations physically export about twice as much as they import – i.e. 440 million tons compared to 242 million tons in 1973). Attempts to expand the fleets of less developed countries to fulfil 40 per cent of the market will, therefore, result in excess capacity in the fleets of the developed countries but more importantly, given the imbalance in the volume of imports and exports, attempts to meet 40 per cent of shipping demand both into and out of LDCs will lead to a 50 per cent excess capacity within their own fleets. Zerby, therefore, feels 'that a rigid adherence to the 40–40–20 principle is likely to be an extremely costly method of reducing the developing countries' dependence on conference services'. Only with co-operation both between the developed and underdeveloped nations and between the LDCs themselves, Zerby argues, will benefits be reaped.

10.3 EEC transport policy

A number of national groupings have emerged in both the developed and less developed world where countries have come together into loose economic unions with the aims of fostering their common economic interests. The objective of the European Economic Community, for example, is 'to promote throughout the Community a harmonious development of economic activities, a continuous and balanced expansion, an increase in stability, an accelerated raising of the standard of living, and closer relations of the member states'. While not central to the policies of such unions, co-ordinated transport policies can facilitate the easier attainment of their basic aims. The difficulties of agreeing on a 'Common Transport Policy' by such unions are numerous. Each member state has its own set of transport objectives which must be modified to conform with commonly agreed goals and objectives and each has its own sets of institutions and policy tools which may conflict with the criteria favoured by the grouping as a whole. Many countries in Europe have traditionally used transport subsidies to protect specific industries or regions, but this may run counter to community objectives of increasing overall economic efficiency or be thought to result in undesirable redistributions of welfare.

The EEC provides a useful illustration of the problems of devising an international transport policy designed primarily to foster economic growth. Attempts to formulate a Common Transport Policy can be traced back to the inception of the older European Coal and Steel Community (ECSC) which, in the Treaty of Paris, explicitly laid out a number of basic requirements regarding comparability of transport charges for carrying coal and steel, publication of rates and the use of discriminatory transport charges during a transition to eventual harmonisation. The Treaty of Rome (signed in 1957) confirmed many of the policies of the ECSC (although not publication of rates) and contains a specific remit for 'the activity of the Community [to include] . . . the adoption of a common policy in the sphere of transport'. While the acceptance of the desirability of a common policy came early, the detailed development of such a policy has been much slower (Button, 1979, Gwilliam, 1979). Early ECSC agreements on non-discriminatory cost-related rail tariffs for intra-community traffic were possible because existing market distortions tended to spread evenly across members and no single country suffered significantly from their removal. Where areas of the Federal Republic of Germany were seen to suffer as a result of such changes specific subsidies were authorised. Subsequent developments in ECSC and EEC policy were less easy.

(1) While the early ECSC policy was concerned primarily with rail transport, the broader EEC policy must encompass all forms of inter-urban freight transport. European railways are heavily regulated and normally state controlled making co-ordination of policies relatively easy. Historical and institutional factors – especially the small size of most operating units – make the regulation of road and water transport more difficult.

(2) There are two broad schools of thought about transport policy within the Community. Countries such as West Germany tend to favour a 'social service philosophy' with transport seen as subservient to wider economic objectives and rigidly controlled to achieve these wider aims. Other countries, notably the Netherlands, argue for a 'commercial philosophy' with the free market determining capacity and price. As the debate over a Common Transport Policy has developed it has become increasingly difficult to find common ground upon which to hang measures.

(2) The EEC has periodically incorporated new members and this has resulted in the need to reconsider the direction of policy as

the balance of views has shifted. The membership of Eire, Denmark and Great Britain in 1973, for example, meant that questions of cross-frontier traffic were effectively superseded by more fundamental questions concerning international trade. It also meant that the commercial philosophy was given added support – the UK being an extreme liberal.

(4) The administrative structure of the EEC means that the Commission is responsible for policy formulation while the Council of Ministers is responsible for adopting regulations. This results in a rather lengthy decision-making process with the Commission formulating many policies that are never adopted. Additionally, the Commission sees its role to be in 'active' policy formulation, designing a framework which prevents transport from distorting the other markets for goods and services. This conflicts with national transport policy formulation which tends to be 'reactive' and responsive to specific problems as they occur. This can lead to difficulties if the Community's policy prevents members responding to specific transport problems within their own boundaries. In such cases members may accept Community policies but operate them half-heartedly and ineffectively (Gwilliam, 1980a).

Until 1972 most policy initiatives within the EEC tended to follow attempts of the ECSC to define detailed operational guidelines. Emphasis, for example, was placed on pricing policies and considerable attention was focused on the idea of 'forked tariffs' (*tarification a fourchette*). This meant the establishment of upper and lower haulage rates within which the actual carriage rate must be set. The underlying idea was that the upper limit would prevent monopoly exploitation of consignors while the lower floor would contain any tendency towards excessive competition among hauliers. Initially, from 1968, a scheme with a 23 per cent fork was applied to a limited range of commodities subjected to international carriage but a subsequent extension did not materialise. The determination and enforcement of such rates proved impossible and this, combined with the logical inconsistency of trying to prevent monopoly exploitation and super-normal competition simultaneously, has led to the adoption (since 1975) of simple reference tariffs. Similarly, there was an initial presumption that intra-community road haulage capacity would need regulating to ensure free competition among members' fleets unhampered by national policies of protection. The existing bilaterial agreements were thought excessively restrictive. A Community Quota of 1200 licences was established in 1968 with the intention that this would gradually expand to replace the bilaterial system. Unfortunately, the Quota has only expanded slowly and by the end of the 1970s it was estimated that 95 per cent of international road freight within the EEC was still carried on bilateral terms. The hope that cabotage rights would become part of the Quota system has failed to be fulfilled.

The limitations of the early phase of a Common Transport Policy were realised in 1973 when the EEC Commission Member for Transport said, 'Without wishing to detract from progress already achieved, particularly when it is reviewed in relation to existing difficulties, we must nevertheless frankly and objectively admit that very few of the aims of the Common Transport Policy have been achieved'. The so-called 'New Impetus', which followed a rapid expansion of intra-Community trade and coincided with the enlargement of the Community in 1973, changed the emphasis from detailed regulation and control of individual transport modes towards the setting of more general guidelines and the establishment of an institutional framework within which transport could operate with maximum efficiency. Progress has, however, been slow. The quota system has been retained (with a small expansion in 1977) but its long-term role is now seen as one of simple supervision of capacity with official interventions limited to situations where the market shows serious economic disequilibrium. Earlier proposals to unify quality licensing arrangements (both in terms of managerial and operational licensing) have been put into practice while the tachograph is fitted to all freight vehicles. There are now uniform working hours within the sector. All members now charge road users at least the short-run marginal road track costs they incur (calculated on common principles) with the long-term intention that a sufficient additional contribution will be made to ensure aggregate long-run marginal costs are recovered (Jennings, 1976). As we have seen in Chapter 4, however, this is hardly a movement forward since such policies were already being pursued by all members anyway. The notion of marginal social cost pricing, embracing external as well as private cost considerations, has become a generally accepted principle but the exact details of such an approach have proved elusive. Compromise is inevitable in the formulation of a Common Transport Policy but to date it has not achieved any results of great significance. Most of the components of the Common Transport Policy, as it now stands, relate to secondary issues.

10.4 Transport and regional development
The inter-regional spread of economic activity within a country is of

major concern to national governments. Geographical variations in unemployment, income, migration and industrial structure are of importance because they both result in spatial inequalities in welfare and, in many cases, reduce the overall performance of the national economy. For these reasons, Britain has pursued an active economic policy for over half a century (McCallum, 1979) in an attempt to stimulate economic activity in depressed areas and to contain damaging explosive growth in prosperous regions. The policies, which have varied both in intensity and in form over time, have generally concentrated on giving direct financial assistance to industry and on improving the mobility of labour. In addition there have been attempts at improving the economic infrastructure of the so-called development areas, with specific emphasis being placed on providing better transport facilities. The policy of biasing transport investment in favour of depressed regions has been subjected to considerable debate (Gwilliam, 1980b). Scepticism about the effectiveness of such a policy as a regional economic development aid was initially expressed by A.J. Brown in a Minority Report of the Hunt Committee Inquiry into the Intermediate Areas (Department of Economic Affairs, 1969) and has more recently been supported by the findings of the Leitch Committee (Department of Transport, 1978). It is now accepted that such a policy must be pursued with circumspection and that, in many cases, improved transport facilities may prove counterproductive for development areas.

A simple hypothetical example illustrates the difficulty (see Sharp, 1980). We have two regions, *A* and *B*, producing a single homogeneous commodity. The centres of the regions (see Figure 10.3) are *M* miles apart and the commodity can be transported over the area at a constant money cost per mile of £t per ton. The markets served by the regions differ, however, because it costs £C_A to produce a ton of

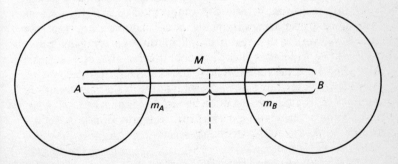

Figure 10.3   Market areas served by regions A and B

the commodity in Region A and £C_B a ton in region B. Consequently, and assuming no production centres exist between the regions, a distribution boundary can be drawn (shown by the dashed line in the figure) which is m_A miles from the centre of A and m_B miles from the centre of B (where $m_A + m_B = M$). The boundary is determined by the relative production costs of the regions and the costs of transport (i.e. $C_A + tm_A = C_B + tm_B$). Basic manipulation of the algebra gives the form:

$$m_A = 0.5 \left[M + \frac{C_B - C_A}{t} \right].$$
(10.1)

If, therefore, production is relatively cheaper in region A then m_A will increase if infrastructure reduces the cost of transport. Thus if A is a depressed area then transport improvements could assist in expanding its potential market and, therefore, generate more income and employment but region A must be a *low cost producer* for this to be automatically true. If region B is the depressed one, then quite clearly investment in improved transport will only worsen the regional problem by contracting the market area served by the region. Indeed, at the extreme (where $(C_B - C_A) \rangle Mt$) region B may be forced from the market entirely by the expansion of the low cost region's market area.

Of course, the model is a considerable simplification. Regions do not normally, for instance, specialize exclusively in the production of a single commodity but produce a range of goods. Thus a transport improvement, while damaging certain industries, may increase the competitiveness of others. The final effect of the improved transport facility will then depend upon relative production costs between regions and the importance of transport *vis-à-vis* production costs in the overall cost functions for the various commodities. Further, costs of production may vary with output and thus (following the 'infant industry argument') it may be beneficial to reduce transport costs if the government's regional policy also involves using grants and subsidies for encouraging the establishment of decreasing cost industry in a depressed area. Supplementary measures of this kind may be necessary if the depressed area is sparsley populated and, to be successful, its industry needs to penetrate the markets of other, more populous, regions to benefit from scale economies. It should be noted, however, that in these circumstances transport improvements *must* be accompanied by other regional aids if the natural gravitation of decreasing cost industries to centres of population is to be counteracted. Additionally, transport costs tend not to increase linearly with distance because of discontinuities and fixed cost elements in the overall cost function (see Chapter 3). Consequently, the influence of any transport infrastructure improvement is much more difficult to predict than the simple analysis implies.

In summary, there is no general case for thinking that investment in transport infrastructure will automatically improve the economic performance of depressed regions. In a country such as Britain, where the transport cost differences between the least and most accessible regions is only about 2 per cent for all industries (Chisholm and O'Sullivan, 1973), the effect of transport investment on regional policy is, in general, unlikely to be substantial. This is particularly true if industrial location is, as many suspect, influenced by objectives other than cost minimisation (for example, on satisficing principles) or where there is a high degree of X-inefficiency.

Empirical evidence on the regional effect of transport policies is scant and that which is available is weakened by the difficulties of isolating transport effects from the effects of other regional policy measures. By conducting a counterfactual exercise Botham (1980) suggests that road investment in Britain between 1957 and 1972 had little effect although there was some tendency for it to have a centralising effect on the distribution of employment in the country. Work by Balduini (1972) attributes the creation between 1958 and 1970 of 53 000 jobs in the heavily depressed Mezzogiorno in Italy to the building of the Autostrade de Sole. This study, however, does not allow for the substantial range of other aid measures then operative, nor for intra-regional movements between sub-regions adjacent to the new facility and those more distant.

10.5 Transport, urban development and redevelopment

Changes in transport technology have, over time, exerted a strong influence upon the shapes and forms of the urban areas in which we live. The development of steam locomotion in the second half of the nineteenth century substantially improved inter-urban transport and permitted urban growth. Local, distributional services evolved much more slowly leading, in most cities, to a concentric pattern of development around the main rail (or occasionally port) terminal. The wealthy tended, because they could afford transport which was available, to live in the outer rings of housing while industry, being dependent upon good inter-urban transport, and the working class poor concentrated near the urban core – the CBD (see Figure 10.4(a) and Chapter 2). The introduction of motorised local public transport (initially the tramcar and later the omnibus) followed by the motorcar encouraged the growth of an axial pattern of urban land-use with

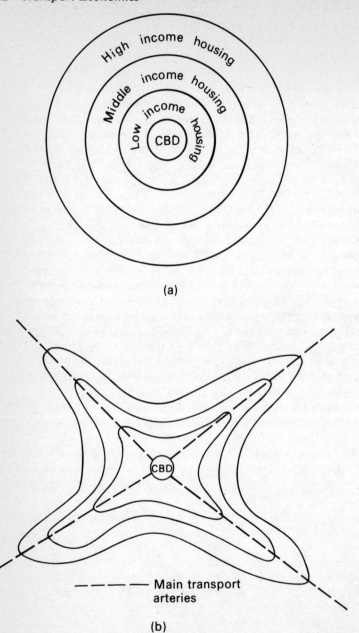

(a)

— — — Main transport
arteries

(b)

Figure 10.4   Transport and (a) concentric city development and (b) axial city development

the former succession of concentric rings of housing being extended (star like) in ribbon developments along the main road arteries (see Figure 10.4(b)). Finally, the widespread adoption of the motor car, combined with improved road systems, limited traffic restraint and more efficient road freight transport has led to the growth of multi-nuclei cities where there are numerous sub-centres and suburbs – Los Angeles is often cited as the extreme example. While this simplified account of urban development misses many important subtleties it serves to highlight the historical role which transport has had in shaping urban growth.

More recently, the difficulties of most large urban areas in the United States and Europe have not been ones of containing or moulding growth but rather of reversing decay. The concern once focused on the role of transport in urban development has been, since the early 1970s, transformed into concern for inner city revitalisation and redevelopment. As can be seen from Table 10.1 there have been substantial outflows of population from the centres of virtually all major cities since the 1960s. This has been accompanied by an even faster exodus of industry. The result of this has been a decay in inner city public economies (the tax base of such areas has fallen while the composition of the population has become increasingly biased towards the old, disabled and poor) and unemployment (not only have firms left faster than population but also it has primarily been manufacturing industry which has left leaving behind large numbers of unemployed, unskilled workers). The causes of the decline of inner city areas are complex (see Button, 1978), regional and urban planning policies are partly responsible but there have also been changes both in the life-styles aspired to by the population (urban life becoming less attractive as incomes have risen) and in the production functions confronting industry (the land–output ratio in

Table 10.1   Net migration from British cities 1966–76

City	Decline in population	
	Number	*% of total population*
Glasgow	205 000	21
Liverpool	150 000	22
Manchester	110 000	18
Inner London	500 000	16
Birmingham	85 000	8
Newcastle	40 000	12
Nottingham	25 000	8

particular has been rising). Improved personal transport, especially higher car ownership levels, has also encouraged more commuting from more distant suburbs.

Official policy to counter the decline of the inner city areas and to stimulate the redevelopment of urban cores has incorporated a substantial transport component. For example, the white paper, *Policy for the Inner Cities* (Department of the Environment, 1977) makes specific reference to the fact that 'Commerce and industry in inner areas need to be served by transport conveniently and efficiently' and points to the need for local authorities 'to give weight to the implications for local firms when designing traffic management schemes to improve access for central traffic, to ensure efficient loading and to provide adequate and convenient parking'. Additionally, it is argued that movement, notably in terms of journey to work trips, needs to be made easier especially for certain groups of travellers.

At the theoretical level, the bid-rent curve analysis set out in Chapter 2 would seem to imply that cheaper and better public transport would lead to a spread of cities (i.e. the residential bid-rent curves would shift up and to the right) while traffic restraint policy would lead to greater concentration of economic activity at the urban core. As Goldstein and Moses (1975) have shown, however, this type of analysis rests upon the assumption of a single central business district with no allowance for possible competing suburban centres. This is unrealistic in the context of most modern conurbations. Figure 10.5 depicts a more typical urban situation with a major urban centre – the Central Business District (CBD) – serving as the focal employment point dominating the suburban centre to which it is linked by road. The urban centre is itself served by good

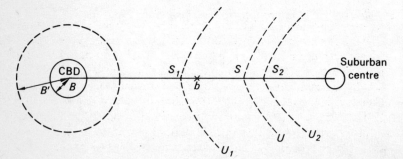

Figure 10.5   The impact of traffic restraint and public transport subsidy policies on the urban core

local public transport with people for up to B miles away travelling into work by bus. The situation is one of equilibrium, with every household achieving the same utility level. Workers may opt for one of three main employment/residential location choices:

(1) live within the immediate commuting area (radius B) and travel to work at the CBD by bus;
(2) live outside of the immediate commuting area and travel to work at the CBD by car; or
(3) commute to the sub-centre by car.

In this situation – and excluding residents of the city who elect to take a fourth option, namely working at home – the boundary U will separate those workers employed at the core and those with jobs at the suburban centre. This state of affairs is one in which no household can improve its utility by changing its place of work, residential location or mode of transport. We now assess the impact of two alternative strategies on the economy of the central core area of the city.

(1) The generalised cost of car travel in the central city area is increased, say by either higher parking charges or the imposition of road pricing. This will tend to cause a rapid decline of the urban core in this model. Higher motoring costs will cause the immediate commuting belt to widen out (say to a radius of B' in Figure 10.5) with a reduction in real income for those living $(B'-B)$ miles from the CBD. This will encourage more people either to work at home or to cease to be active in the labour force (if there are other cities in the economy, there may also be some out-migration) leading to a decrease in the labour supply function at the CBD. Also car travellers confronted by higher costs will seek work at the suburban centre shifting the employment boundary to, say, U_l. The increased competition for jobs at the sub-centre will depress real income there leading, once again, to a general reduction in the overall labour supply in the city. Generally, therefore, traffic restraint in the CBD makes labour conditions less favourable which will, in the long term, make non-core sites more attractive for industry. The empirical fact that skilled labour tends to be more mobile (both between jobs and locations) is likely to magnify this effect on industrial location.

(2) A subsidised express bus service running in bus only lanes is

introduced from a depot at location *b* to run non-stop into the urban core. This is unlikely to have an effect on those using the existing commuter public transport services around the CBD – although if fewer car trips and less congestion result the speed of their journeys may rise – but if the service is, in general cost terms, cheaper than car travel this will widen the employment market for the urban core. Former car travellers from as far out as S_2 will find that by driving to *b* and transferring to the express service they reduce the overall cost of travelling to the CBD. Consequently, the boundary marking employee catchment areas will shift to U_2. People living to the left of U_2 will find their real income has risen as a result of lower transport costs (indeed, many people to the left of *b* may drive *out* to the depot to catch the bus into the core) and the labour supply function at the core will have shifted out making the CBD a more attractive place for industry. People formerly inactive or working at home may also now find it attractive to seek employment at the CBD. The labour supply for the sub-centre has fallen, and wages will have to rise to generate the real income increase anticipated by employees there. In the long term the sub-centre will become less attractive for employers.

This theoretical analysis suggests that while one common effect of both the traffic restraint policy and the public transport improvement policy is to increase local bus service utilisation, the long-run effects on the distribution of population and economic activity are likely to be quite different. Goldstein and Moses (1975) argue, therefore, that even if transport policy in itself cannot cure the malaise of inner city areas, improved public transport provision can at least slow down the decline.

The abstract theoretical framework above relies upon a large number of rather stringent assumptions but the general conclusions that flow from the model have been substantiated to a considerable extent by empirical work. Mackett (1980), for instance, has assessed the effects of four alternative transport options for the inner area of Leeds. The policies considered were:

(1) Adjusting public transport fares, so that revenue remained constant and no mode switch resulted, but so that short trips are cheaper;
(2) Removing parking charges in the inner city;
(3) Introducing more cross-city bus services so that all parts of the

city can be reached from zones in the inner city without changing buses; and

(4) Reducing private transport access times to inner city zones by 10 per cent.

The effects of the alternatives, together with a composite policy, were assessed on a variety of criteria including population shifts, employment changes, effects on retail sales and changes in travel patterns. The main locational findings are summarised in Table 10.2. The general conclusion reached was that by 1991:

Policy A, the introduction of a new fare structure, would provide the lowest mean cost of travel to work by bus for inner city residents, but would lead to a loss of jobs in the inner city. Policy B, the removal of parking charges, would induce most employment into the inner city, including manufacturing, and provide the overall lowest mean cost travel for inner city residents; but there would be a cost since considerable bus revenue would be lost, and this might not be the best way of spending that money. The introduction of more cross-town bus routes (Policy C) would permit inner city residents to commute further out and increase public transport revenue, but would have a detrimental effect on scales of convenience goods in the city centre. The reduction of private transport access time (Policy D) would have the least effect of the four policies.

Table 10.2   The impact of alternative transport policies on the economy of the inner city of Leeds by the year 1991

	Residential location of those working in inner Leeds, 1991			
Transport policy option	*A*	*B*	*C*	*D*
Inner City	12 176	12 033	11 439	11 918
Inner Suburbs	28 538	28 653	29 642	28 558
Outer Suburbs	40 100	41 478	42 295	40 820
Outside Leeds	42 565	46 876	43 715	43 975
Total	123 378	129 040	127 092	125 271
	Employment location of those living in inner Leeds, 1991			
Transport policy option	*A*	*B*	*C*	*D*
Inner City	12 176	12 033	11 439	11 918
Inner Suburbs	2 817	2 844	2 954	2 827
Outer Suburbs	1 839	1 900	2 054	1 920
Outside Leeds	1 593	1 616	1 677	1 653
Total	18 425	18 393	18 124	18 318

Source: Mackett, 1980

While this study highlights the differing effects of traffic restraint (or at least their relaxation) policies and public transport subsidies, it also shows that the objectives of inner city redevelopment need to be carefully defined. More specifically, it reveals that while one transport policy may be the best for increasing employment in inner city areas it may not provide more work opportunities for inner area residents – the jobs being taken up by long distance commuters. Consequently, the policy-maker must be explicit in what he is attempting to do in this situation and recognise the complexity of the local economy in which he is operating.

10.6 Further reading and references
The importance of transport in encouraging the development of third world economies is looked at in Prest (1969) which offers a good, general, if dated introduction to the subject. Little and Mirrlees (1974) is difficult, but fruitful reading, and provides a comprehensive treatment of investment appraisal (including transport) in less developed countries. The EEC periodically publishes pamphlets outlining changes in its transport policy, but for further analysis of the philosophy underlying the Common Transport Policy and also for some critical comments on its development to date see Gwilliam (1980a). Transport and regional policy is well assessed in Gwilliam (1979) and Sharp (1980), both of which contain careful theoretical arguments outlining conditions where transport policy may affect regional economic performance as well as reference to a body of applied literature. Mackett's (1980) paper referred to in the text is recommended as being a rather rigorous analysis of the role of transport in reviving inner city economies.

References
Ahmed, Y., O'Sullivan, P., Sujono and Wilson, D. (1976), *Road Investment Programming for Developing Countries: An Indonesian Example*, Evanston, Northwestern University.
Balduini, G. (1972), *Autostrade et Territorio in Quadermi de Autostrade*, Rome.
Baxter, R.D. (1866), 'Railway extension and its results', *Journal of the Statistical Society*, Vol. 24, pp. 549–95.
Botham, R.W. (1980), 'The regional development effects of road investment', *Transportation Planning and Technology*, Vol. 6, pp. 97–108.
Button, K.J. (1978), 'Employment and industrial decline in the inner city areas of British cities: the experiences of 1962–1977', *Journal of Industrial Affairs*, Vol. 6, pp. 1–6.
Button, K.J. (1979), 'Recent developments in EEC Transport Policy', *Three Banks Review*, no. 123, pp. 52–73.
Chisholm, M. and O'Sullivan, P. (1973), *Freight Flows and Spatial Aspects*

of the British Economy, Cambridge, Cambridge University Press.

Department of Economic Affairs (1969), *The 'Intermediate Areas'*, London, HMSO.

Department of the Environment (1977), *Policy for the Inner Cities*, Cmnd 6845, London, HMSO.

Department of Transport (1978), *Report of the Advisory Committee on Trunk Road Assessment* (Leitch Committee), London, HMSO.

Devanney, J.W., Livanos, V.M. and Stewart, R.J. (1975), 'Conference rate making and the west coast of South America', *Journal of Transport Economics and Policy*, Vol. 9, pp. 154–77.

Evans, J.J. and Benham, A. (1975), 'A forked tariff system for liner freight routes', *Journal of Transport Economics and Policy*, Vol. 9, pp. 62–6.

Fogel, R.W. (1964), *Railroads and American Economic Growth, Essays in Econometric History*, Baltimore, John Hopkins University Press.

Fromm, G. (1965), 'Introduction: an approach to investment decisions', in G. Fromm (ed.), *Transport Investment and Economic Development*, Washington, Brooking Institute.

Gauthier, H.L. (1970), 'Geography, transport and regional development', *Economic Geography*, Vol. 46, pp. 612–19.

Goldstein, G.S. and Moses, L.N. (1975), 'Transport controls and the spatial structure of urban areas', *Papers and Proceedings of the American Economics Association* (87th Meeting), pp. 289–94.

Gwilliam, K.M. (1979), 'The transport policy', in A.M. El-Agraa (ed.), *The Economics of the European Community*, London, Philip Allan.

Gwilliam, K.M. (1980a), 'Realism and the Common Transport Policy of the EEC', in J.B. Palack and J.B. Van der Kamp (eds.), *Changes in the Field of Transport Studies*, The Hague, Martinus Nijhoff.

Gwilliam, K.M. (1980b), 'Transport infrastructure investments and regional development', in K.J. Bowers (ed.), *Inflation, Development and Integration – Essays in Honour of A.J. Brown*, Leeds, Leeds University Press.

Hirschman, A.O. (1958), *The Strategy of Economic Development*, New Haven, Yale University Press.

Hunter, H. (1965), 'Transport in Soviet and Chinese development', *Economic Development and Cultural Change*, Vol. 14, pp. 71–72.

Jennings, A. (1976), 'Infrastructure pricing and the EEC Common Transport Policy', *Journal of Transport Economics and Policy*, Vol. 10, pp. 177–95.

Little, I.M.D. and Mirrlees, J.A. (1974), *Project Appraisal and Planning for Developing Countries*, London, Heinemann.

Lugard, F.D. (1922), *The Dual Mandate in British Tropical Africa*, Edinburgh, Blackwoods.

McCallum, J.D. (1979), 'The development of British regional policy', in D. MacLennan and J.B. Parr (eds.), *Regional Policy – Past Experience and New Directions*, Oxford, Martin Robertson.

Mackett, R.L. (1980), 'The relationships between transport and the viability of central and inner urban areas', *Journal of Transport Economics and Policy*, Vol. 14, pp. 267–94.

Millard, R.S. (1959), 'Road development in the overseas territories', *Journal of the Royal Society of Arts*, Vol. 107, pp. 270–91.

Nath, S.V. (1962), 'The theory of balanced growth', *Oxford Economic Papers*, Vol. 14, pp. 138–53.

Neff, S.C. (1980), 'The UN code of conduct for liner conferences', *Journal of World Trade Law*, Vol. 14, pp. 398–423.

Owen, W. (1964), *Strategy for Mobility*, Washington, Brookings Institute.

Prest, A.R. (1969), *Transport Economics in Developing Countries*, London, Weidenfeld and Nicolson.

Rostow, W.W. (1960), *The Stages of Economic Growth*, Cambridge, Cambridge University Press.

Sharp, C.H. (1980), 'Transport and regional development with special reference to Britain', *Transport Policy and Decision Making*, Vol. 1, pp. 1–11.

Shneerson, D. (1977), 'On the measurement of benefits from shipping services', *Maritime Policy and Management*, Vol. 4, pp. 277–80.

UNCTAD (1969), *Level and Structure of Freight Rates, Conference Practices and the Adequacy of Shipping Services*, New York, United Nations.

Wilson, G.W. (1966), 'Towards a theory of transport and development', in G.W. Wilson, B.R. Bergmann, L.V. Hirsch, M.S. Klein (eds.), *The Impact of Highway Investment on Development*, Washington, Brookings Institute.

Zerby, J.A. (1979), 'On the practicability of the UNCTAD 40-40-20 code for liner conferences', *Maritime Policy and Management*, Vol. 6, pp. 241–51.

11. Economics and Transport Policy

11.1 The reasons for government intervention and the methods employed

Chapter 1 highlighted the considerable growth of interest in economic policy-making in transport which has occurred over the past twenty years. This brief concluding chapter looks in more detail at the validity of some of the arguments presented in support of the types of policy, in very broad terms, as they have developed in the United Kingdom. It is not intended to offer a catalogue of policy measures nor a chronology of their application but, instead, the approach is one of looking at the way different philosophies have emerged, usually in response to changing conditions in the transport market and as a consequence of evolving socio-political ideas.

Initially it seems sensible to outline briefly the main reasons which have been advanced for government intervention in the transport market. Some of these have already been subjects of detailed discussion in previous chapters, but a listing offers a chance to show the diversity of arguments. Broadly, government has explicitly intervened for the following reasons.

The containment of monopoly power This was particularly so in the case of the railways, which dominated inland transport for nearly a century from the late 1830s, but while some monopoly power still persists today in certain areas of transport activity, especially passenger transport, technical advances have reduced the potential of monopoly exploitation, at least in most developed countries.

The control of excessive competition Unregulated competition may limit the *quality* of service offered to customers and result in instability in the industry. In general, the problem is not the competition *per se* but rather the possibility that externalities may result or that certain sections of the community may not be provided with adequate services. Additionally, in some instances, notably road haulage and inter-urban passenger transport the potential for conditions of monopolistic competition developing also poses problems of possible excess capacity being supplied.

The regulation of externalities Imperfections in the market mechanism may result in transport activities imposing costs which are not directly included in the private sector's decision-making – pollution and congestion being the main causes for concern. This subject has been explored fully in Chapters 5 and 7.

The provision of public goods   Because certain items of infrastructure, such as roads, exhibit public good characteristics (i.e. non-excludability and non-rivalness) their provision would be at best inadequate without government intervention.

The provision of high cost infrastructure   The sheer cost and long pay-back period, combined with possible high levels of risk, makes it unlikely that major pieces of infrastructure would be built or expensive transport engineering research undertaken without some form of government involvement.

The assistance of groups in 'need' of adequate transport   As was seen in Chapter 3 this embraces the notion that, for a variety of reasons including faults in the existing pattern of income distribution, effective demand is not an adequate guide to transport resource allocation and wider, social criteria should, therefore, be sought.

The integration of transport into wider economic policies   Land-use and transport are clearly interconnected and some degree of co-ordination may be felt desirable if imperfections exist in either the transport or land-use markets. Additionally, intervention in the transport sector may form part of a wider, government macro-economic strategy (e.g. price controls or investment programmes) or industrial policy.

The need to reflect the genuine economic resource costs of transport   In the case of certain finite, non-renewable resources (e.g. mineral fuels) the market mechanism may fail to reflect the true social time preference of society. The government may, therefore, intervene to ensure that the decision-maker is aware of the true shadow price.

The improvement of transport co-ordination   Because there are numerous suppliers of transport services, inefficient provision may result if their decisions are made independently. There is also the prospect of duplication of transport facilities and consequential wastage of resources, without some degree of central guidance.

Of course, most official policies claim to cover a range of different problems although conflicts may, and do, emerge. For example, policies designed primarily to contain externalities may have adverse effects on income distribution or could run counter to a national economic policy that is pursuing a course of maximising gross national product. Similarly, measures to ensure that adequate high cost research is conducted may mean conferring monopoly powers on private suppliers (e.g. through the patent system or in terms of government contracts to purchase the fruits of a new technology). Consequently, there is an inevitable blurring across these justifications for government involvement when various policy measures are discussed or introduced. Even more uncertain than the exact justification or objectives underlying some policies is the exact effect the different policy tools employed by policy makers are likely to exert. One can usefully classify these various policy instruments under the following headings:

Taxes and subsidies The government may use its fiscal powers either to increase or to decrease the costs of various forms of transport or services over different routes. Or, indeed, the cost of transport in general. It may also influence the factor costs of transport inputs.

Direct provisions Local and central government are direct suppliers, via municipal and nationalised undertakings, of a wide range of transport services. They are also responsible for supplying a substantial amount of transport infrastructure, notably roads, and supplementary services, such as the police.

Laws and regulations Government (and to a lesser extent, local authorities) may legally regulate the transport sector and there has grown up an extensive body of law which, in effect, controls and directs the activities of both transport supplies and users.

Licensing The government may regulate either the quality or quantity of transport provision by its ability to grant various forms of licences to operators, vehicles or services. The system of driving licences also influences the demand for private transport.

The purchase of transport services Various non-transport activities of government require the use of transport services. Hence, by means of its position as a large consumer government may exert a degree of countervailing power over transport suppliers.

Moral suasion In many instances this is of a weak form, usually being educational or the offering of advice on matters such as safety (e.g. advertising the advantages of the wearing of seat belts) but it may be stronger when the alternative to accepting advice is the exercise, by government, of others of its powers (e.g. the refusal of a licence or withdrawal of a subsidy).

Research and development Government may influence the long-term development of transport through its own research activities. These are, in part, conducted by its own agents (e.g. the Transport and Road Research Laboratory) and, in part, through the funding of outside research.

Provision of information The government through various agencies offers certain technical advice to transport-users and provides general information to improve the decision-making within transport. Many of these services are specific to transport (e.g. weather services for shipping) while others assist the transport sector less directly (e.g. information on trading arrangements overseas).

Ideally, policy-makers like to match one policy instrument with one objective but this is seldom possible in transport. The problem of interdependence of objectives have already been alluded to but, in addition, the instruments themselves frequently have diverse effects. Taxation policies to reduce the use of a specific mode of transport may prove regressive while licensing to contain externalities may result in quasi-monopoly powers being given to certain suppliers. Actually forecasting, monitoring and appraising the effects of alternative policy instruments also usually proves difficult. Transport policy is pursued through a package of instruments and policy changes usually resulting in several of these instruments being varied in their intensity at once. The effects of such changes is also only likely to be fully felt after a lag as agents in the transport market gradually respond and adjust to the new situation. In the short term a road haulier, for instance, may do little in response to higher fuel taxation (save pay the additional money) but in the longer term he is likely to modify the method of operation employed and, in the very long term, he may even change the type of vehicle fleet used. Even if one could isolate occasions when a change is made to a single policy instrument it is unlikely that the full effect could be recorded before further changes take place. Finally, there is the problem of determining the counter-factual – the course of events which would have ensued if policy had not been changed. Government is frequently reactive in its approach – suggesting that changing circumstances are already observable by the time policy is enacted – but on other occasions policy changes represent initiatives and actually anticipate change. One can never simply assume that events would have continued on the course set prior to a major policy change.

It now seems appropriate to examine the various landmarks and phases of UK transport policy. This is intended to highlight the way in which transport policy has evolved to match both the changing technical and organisational structure of the sector and also the differing attitudes that society has had to transport over the past century and a half. It is in no way intended as a comprehensive piece of economic history.

11.2 Priorities in transport policy

The anti-monolopy phase, pre-1930
Government has always taken some interest in transport. Historically, military, political and fiscal factors were the prime motivation but over the past century and a half this concern has broadened out. Previously, it was not the efficiency of the transport market which was the principal concern but rather the insurance that adequate transport was available to permit the fulfilment of the major commitments of defence, administration and internal stability. The Industrial Revolution placed greater emphasis on the need for an economically efficient transport system which, combined with the rapid technical changes that took place in transport during the later years of the eighteenth and, more importantly, the early decades of the nineteenth centuries, resulted in rather more official intervention. (Indeed, even the Duke of Wellington called for a National Transport Plan at one stage.) While much of the early involvement was to permit canal and railway facilities to be constructed, there was also a political awareness of the potential monopoly powers which canals, but railway companies in particular, could exercise. The 1844 Railway Act, for example, gave government the option of purchasing newly formed companies after twenty-one years (a power never exercised) and maximum rates were normally included in the enabling acts. In all over two hundred regulatory acts were passed before 1930 to appease public concern over the private control exercised over the monopoly of the railway companies. By the 1920s the railway companies had to publish their rates, were subject to common carrier obligations, were not allowed to show undue preference, had to present accounts in a prescribed manner and were subjected to controls over wage bargaining. An element of social service obligation was also apparent in some of this legislation with, initially, railway companies required by law to provide specified cheap services and, subsequently, workmen's tickets.

The anti-competition phase, 1930–45
The advances in road haulage and passenger transport in the period after the First World War substantially eroded the near monopoly that had been enjoyed by the railways for the previous eighty or so years. The nature of road transport, and especially the relative ease of entry, and low capital requirement necessary, changed the

emphasis of transport policy away from monopoly control and towards the regulation of dangerous operating practices and 'excessive competition'. The political pressures of the railway companies, still hampered by numerous restrictions on their commercial freedom, to contain cheap road transport added emphasis to the debate. Besides the financial strains on the regulated railway industry, fears were expressed that excessive competition produces dangerous operating practices and results in inadequate and unreliable services for those situated away from the main transport arteries. The Salter Conference, for instance, which reported on the road haulage industry in 1932 found that, 'Any individual at present has an unlimited right to enter the haulage industry without any regard to the pressure on the roads or the existing excess of transport facilities ... This unrestricted liberty is fatal to the organisation of the industry in a form suitable to a carrier service purported to serve the public.' (It should perhaps be said that the composition of the Salter Conference – it was made up of railwaymen and representatives of *established* hauliers – may have coloured its conclusions!)

The legal manifestations of this policy were the passing of the Road Traffic Act, 1930 and of the Road and Rail Traffic Act, 1933, which introduced, respectively, quantity licensing into road passenger transport and public road haulage. In addition to trying to temper the competitive environment of road transport the operation of the licensing system for road passenger transport also encouraged the provision and cross-subsidisation of unprofitable social bus services by virtue of the method of licence allocation. Other measures designed to produce greater equality in the operating conditions encountered on the roads and railways included relaxation of certain constraints on railway pricing and the introduction of minimum wage rates and specified employment conditions into the road haulage industry.

Central control and nationalisation, 1945–51

The years immediately following the end of the Second World War saw, under the newly elected Labour government, a period of reconstruction and an industrial policy emphasising the nationalisation of industry. The 1947 Transport Act, for the first time outside of war years, brought a substantial part of the British transport system under direct government control. (Although it should be pointed out that peace time nationalisation was not entirely new nor a Labour Party monopoly and, indeed, the British Overseas Airways Corporation was formed in 1939 by a Conservative administration.) The objectives of the 1947 Act were clearly stated, namely to 'secure the provision of an efficient, adequate, economical and properly integrated system of public inland transport and port facilities'. The earlier success of the London Passenger Transport Board gave credence to this view and the British Transport Commission (with five functional executives) was established to emulate this success. It was given the responsibility of co-ordinating the newly nationalised railways, long distance road haulage, sections of public road transport, London Transport and publicly owned ports and waterways.

Unfortunately, the BTC was given no rules of economic behaviour as guidelines. It was recognised that, for the railways to compete efficiently, a much closer price–cost relationship was required but it was impossible for a new set of freight charges to be set before 1955 and, in the meantime, the BTC was impotent to detail traffic to the mode of transport for which it thought it was best suited. The difficulty was compounded by the fact that consignors had a free choice of transport mode, and that own account road haulage vehicles were free from government control. Further, the 1947 Act had little opportunity to work because of, firstly, the lack of sufficient time needed to develop the necessary administration and to reorganise the newly nationalised undertakings and, secondly, the inadequate funds available to carry out the necessary investment required in the rail sector.

A competitive framework, 1951–64

The period of successive Conservative administrations between 1951 and 1964 witnessed a movement away from a regulatory approach to transport co-ordination towards one based upon competition, i.e. by making use of 'the natural interplay of economic forces'. A policy of decentralised control was pursued and, under the 1953 Transport Act, the railways were freed from many of their long-standing statutory obligations (e.g. they were relieved of the status of 'common carrier' and the burden of having to publish their rates and charges). Large sections of nationalised road haulage were also returned to private ownership. The basic argument for this competitive approach was that 'even if integration in the fullest sense were practicable, it would result in a large unwieldly machine, ill-adapted to meet with promptitude the varying and instant demands of industry' (Ministry of Transport, 1952).

The culmination of these policies was the 1962 Transport Act which freed the railways from most of their remaining legal constraints, regionalised their boards, separated their overall administration from that of road haulage and recognised that commercial viability required some rationalisation of the rail network. Nationalised road haulage (which was composed of British Road Services and several specialist undertakings) was given terms of reference requiring it to perform as though it was a 'private enterprise concern'.

The general policy of 'co-ordination by competition' pursued by the Conservative government met with considerable problems after 1962. The railways and public transport in general ran into increasing financial difficulties while public concern began to grow about both the need to provide additional road space for the growing number of motor vehicles and the actual environmental effects of this growth, especially on urban areas. The established method of providing social services by cross finance from profitable services ceased to be financially viable. Further there were questions arising concerning the most appropriate ways of exploiting new transport technologies, especially containerisation.

Controlled competition, 1964–74

The Labour administration elected in 1964 undertook a series of detailed policy studies in transport which culminated in the passing of the 1968 Transport Act. This, in conjunction with the 1968 Town and Country Planning Act, attempted to produce a policy based upon 'controlled competition' (see Munby, 1968). It hoped to combine the advantages afforded by the automatic processes of the market mechanism with those of direct control. The policy was comprehensive, setting up authorities (Passenger Transport Authorities) to control and co-ordinate urban public transport, devising new systems of quality licensing for road haulage, providing specific finance to support socially necessary transport, drawing up a national road-building programme and reconstructing the accounts and activities of the railways. It used all means of policy; market measures, such as taxation and subsidy, as well as 'administrative' measures such as licensing and the establishment of new institutions. The Act was also liberal in the sense that the framework of legislation and licensing which was introduced was intended to provide a basis for 'fair' competition, leaving the actual co-ordination of modes, in the majority of sectors, to market forces. The PTAs were introduced in the major conurbations to control urban public transport, but this was in a market where externalities are widespread and competition felt to be unlikely to solve problems of congestion and environmental decay. The inter-urban market was left to competitive forces with intervention limited to preventing excess instability or dangerous practices.

The Conservative government returned to office in 1970 pledged themselves to the repeal of many of the measures contained in the

1968 Act although, in practice, few of the measures they found exceptionable – such as quantity licensing for long distance road haulage – had in fact been implemented (see Button, 1974). Indeed, the 1972 Local Government Act set up authorities which logically extended the PTA concept and further integrated the long-term planning of overall urban development (see Chapter 10). The Civil Aviation Authority, which was set up in 1971, rather than reverse the philosophy of the 1968 Act, was designed to control operating practices and improve the stability of the sector. As the Minister said at the time, 'There are close links between the economics and the financial health of the airlines and the safety of their operations and between operational safety, airworthiness, air traffic control and navigational services.'

The search for efficiency, 1974–80s

The policy emphasis of the Labour government from 1974 to 1979 was spelt out in their White paper on *Transport Policy* (Department of Transport, 1977). They were, 'First, to contribute to economic growth and higher national prosperity... Second, to meet social needs by securing a reasonable level of personal mobility, ... Third, to minimise the harmful effects, in loss of life and damage to the environment, that are the direct physical results of the transport we use.' In many ways the policies, which reduced government expenditure considerably, moved further towards the free market than the 1968 Transport Act, with greater emphasis now placed on allocative efficiency. Although government expenditure on 'roads and transport' fell from £3820m to £3023m per annum (at 1978 prices), between 1974 and 1978, this does not mean official intervention was ignored. The 1974 Railway Act, for example, had already introduced the idea of a 'Public Service Obligation' and subsidies were made available to provide services 'comparable' to those existing at the time of the legislation. Methods of allocating public monies were also modified with the introduction of transport supplementary grants and the need, from 1974, for the production of transport policies and programmes by local authorities to demonstrate the evolution of coherent local transport policy. This latter idea was later extended in the 1978 Transport Act to embrace public transport services (the Public Transport Plans) at the shire level. But, on the other hand, grand strategies for road-building were replaced by piecemeal assessments emphasising a further shift from the active policy of the Labour administration of the 1960s to rather more reactive policy-making (Gwilliam, 1979).

The emphasis on allocative efficiency and market mechanisms was further strengthened in the 1980 Transport Act introduced by the Conservative government returned the previous year. Quantity licensing in the express coach sector was abolished and free competition (with quality controls) was permitted. Further relaxation of sharing and lift-giving laws also allowed more opportunity for private transport to offer limited forms of public service in rural areas, while policies of denationalisation have resulted in sales of limited amounts of publicly owned transport assets to private industry. (It is interesting to compare this trend towards both reactive policy-making and a greater reliance on market forces with the developments in the EEC Common Transport Policy discussed in Chapter 10.)

Despite the removal of some transport assets from public ownership, it became clear in 1980 that government involvement in transport finance may require some further injections to achieve longer-term, wider objectives. More specifically, the need to replace ageing railway equipment raises the question of increased electrification of the network. Such a step would (i) reduce to some extent the demand for scarce oil fuels (although not energy as a whole); (ii) provide a service more suited to the needs of UK industry; and (iii) contain rising labour costs. At the time of writing a Department of Transport–British Rail (1981) study offers in evidence the most up-to-date information on the desirability of additional electrification (see Table 11.1). The indications are that a positive rate of return is likely to be earned (an 11 per cent internal rate of return in the case of larger options) although the exact length of payback and the effect on rail transport differs among schemes.

Table 11.1   Alternative options for railway electrification

Option	Additional electrification over present day (1981)		Completion date	Payback year	% of rail traffic hauled electrically	
	Route miles	Track miles			Passenger	Freight
Base	240	490	1988	–	52	23
Small	1120	2870	1995	2009	62	38
Medium (slow)	2280	5550	2005	2009	75	54
Medium (fast)	2280	5550	1995	2006	75	54
Large (slow)	3410	7710	2010	2010	83	68
Large (fast)	3410	7710	2000	2007	83	68

Source: Department of Transport, 1981

11.3 Co-ordination via the market, or by direction?

These very important facts emerge from the previous section. Firstly, government finds the transport sector extremely difficult to handle; this is perhaps most clearly seen if one reflects on the fact that *major* pieces of transport legislation have appeared on the statute books every seven or eight years during the past half-century (i.e. 1930, 1933, 1947, 1953, 1962, 1968, 1974, 1980). These have been supplemented by numerous pieces of minor legislation. There have been substantial shifts both in the way that transport has been viewed and the type of policy approach pursued.

Secondly, the changes in policy have exhibited systematic swings between attempts at making greater use of market forces and a more comprehensive level of central control or direction. Intervention has always existed but the degree and nature of this intervention has differed according to whether more or less confidence was felt in market processes. Recent changes in policy, from the late 1970s, have reflected a greater market orientation while the nationalisation of the immediate post-war period followed philosophies of direction. The respective merits of market oriented policies *vis-à-vis* ones of planned allocation of resources are subjects of considerable debate. While much of the discussion is political (often doctrinal) there is, nevertheless, an important area of economic controversy involved.

It is quite possible that in theory a variety of approaches with quite significant differences in their degree of market orientation could achieve the basic objectives of transport policy but the standard economic problem of integration or 'co-ordination' remains practically difficult. (Co-ordination is here used in its economic context and is best defined by Peterson (1930), 'Co-ordination is the assignment by whatever means of each facility to those transport tasks which it can perform better than other facilities, under conditions which will ensure its fullest development in the place so found.') In practice, reliance is never placed entirely on the market mechanism to achieve the desired co-ordination, nor upon direction. The issue is rather one of degree and emphasis. It seems useful, however, to look initially at some of the arguments that are advanced for adoption of the extreme position.

The price mechanism is the main instrument of the market and offers an obvious method of co-ordination – each consumer being in a position to purchase transport services at the lowest cost. Arguments that transport is a public utility, on a par with street lighting or the police force, are dismissed by advocates of this school who point out that transport, unlike genuine utilities, would be provided even if government did not exist. There may be cases (e.g. quasi public goods) where government must act as the supplier, if provision is to be optimal, but providing the rules of marginal cost pricing are pursued no difficulties arise. If externalities exist then these can be handled adequately by means of ensuring that property rights are allocated according to fairly accepted rules while social difficulties associated with hardship should be tackled by lump sum transfers. (At the extreme one may argue that income differences are themselves the result of market forces and should, therefore, be left.) The longevity of transport infrastructure and associated risks would be handled by insurance markets. Safety would be ensured by travellers/consignors selecting operators with good safety records or alternatively they may prefer a higher risk but at a lower charge for the trip. Perfection in the 'safety market' may require government intervention to ensure that users are cognizant of the dangers involved – in this sense information becomes the only 'merit good' to be provided in the transport sector (see Charles and Westaway, 1981 for a discussion of this aspect of merit goods).

Advocates of the market approach to co-ordination point to the automatic mechanisms involved and the freedom of the system from political manipulation. Hibbs (1976), in particular, suggests that the direction of resources by some overriding body is likely to be less efficient at co-ordination because 'The administrative mind is not likely to possess the qualities of imagination and flair that are necessary if the consumer's interest is to be served.' Cooter and Topakin (1980) produce evidence from the Bay Area Rapid Transit system of San Francisco that provides tentative confirmation of this type of bureaucratic hypothesis; namely, that the technostructure places *its* interest before that of customers. The validity of this view is, however, debatable and it has been suggested by Galbraith (1967) that the managers of any large undertaking, irrespective of the type of purpose they are charged to pursue, will be motivated by their own self-interest – in particular they will attempt to maximise their power and security. Self-interest at the expense of customer interest, therefore, seems to be a function of the scale of management rather than of ownership or the objectives which are set it.

But even if there are potential managerial problems associated with the central direction of resources, these may well be outweighed by the possible benefits. Strictly, planned resource allocation involves the direction of traffic as well as factors of production actually employed in providing transport services. In general, however, UK policy has seldom attempted to direct traffic, leaving the consumer free to choose his mode, route, service, etc. (There are exceptions such as one-way streets, barriers to lorry traffic, etc. but these are rather outside of the main thrust of the debate.) The most important case, where some degree of direction was intended, concerned the proposed introduction of quantity licensing into long-distance road haulage under the Transport Act, 1968. The broad argument here was that it was the consignor's benefit to be directed to rail in certain instances because of his own misperceptions. ('Inertia and habit will play their part and some consignors may not even be aware of the advantage to them of the new rail services, nor of the true economic cost of their present arrangements' according to the Ministry of Transport, 1967). The difficulty with this line of argument, and possibly one of the main reasons the system was never implemented, is that the administrators, in makng their allocation, may misperceive the priorities and needs of the consignor.

On the more central issue of service provision it has been suggested that without directed co-ordination it is often impossible or prohibitively wasteful for many of the wider goals to be fully achieved. Direct income transfers, for example, may rectify differences in the spending power of households but it is often a sub-group within a household (e.g. housewives) whom one is trying to assist and direct transfers may not reach them. Further, with so many operators in the transport market, there are suggestions that technical co-ordination of services would be less efficient (e.g. bus services would not act as local distributors to trunk rail services). Private firms may not be willing to undertake substantial capital projects because unlike government, they cannot spread risk adequately, even where insurance markets do exist. In more simple terms, advocates of direction feel that it is likely to prove overall to be more efficient than an optimally maintained market environment.

Quite clearly the substance of these lines of argument is likely to vary among transport sectors. It is not surprising, therefore, that in general the allocative mechanism favoured for inter-urban transport (especially freight) is that of the market and of price while intra-urban transport tends to be subjected to considerable planning and control. The widespread occurrence of externalities, the more immediate distribution issues, the interaction of an imperfect transport market with that of an imperfect land market, etc. make it particularly difficult to remove the impedences that exist to the efficient function of a pure market for urban transport. One exception, which should be noted, to the dominance of the market in allocating inter-urban resources is the public provision of roads. Here, as we saw in Chapter 4, there are important differences between the way road and rail track cost are passed on to users. Comparable pricing policies are the clear market solution, but it is worth noting that some economists have taken the argument further and suggested that both sets of track should be publicly owned and then users should pay on an identical basis for the services rendered (e.g. Mance, 1940).

Finally, it is becoming increasingly apparent that the tools of direction or control are, in effect, so numerous, sophisticated and subtle that the distinction between market-oriented policy and control is rapidly ceasing to be a meaningful one. By manipulating price, licensing, operating laws, and work conditions, the government is in effect directing resources and ultimately influencing the traffic patterns that evolve. The tools of policy outlined in section 11.1 are all, in effect, tools of direction but at the same time they may operate as tools to improve the workings of the market. Would road-pricing, for example, be extending the market to embrace congestion or would it be a direction of traffic? In this context the extremes of market versus direction cease to be helpful; one removes to a rather more basic debate concerning the desirability of goals and the relative merits of different policy tools for achieving them.

11.4 Further reading and references
The most comprehensive reference on the economics of transport policy is Gwilliam and Mackie (1975) but for readers more interested in the underlying basis of policy Gwilliam (1979) offers a particularly penetrating analysis. Details of actual United Kingdom transport policy is set out in a series of white and green papers which are referred to in the text. Readers interested in keeping up to date are recommended to be alert for future official white papers both directly dealing with transport policy and public expenditure policy.

References
Button, K.J. (1974), 'Transport policy in the United Kingdom 1968–74', *Three Banks Review*, no. 103, pp. 26–48.
Charles, S. and Westaway, A.J. (1981), 'Ignorance and merit wants', *Finanzarchiv*, Vol. 39, pp. 74–8.
Cooter, R. and Topakin, G. (1980), 'Political economy of a public co-operation – pricing objectives of BART', *Journal of Public Economics*, Vol. 13, pp. 299–318.
Department of Transport (1977), *Transport Policy*, Cmnd 6845, London, HMSO.
Department of Transport (1977), *Review of Main Line Electrification – Final Report*, London, HMSO.
Galbraith, J.K. (1967), *The New Industrial State*, Boston, Houghton Mifflin.
Gwilliam, K.M. (1979), 'Institutions and objectives in transport policy', *Journal of Transport Economics and Policy*, Vol. 13, pp. 11–27.

Gwilliam, K.M. and Mackie, P.J. (1975), *Economics and Transport Policy*, London, Allen & Unwin.

Hibbs, J. (1976), 'Transport-accountability and consumer choice', *National Westminster Bank Quarterly Review*, pp. 58–68.

Mance, H.O. (1940), *The Road and Rail Transport Problem*, London, Pitman.

Ministry of Transport (1952), *Transport Policy*, Cmnd 8538, London, HMSO.

Ministry of Transport (1967), *The Transport of Freight*, Cmnd 3470, London, HMSO.

Munby, D.L. (1968), 'Mrs Castle's transport policy', *Journal of Transport Economics and Policy*, Vol. 2, pp. 135–73.

Peterson, G.S. (1930), 'Transport coordination: meaning and purpose', *Journal of Political Economy*, Vol. 38, pp. 660–81.

Index